SamBop NYC

SamBop NYC

Brazilian Jazz in New York City during the New Millennium

MARC GIDAL

OXFORD

UNIVERSITY PRESS

OXFORD
UNIVERSITY PRESS

Oxford University Press is a department of the University of Oxford. It furthers
the University's objective of excellence in research, scholarship, and education
by publishing worldwide. Oxford is a registered trade mark of Oxford University
Press in the UK and certain other countries.

Published in the United States of America by Oxford University Press
198 Madison Avenue, New York, NY 10016, United States of America.

© Oxford University Press 2024

CIP data is on file at the Library of Congress

ISBN 978–0–19–761905–6 (pbk.)
ISBN 978–0–19–761904–9 (hbk.)

DOI: 10.1093/oso/9780197619049.001.0001

Paperback printed by Marquis Book Printing, Canada
Hardback printed by Bridgeport National Bindery, Inc., United States of America

MIX
Paper | Supporting
responsible forestry
FSC® C103567
FSC
www.fsc.org

*To Jessica, Noa, and Max, and to the musicians
and supporters of Brazilian jazz.*

Contents

Preface

This book is intended for multiple audiences who share overlapping interests in Brazilian jazz yet probably prioritize different topics. While musicians and music fans want to learn about the music and musicians, scholars of music and culture expect an informed critical analysis that aims to advance our collective knowledge about the world. Balancing subjects to address these two readerships was less challenging when drafting chapters than it was during the editing stages, as topics increasingly competed for limited space and attention. The book is not a chronological history but a collection of interrelated subjects. So, dear reader, depending on your vantage point and interests, feel free to skip around the book, as the order of chapters and sections within them is not critical to follow. The footnotes are often succinct, pointing readers to relevant sources for further study.

I encourage readers to listen to Brazilian jazz, both at live events and through recordings. Most of the recorded music discussed in this book is on widely available albums and online services. Included is a discography with a selection of recordings by artists in this book made between 2000 and 2020.

When condensing a book for space, an unfortunate consequence is the removal of sections and chapters. It was especially heartbreaking to cut parts about specific people who were invaluable to the local scene or my research. The choices of musicians to feature in the book were not entirely based on relative merit, popularity, or even personal tastes; often their music, careers, experiences, or perspectives helped to explain larger points. To provide future readers insights about other musicians and subjects than this book highlights, I created a website with basic information about musicians who were engaged in New York's Brazilian jazz scene during the 2000s and 2010s. Currently the website resides at newyorkbrazilianjazz.com.

This book primarily contributes to the academic fields of ethnomusicology, jazz studies, and Brazilian music studies. Ethnomusicology was named in the mid-twentieth-century to combine musicology with ethnography and ethnology, studies of music and people.[1] As an interdisciplinary approach to research and interpret music in relation to cultural contexts, ethnomusicology combines music history, performance, and analysis with methods and concerns of social sciences, here, anthropology and sociology. Interviewing musicians and attending music performances were key research activities that provided me insightful experiences and connected me personally with the musicians. As an amateur jazz musician who researches and teaches jazz and Brazilian music, I also tried to balance multiple musical perspectives in this book, as do the professional musicians who create Brazilian jazz. I hope that readers enjoy learning about the musicians, music, and critical issues discussed in this book.

South Orange, New Jersey
August 2023

Note

1. Nettl 2005, 11, Chapter 17.

Acknowledgments

My experiences researching Brazilian jazz in New York over the past decade have been intellectually fascinating, musically invigorating, and personally enriching, especially when studying the music closely and meeting so many wonderful individuals engaged in creating and promoting it. I am tremendously grateful to have received support from different groups of people and institutions.

Musicians are of course at the top my list of people to thank because this book is about them and the music they create for all of us to enjoy. Every musician I interviewed shaped my understanding of the broader music scene and issues, whether or not they are quoted or mentioned in the prose. I am appreciative to everyone who granted me interviews and conversed with me after shows, and several musicians, in particular, who generously shared insights on numerous occasions: Lívio Almeida, Clarice Assad, Cyro Baptista, Jorge Continentino, Amarildo Costa, Duduka Da Fonseca, Eumir Deodato, Vitor Gonçalves, Scott Kettner, and Amanda Ruzza.

I am fortunate to have a supportive family, especially my wife Jessica, whose time and finances were impacted whenever I interviewed people and attended shows. I also thank my close friends with whom I discussed my research and those who attended shows with me and shared their observations.

Editor Norman Hirschy and the staff at Oxford University Press deserve tremendous gratitude for publishing, editing, designing, and marketing this book, and especially Norman for his many insightful and supportive consultations at tough junctures.

The faculty, administrators, and staff at Ramapo College of New Jersey, where I have taught music history and culture courses since 2010, have my appreciation for supporting this research project, both collegially and financially through research grants and conference travel support. I received valuable assistance from the librarians at Ramapo College and use of the Seton Hall University Library and the New York Public Library. Ramapo's Faculty-Student Research Fund helped to compensate students for meticulously transcribing recorded interviews and other tasks; thank you to Khalisah Hamed, Rosa Javier, Gwen Manley-Muller, Joseph Morrongiello, Kenneth

Rapsas, Hannah Reasoner, Laura Veloso, and Adam Witkowski. Professional Portuguese-English translators Nadja Batdorf and Cássio Barth provided their expertise for a few transcriptions and translations. The services of Scribie.com and Temi.com assisted the transcription process.

The photographers who contributed work to this book deserve all of our gratitude: Christopher Drukker, Samuel Elijah, Kim Fox, Fran Kaufman, Bob Plotkin, Poby, Nick Suttle, Maria Traversa, and Janis Wilkins.

Fellow scholars in diverse fields have shaped my research and resulting book. Many scholars of Brazilian music and Brazilian studies have indirectly guided this project through their publications, as cited throughout the book. I want to recognize the late John Murphy, author of *Music in Brazil* (Oxford University Press, 2006); Jason Stanyek and Frederick Moehn, whose research collaboration about bossa nova in the United States sparked my project; Andrew Connell, Acácio Tadeu de Camargo Piedade, Marília Giller, Eduardo Lis, Abelita Mateus, and Bryan McCann, for their informative research about Brazilian jazz; and K. E. Goldschmitt, whose book *Bossa Mundo* (Oxford University Press, 2020) has been a continual reference. I am appreciative to the anonymous readers of the book proposal and complete manuscript, who volunteered precious time to offer support as well as critical notes for improvement. My work also benefited from feedback of anonymous readers of related research articles and several scholars who commented on chapter drafts: Erin Augis, William Bares, Gilad Cohen, Ben Neill, and my mentor Ingrid Monson. A final thanks to the Society for Ethnomusicology, the Latin American Studies Association, and other learned societies and academic institutions that cultivate intellectual growth and exchange.

Introduction

"New York Brazilian Jazz"

"It's New York Brazilian jazz," Amanda Ruzza answered.[1]

The electric bassist—a female, young adult from São Paulo, Brazil—recalled producing the album *Phantom Fish* with Sérgio Galvão, a middle-aged, male saxophonist-composer from Rio de Janeiro.[2] Galvão had been visiting Ruzza in New York City, in February 2013, when they decided to arrange and record his works that same month, during his stay. She released their record through her business Pimenta Music; distributed it through the online platforms CD Baby, iTunes, Spotify, and Amazon; and marketed it to the music press.

I had asked Ruzza, "How would you describe the sound of the album?" She continued:

"That is the ultimate New York–sound album. I made sure. I said, 'Okay, the drummer's going to be Brazilian, but the piano players are not going to be Brazilian. I don't want them to groove like a Brazilian.'" A Brazilian, Maurício Zottarelli, played drums. "But then you have Leo Genovese from Argentina playing piano and Aruán Ortiz from Cuba playing piano. And then you have Leni Stern playing the Senegalese blues groove, and you also have an American guitar player Alex Nolan" (see Figure I.1). Brazilian-American trumpeter Claudio Roditi and American trombonist and music scholar Chris Stover joined them for one track each. Ruzza noted some of their nationalities to emphasize the international makeup of ensemble members and their diverse musical influences, which contribute to intercultural musical fusions in New York City. Stern is a female, German-immigrant guitarist who regularly fuses jazz with Senegalese music and, when collaborating with Genovese, Argentine music.[3] Because this book discusses demographic diversity, I have noted gender and racial categories of musicians in this mixed-gender (three female and six male), mostly white ensemble.[4]

SamBop NYC. Marc Gidal, Oxford University Press. © Oxford University Press 2024.
DOI: 10.1093/oso/9780197619049.003.0001

Figure I.1. Ensemble of Sérgio Galvão and Amanda Ruzza at the Blue Note Jazz Club, New York, on March 14, 2014. Left to right: Alex Nolan (guitar), Leni Stern (guitar), Galvão (saxophone), Ruzza (bass), and Maurício Zottarelli (drums). Photograph captured from video. Reproduced courtesy of Sérgio Galvão.

We were having lunch outside the Rogue restaurant on Sixth Avenue and West 25th Street in Manhattan, next to a bustling sidewalk and roaring traffic. Ruzza explained:

> That is New York Brazilian jazz, because it was like, you got to get out of this whole easy solution that people in Rio de Janeiro have. "I know what feels good. I know what sounds good. Let's do always the same recipe." [...] I think that the music that Brazilians [have] done in New York is something very unique and only happens here, with certain musicians. [...] Because some people—I include myself in this pile—we walk in here to New York with this mentality—and this is my mentality and I've spoken with a lot of these people in this pile—saying like, "Well, if I want to play Brazilian music, I might as well just be in Brazil." It's too easy. I'm here, I love music, and I want to learn from people. So, we start playing all these gigs. And like what happened to me? I came with that mentality, but also, I needed to pay my rent.

She recalled in dialogue her experiences with other musicians:

And people were like, "Where are you from?"

"I'm from Brazil."

"That's so cool. Do you want to play this gig from Morocco?"

"Sure." Then you kill yourself to learn this Morocco music so you can fake it at the gig. And then you play the gig. And then they go like, "Oh, where you from?"

"I'm from Brazil."

"Oh, there's a Colombian gig."

And then you have to learn entire new like Colombian music, which is not salsa, it's not Brazilian, and they have their own *clave*. And you have to learn this stuff and you kill yourself, and then you learn a thing. Like, I worked with Leni Stern a lot. And it seems an easy gig but it's very hard for me. It drives me crazy because I have to un-Brazilianize myself. Some of the rhythms are kind of the same, but if I walk in there with a Brazilian spirit, I kill the percussionists. But you see, I'm bringing all these aspects. And then, you love jazz [Ruzza was addressing me, a jazz bassist, fan, and educator] and for us, it's fun to play jazz standards, even though Americans don't like to because all they do is play that. For us, it's fun because we don't play it. So, then we mix all this stuff and we go like, "Oh, now let's play samba." And it sounds different and we like it. But we already walked in this town with this mindset. Some people didn't. Some people, they just want to be in their comfort zone and just do that. They want to be authentic. And you know, I respect that, but in my opinion, if I would be like that, I would—that's not what I'm about—I would be an unhappy person. And that's maybe one of the reasons why I ended up leaving Brazil. Because as much as I was playing every possible gig you can imagine, from reggae to rap to samba to every possible thing, I always wanted to learn music from the world. You know what I mean?

This book explores an intersection of subjects: jazz, Brazilian genres (especially bossa nova and samba), and musical fusions as played by professional specialists based in New York City during the first two decades of the twenty-first century.[5] In this time period, I estimate that over 200 resident musicians regularly played Brazilian jazz locally, nationally, and internationally.[6] There are countless more jazz singers and instrumentalists who incorporate Brazilian works into their repertoires, at least the bossa nova hits. Here, the focus is on the experts, from the best known among them—such as Eliane Elias, Dom Salvador, Maúcha Adnet, Vinícius Cantuária, Duduka Da

Fonseca, Luciana Souza, Romero Lubambo, and Anat Cohen—to anchors of the local scene, swiftly ascending virtuosi, workaday professionals, and aspiring artists.[7]

As one of these expert professionals, Ruzza's reflective explanation overflowed with topics explored in this book. She creatively navigates competing values and pressures in order to develop her career as a musical artist in an internationally diverse city. Work opportunities abound, but in an extremely competitive industry. To generalize from Ruzza's experiences, the musicians in the book move back and forth between Brazil and the United States, as well as Europe and parts of Asia, as they collaborate, tour, and record internationally. The technologies, recording studios, distribution, and publicity have been easier for musicians to access in the United States than in Brazil. They adopt an entrepreneurial approach necessary to jumpstart a career in music, up to the point that music-industry and media professionals can add significant boosts. They need tremendous personal drive to create art while working within and beyond conventional repertoires, styles, and performance practices. They intentionally collaborate with Brazilian and non-Brazilian musicians, usually favoring Brazilians in the rhythm section to ensure authentic Brazilian grooves. Musicians of various ages who have developed individual voices in contemporary styles collaborate to develop novel collective sounds. They need to work flexibly and eclectically in order to establish themselves professionally. They experience the challenges and rewards of playing genres outside their comfort zones that reflect New York's cultural demography and its strength in jazz. New York's multicultural musical sounds and values affect Brazilians, whether they play Brazilian music or create new fusions. The *Phantom Fish* project had a female co-leader and multiple female musicians in the ensemble, traits that are unusual in the male-majority Brazilian jazz scene and the larger jazz industry; and the ensemble included one Black musician among otherwise white musicians, which also reflects the low numbers of African descendants who specialize in Brazilian jazz in New York. The immigrant musicians, who speak Portuguese and other languages natively, may speak colloquial English fluently, as Ruzza does, while other musicians speak English with less fluency and maintain strong spoken accents, which affects their assimilation into American society. In sum, the musicians featured in this book develop and apply competencies in multiple music systems, languages, and cultures while working with collaborators who are diverse musically and demographically, all of which affects their art and careers and collectively shape what Ruzza calls "New York Brazilian jazz." While Ruzza is the only person I met who uttered this catchy phrase, it encapsulates many musicians' musical practices and experiences.

Musicians move to New York City to advance their musical art and careers because of its myriad opportunities, yet they face an extremely challenging music industry that has continued to worsen for them. They include younger and older, queer and straight, female, male, and possibly also non-binary musicians; usually from a middle economic class, they have different national, ethnic, and racial ancestries; and they move to New York not only from Brazil but also from elsewhere in South America, around the United States, Canada, Japan, Israel, and Europe. During rehearsals, shows, tours, and recording projects they collaborate and experiment to create wide-ranging music that combine influences from Brazilian genres, jazz, and other music, notably classical (i.e., Western art music), funk, and rock music. Their works combine Afro-Euro-American fusions from Brazil and the United States as well as eclectic influences from their personal backgrounds and other local scenes. In the process, they grow as artists and people. As the musicians interact with each other, study new music, perform in a musical culture that values diversity and stylistic fusions, and appease market preferences and demands, they expand their musical competencies, original music, often their foreign-language skills, cross-cultural understandings, and, in turn, perspectives about the world and themselves. When they tour internationally, they share new music with local musicians and audiences as well as absorb local trends when they can, which they then spread further. Many of the successful musicians from outside the United States have extraordinary talents that, in addition to delighting audiences, have brought them privileged access to international mobility through special visas in order to live and work in the United States.

Despite the creative outcomes of these global circulations, for New York–based musicians to earn a living in the local and international music markets poses significant challenges that have been exacerbated since the turn of the millennium by declining revenues in the recording industry. By the 2000s, most musicians had to tour nationally and internationally in order to earn enough money to live comfortably in New York due to the high cost of living as well as the particularities of its live music industry and decreased revenue from record sales. The economic crises of 2001 and 2008, and stricter US immigration policies since September 11, 2001, made their careers more challenging financially and logistically. Yet, I have found that many musicians still moved to New York City in order to advance their art and careers; the musicians in this book moved to New York in each decade since the 1960s.

Then the Covid-19 pandemic struck the United States in March 2020, bringing live performances and most recording studios to a standstill, thereby obliterating the remaining major sources of income for musicians. The musicians I had interviewed who had already been teaching or composing music tried to increase those activities, while most others relied on public assistance, aid from nonprofit organizations, meager savings, spousal income and limited family support, or non-musical work. If they avoided catching the virus itself, most suffered in their mental health to varying degrees. Some took a break from music to attend to their health and financial well-being, moved away from New York, or pivoted with new technologies. All the musicians I contacted during the pandemic who had US citizenship were able to survive financially with the help of federal relief checks and state unemployment aid in combination with other financial support, minimal income, and reduced or deferred rent. The musicians worst affected economically were those with immigration statuses coincidentally in flux during the pandemic. Ruzza, for example, had a permanent resident visa (a "green card") when the pandemic hit New York City, but she had received it within a couple of years and therefore could not utilize all its benefits, importantly food subsidies. She accepted free food from community handouts, successfully applied for small grants from nonprofit organizations supporting musicians, and negotiated a lower rent with her landlord. Though too depressed to practice and compose music, she voluntarily organized outdoor performances on commercial strips in Brooklyn, discovering the structural obstacles such endeavors face. With minimal prospects for income, she reluctantly accepted work that felt demeaning and demoralizing. By 2022, however, freelance work playing bass slowly resumed, notably in pit orchestras as Broadway shows reopened.[8] New York was barely a financially sustainable destination even before the pandemic. Advancements in technology, media, and mobility have made it unnecessary for musicians around the world to play music together in person and record outside their home or with others in a single location. This was already true before the pandemic forced the mass adoption of remote collaboration technologies. Nevertheless, I find that musicians still value in-person music-making, from which they benefit financially.

The musicians in this book with expertise in Brazilian jazz actively cultivate their own musicianship, intercultural competencies, and self-identities while contributing to the development of collective musical practices, repertoires, and aesthetics associated with two countries. The necessity to incorporate individuals into a culture concept is crucial for this study of musicians with talent, skills, and determination to shape genres through their creativity, as did countless musicians before them. I understand culture and cultivation (used without moralistic implications) as co-developments between shared ideas, values, practices, and behaviors—including music— and individuals' education, socialization, participation, innovations, and, in turn, contributions.[9] While studying, playing, and composing Brazilian-jazz fusions, musicians learn and adapt to multiple genres associated with the United States and Brazil, which shape their own personalities. They also participate in global circulations of new music, changing musical conventions, and global music markets, which includes the music they share with each other and audiences in multiple countries. These cumulative experiences— intercultural and international, local and translocal—alter how they understand the world and see themselves. Whether immigrant or US-born, and regardless of their musical backgrounds, through prolonged engagement with Brazilian jazz, the musicians' changing self-identities are influenced by the social institutions, commercial markets, and cultural aspects of multiple nations. This phenomenon is what this book will explain primarily through the lens of *transnational polymusicality*, the simultaneous development of multiple musical competencies and national-cultural identifications. They are learning and shaping culture, cultivating themselves, and influencing others.

Brazilian Jazz in New York and Its Jazz Industry

What Is Brazilian Jazz?

Brazilian jazz can mean any combination of Brazilian music and jazz, with bossa nova as the most famous example. Historians of Brazilian jazz, usually called "instrumental music" or "Brazilian instrumental music" in Brazil, have highlighted jazz influences since the early twentieth century as well as parallel developments to bossa nova and expanding directions after the 1960s.[10] This book will discuss parts of this history when relevant, particularly its interpretive history, in this chapter; bossa nova in Chapter 3; and samba jazz in Chapter 4. Here is a whirlwind summary: the early history of jazz in Brazil included dance bands that played jazz to accompany the fox-trot as well as Brazilian genres that included cousin Euro-Afro-Brazilian dance genres *maxixe*, Brazilian tango, and later *choro*.[11] Jazz also paralleled and occasionally influenced developments of *choro*, a semi-improvised practice that is often considered a precursor to, and continuous influence on, Brazilian jazz.[12] During the 1920s, Brazilian musicians at home and abroad adapted jazz into Brazilian genres.[13] The most famous of these musicians was woodwindist Alfredo "Pixinguinha" da Rocha Viana Jr., a Black Afro-Brazilian who infused *choro* with jazz after sojourning in jazz-enamored Paris.[14] The blues, from the United States, began influencing Brazilian musicians at least as early as the 1950s, via live performances by American musicians and recordings;[15] *baião* from Northeastern Brazil and the blues already shared scales.[16] In the late 1950s and 1960s, bossa nova emerged along with instrumental music later called "samba jazz" in urban settings where musicians were also playing American jazz.[17] These scenes in Rio de Janeiro and São Paulo nurtured a few musicians featured in this book, who eventually migrated to the United States: Dom Salvador, Cidinho Teixeira, and Eumir Deodato as well as Antônio Carlos Jobim. Among the American jazz musicians who were highly influential for Brazilians during the 1950s, Salvador and Teixeira singled out Nat King Cole, George Shearing (English American), and the originators of bebop and cool jazz.[18] The early 1960s marked the international explosion of bossa nova; although it began in Brazil, collaborations with Americans produced smash recordings that shaped the transnational nature of Brazilian jazz. As Brazilian musicologist Acácio Tadeu de Camargo Piedade summarized this pivotal moment:

> In the midst of these various waves [of Brazilian popular music], the emerging Brazilian jazz was growing, sustained mainly by *bossa nova* and its reflections in the United States, where the celebrated meeting of João Gilberto and Stan Getz symbolized the encounter between the Brazilianess [sic] of *bossa nova* and the Americanness of jazz, launching a dialogue of musicalities that would become central to Brazilian jazz.[19]

Also during the 1960s, pianist Sérgio Mendes combined Brazilian songs, up-tempo bossa nova, jazz, and popular styles to shape a Brazilian pop sound for international audiences.[20] In 1970s Brazil, the innovators Hermeto Pascoal and Egberto Gismonti took instrumental music in new directions, for example, by incorporating further aspects of Northeastern Brazilian folk music; their international popularity surged during the 1980s, as have the careers of their disciples.[21] Brazilians abroad who played jazz fusion in the 1970s, notably Airto Moreira, Flora Purim, Naná Vasconcelos, and Milton Nascimento, contributed Brazilian grooves, percussion timbres, repertoire, and other elements.[22] Meanwhile, a national and international *choro* revival movement has distanced itself from, yet continues to influence, Brazilian-jazz fusions.[23] These are the major developments and trajectories, while musicians have continued to expand Brazilian-jazz fusions.

Brazilian jazz can be explained in multiple ways: as a fusion of cousin Afro-diasporic traditions (jazz, samba, *choro*, *baião*, etc.); as a hemispheric hybrid of these already hybrid Afro-Euro-American genres; as a combination of nationalized Brazilian and US genres (jazz and samba) that co-developed with some interactions and collaborations along the way; and as its own genre that has been embraced by musicians and audiences worldwide. Brazilian jazz features innovations and cultural practices of Afro-Brazilian and African American musicians, racialized and oppressed people in both countries. The music often shows European qualities and aesthetics, and is performed and composed by white musicians with European ancestry who have benefited from white privilege in the two racially hierarchical countries, including their music industries. Musicians with neither African nor European ancestry also create Brazilian jazz and may contribute their own cultural conventions or interpretations. While some musicians and audiences may associate Brazilian jazz with African-descended musicians in the Americas, other people might associate the music with Brazilian nationals or Latin Americans in general; still others may view it as one of many globally performed genres available for anyone to perform, compose, and enjoy regardless of ethno-racial or national identities or associations. All these perspectives may coexist within audiences interpreting the same musical performance; I did not survey audiences about this topic. Interpretations of the music may also depend on the audience's location—explored later in this chapter—such as a concert in São Paulo with more nationalist associations, a concert in New York City with broader associations, or a festival performance in Europe or Asia with universalist interpretations of the music.

Regarding key terms, sometimes I write "Brazilian jazz" as a shorthand and to imply a somewhat unified genre of conventional approaches and related cultural aspects, while other times I write "Brazilian-jazz fusions" to emphasize a wide range of creative practices and products with eclectic influences. I consider "fusion" an approach and sometimes a genre itself that includes stylistic qualities and cultural aspects, discussed in Chapter 4 with regard to samba jazz. Some labels in Brazil seem to hide the significant jazz influences in the music. American ethnomusicologist Andrew Connell summarized the situation, which he studied in Brazil: "Sometimes known as Brazilian jazz, *música improvisada* (improvised music), *música instrumental brasileira contemporânea* (contemporary Brazilian instrumental music), hard-bossa, jazz-samba, or *samba novo* (new samba), *música instrumental brasileira* is an umbrella term which covers a number of musical styles, rhythms, and forms and thus eludes exact definition. The term Brazilian jazz is more commonly used in the United States."[24] Add to these terms "*música popular instrumental brasileira*" (Brazilian instrumental popular music), for Piedade views the genre as a subset of Brazilian popular music (*música popular brasileira* or *MPB*).[25] I use "Brazilian jazz" as an umbrella term that includes bossa nova and samba jazz as well as jazz renditions of popular Brazilian songs and even some jazz-influenced renditions of other Brazilian genres like *choro, baião, frevo, toada, afoxé, maracatu*, and *MPB*. Curiously, the Brazilian terms omit singing, which reinforces a recurring notion that Brazilian jazz is instrumental music that features improvisation, even when adapting songs, whereas songs with vocalists are considered something else. For instance, samba jazz is often distinguished by encompassing instrumental and improvisatory renditions of bossa nova songs and other repertoires, and therefore also known as "instrumental bossa nova."[26] Discursive distinctions between popular song and Brazilian instrumental music, and between sung bossa nova and instrumental bossa nova, or samba jazz, parallel a tendency in jazz histories to misrepresent jazz as instrumental music at the expense of vocalists and female musicians.[27]

If Latin jazz is "the other jazz" when compared to mainstream jazz, as ethnomusicologist Christopher Washburne stated, then Brazilian jazz is one of many other Latin jazzes.[28] The label "Latin jazz" can include Brazilian jazz, though it most often refers to Afro-Hispanic-Caribbean-influenced jazz fusions.[29] Brazilian jazz covers diverse sub-styles, while it generally implies the use of rhythms and grooves from Brazilian genres and the harmonies and approaches to improvisation typical of jazz. "Lemon merengue pie" was musician Mario Bauzá's analogous summary of Caribbean-styled Latin jazz: "Jazz in the top and Afro-Cuban rhythms in the bottom."[30] Ruzza described *Phantom Fish* similarly, adding the metaphor of a story:

The main idea of this album was to keep the bottom of it (bass and drums) Brazilian, but everything else a collection of different musicians that all had one passion in common: groove, harmony and an open mind. [. . .] I wanted every melody and every groove to be specifically connected to each other, as if the listener would be reading a wonderful novel and feeling that he or she was being told a beautiful story. And that's the story of Sérgio Galvão, the man who went on a trip from Rio de Janeiro to New York and decided to tell his life story (his melodies) with a New York spirit.[31]

In Brazil, improvisation is strongly associated with jazz, though not uniquely, since *choro* also features improvisation.[32] The conventional instrumentation of American jazz bands helped to differentiate Brazilian-jazz fusions from other Brazilian genres. Pixinguinha adopted jazz instrumentation he observed in Paris, and the combination of piano, bass, and drum set influenced the development of piano trios in Brazil, which became central to the bossa nova and samba jazz scenes in Rio de Janeiro and São Paulo in the 1960s.[33] When combining two musical worlds, however much they have already been intertwined, there are issues of styles, conventions, melodies, approaches to phrasing, song forms, swing feels, and other subtleties. Sometimes these stylistic characteristics overlap, other times they are complementary, and on other occasions they sound jarring. Piedade calls this tension a "friction of musicalities" between Brazilian and North American approaches, a recurring point for discussion in this book.[34] I generally agree with Piedade's interpretation, yet friction is one of many ways that two related musical traditions interact as musicians create fusions, discussed in Chapter 4. The complexities within and beyond these generalizations are explored through descriptions and analyses of musical examples, which incorporate the musicians' backgrounds and intentions.

New York City circa 2000–2020

This book's title and Ruzza's clever phrase beg a key question: is Brazilian jazz in New York particularly different from Brazilian jazz composed, performed, or recorded anywhere else? There are recording projects similar to *Phantom Fish* made in Rio de Janeiro, Los Angeles, and Tokyo; and probably in Berlin and Buenos Aires, Lisbon and London, Tel Aviv and Toronto. Indeed, some recordings by musicians in this study were made in both New York and Brazil.

I am comfortable saying that the music is *of New York* without being *unique to New York*. Moreover, Brazilian jazz seems to have different cultural significance in New York than it does in Brazil. Some aspects of contemporary New York that are intertwined with the music and musicians in this book are extra-musical, meaning outside musical technicalities and instead based in cultural and societal contexts. Also influential are the values and desires that circulate in New York: to create original artworks and not solely commercially viable works; to draw on the myriad nationalities and subcultures present, that is, a value in multiculturalism and intercultural collaboration; to live and work in an epicenter of jazz, instrumental music, and experimental music; to live in a region with large numbers of other Brazilians; and to embrace a level of music professionalism less common elsewhere. These characteristics are all part of New York's appeal and influence for the musicians I met. Further, these values can affect their musical creations that distinguish them from projects created elsewhere. Ruzza, for example, has lived in several metropolises that she contrasts with New York: she grew up São Paulo, where she already had eclectic musical tastes and activities. She moved to the United States to study at Berklee College of Music in Boston, though she completed her bachelor's degree at the New School in New York City. In between schools, she toured with the country band Mustang Sally, based in Nashville, and visited Los Angeles, where she once predicted she would work in the pop-music industry. Based on these experiences, she finds New York unique enough a setting to settle there and say confidently that her sound is "New York Brazilian jazz."

New York has provided me a location to observe the creation and global circulation of Brazilian-jazz fusions. The frame of the city helps to provide one view of a larger situation, a local hub in a trans-local paradigm. Pragmatically, narrowing the research focus to contemporary New York afforded me a depth and breadth within a smaller collection of musicians, venues, and audiences than if my research frame had been the United States, North America, the Americas, the Atlantic world, or the world. Likewise, the temporal focus on the first two decades of the new millennium narrowed the study to a manageable scope rather than trying to analyze the entire history of Brazilian jazz in New York. Luciana Souza has called her songs "snapshots" of larger stories; likewise, this book is a snapshot of a long and wide international history well beyond the confines of the book.

The ethnographic examples in this book took place in New York City during the 2010s. The specific musicians I witnessed, interviewed, or analyzed on record were primarily from this time and place because they were accessible to me. Had I conducted research in the early 2000s, I would likely have researched several different musicians who lived in New York then and were more prominent: perhaps Badi Assad instead of her niece Clarice Assad; Marianne Ebert, who sang weekly at the Zinc Bar, instead of Monika Oliveira, who replaced her; and record producer Rick Warm of Malandro Records, before he moved to Ohio and changed professions. The lessons learned from the musicians I interviewed or studied from afar are likely similar to lessons I would have learned a decade earlier and similarly informative about changes in the new millennium. Many musicians I interviewed have lived in New York since the 1970s through the 1990s. So, for comparison, I have used their reflections on the situation during those decades as well as their recordings and other documentary evidence.

My research focuses on New York City instead of other US centers for Brazilian musicians, so it reflects issues more specific to New York than elsewhere. It may be impossible to know what these are without comparative data, but my suspicion is that the dynamics of the local music scenes—specifically for jazz, Latin jazz, Latin music generally, and experimental art music, artistically and economically—have shaped the Brazilian music scene and the Brazilian-jazz fusion projects. Most Brazilians, Japanese, and Israelis I spoke with said they moved to New York in part to be in the jazz Mecca, for they self-identified as jazz musicians in their home countries. Except for New Orleans, other US cities do not have the intensity of tourist interest in jazz, abundance of jazz clubs, and draw for international musicians primarily interested in jazz. Those interested in film scoring, studio work, or commercial music are more likely to settle in Los Angeles; those interested in the blues, Chicago; those interested in Latin pop, Miami; and those interested in higher education may go to Boston. Personal and family ties may bring musicians to any of these cities as well as San Francisco, Seattle, Texan cities, and elsewhere with sizable Brazilian populations.

The Jazz Market

The jazz scene and industry, in New York and elsewhere, is the main market within which Brazilian jazz can be heard. Brazilian jazz is peripheral to traditional jazz styles and is more marginal than Afro-Hispanic-Caribbean-derived Latin jazz. Many of the nightclubs that hire Brazilian jazz acts are jazz clubs. The venues and festivals in Europe in which these musicians perform focus on jazz. The companies that record the local musicians are often jazz labels. This does not mean that Brazilian-jazz fusions are central to jazz, however. Sometimes they are categorized as world music. Two bossa nova singers, Bebel Gilberto and Luciana Souza, have received Grammy Award nominations in different categories: world music for Gilberto and jazz for Souza.

A main reason for the connection between jazz and these Brazilian-jazz fusions is because of bossa nova, the style that coalesced in Brazil during the late 1950s and made a huge impression on US jazz musicians and audiences in the early 1960s before Beatlemania seized mainstream attention and Brazilian popular music styles changed. Bossa nova continued to be popular outside Brazil as an adult-oriented music through the popular jazz-oriented singers, so-called big singers from Frank Sinatra, Nat King Cole, and Tony Bennett in the 1960s to Diana Krall and John Pizzarelli in the 2000s. At the turn of the millennium, Bebel Gilberto's electronica–bossa nova fusion boosted the interest of audiences and thus venues and musicians in bossa nova and other Brazilian-jazz fusions.[35] Bossa nova, and the related samba jazz, have stayed the main focus of Brazilian music in international jazz scenes even though musicians I interviewed who are deeply familiar with other Brazilian genres try to play them professionally and introduce audiences to them. This is an uphill battle and causes frustrations and tensions in the Brazilian music scene of New York, especially because presenters find that shows of bossa nova are more likely to attract audiences. I call this tension "bossa nova anxieties": although musicians enjoy playing bossa nova, they also want to play other styles and repertoire, and some resent the industry's bias for bossa nova, explained in Chapter 3.

Most musicians I studied, whether US-born Americans or international immigrants, had considered themselves jazz musicians before becoming involved with the Brazilian music scene. Musicians moved to New York in order to play jazz but found more work and personal interests combining jazz with Brazilian music. Their trajectories resulted from artistic, pragmatic, and nationally overdetermined forces. Just as bossa nova and other Brazilian jazz fusions hover in the periphery of the jazz scene, so do most musicians in this book because their aspirations have been curtailed or redirected. Notable exceptions are Eliane Elias and Anat Cohen, immigrants who established themselves within the jazz industry before professionally expanding into Brazilian jazz.

Relevant to this book, jazz history has been presented through at least three cultural frames that are sometimes isolated and debated yet are more productively considered together: First, jazz is first and foremost an African American genre, an Afro-diasporic music, created and developed primarily by musicians racialized and oppressed as Black in the United States. Second, jazz also became embraced nationally, even patriotically, in the United States as an American genre, over a gradual process of dismissal then acceptance bolstered by continual integration and appropriation by white musicians and audiences. Third, jazz is a prominent international genre that spread globally and became localized in many countries as it was interpreted though local perspectives or was fused with local music. Many have described jazz through these three frames, in which identity politics regarding race, gender, and sexuality also played out.[36] Taken together, these frames can account for much of jazz's history, key originators and innovators, wide dissemination and popularity, a heterogeneity of contributions, contextualized sub-styles, and myriad cultural interpretations.

To add details to this history, jazz was created and developed by African Americans, an extremely oppressed racialized minority in the United States.[37] It became distinguished from progenitor genres around the turn of the twentieth century as a musical language and constellation of performance practices that included elaborating on contemporary music: the blues and other African American genres, dance music, brass band music, popular songs, show tunes, European art music, folk music, religious music, Latin American music, and so on. US economic and military might during and after World War I helped to spread jazz around the world via touring musicians, recordings, sheet music, and radio broadcasting as well as foreign interests in a music that often represented modernity, progress, freedom, and counterculture.[38] Paradoxically, while jazz was usually promoted or received internationally as a positive sign of ingenuity, modernity, progress, freedom, and democracy (especially during the Cold War), African Americans continued to suffer oppression and the music suffered stigmatized associations in the United States as well as sometimes internationally, notably in Nazi-era Germany.[39] Although jazz had been associated with femininity and modern womanhood in the 1920s, at some point jazz became linked to masculinity, in particular Black masculinity.[40] The Cold War of the 1950s brought ire from empowered, socially conservative politicians in the United States that pushed underground the queer culture in jazz scenes, one of many such eras in that country.[41] During the same decade, however, the racialized and sexualized stigmatizations contributed to the image and popularity of jazz for young, countercultural, non-Black audiences and musicians.[42] Meanwhile musicians other than US Americans and African Americans have played jazz as amateurs and professionals throughout its history and contributed to stylistic developments. Compared to African American musicians, white jazz musicians experienced greater access to mass media, promotion, and employment opportunities, although had different (usually less) confidence in their abilities, receptions as authentic, levels of contribution, and claims to authority.[43] For chauvinistic reasons, female jazz musicians in the United States have long been marginalized, discouraged, belittled, and excluded from jazz histories throughout the twentieth century and into the twenty-first.[44] By the end of the twentieth century, jazz had been transformed into the category of art music in the United States with diminished racial stigmatization, long replaced by other African American secular genres as popular idioms, from rhythm and blues and rock 'n' roll to soul and funk, and then hip-hop and electronic dance music with various labels.[45] Yet, sexism and homophobia in jazz scenes, industries, and education still persist.[46] Jazz musicians around the world have self-identified with the music, fused aspects with local music traditions, and shared their individual innovations with the jazz world, with minimal influence in the United States.[47] The flexibility and accessibility of jazz, despite its musical complexities, may have helped musicians fuse it with other music, notably folk music in non-US locations.[48] In addition to recognizing the historical expansion from the United States to international cultural frames for jazz participation and interpretation, central to jazz have been its African American origins, practices, innovations, aesthetics, and cultural meanings as well as its associations with the United States, in addition to nationalistic discourses abroad.[49] The next section elaborates on the contrast between nationalistic associations of Brazilian jazz in Brazil and the United States.

Cultural Meanings Fit Contexts

Brazilian jazz carries different cultural meanings regarding international politics in Brazil than in the United States, even though the music made in both countries may sound generally the same. According to scholars of music in the Brazilian setting, bossa nova, samba jazz, and Brazilian jazz in general have evoked strong feelings about relations between the United States and Brazil. Even though the countries are allies and cooperate politically and economically, jazz has been associated with the outsized prominence of American cultural products in Brazil and therefore can represent American cultural dominance, even imperialism, and political-economic intervention; meanwhile in Brazil, samba has continued to epitomize Brazilian nationalism.[50] Influences of jazz in Brazilian music have often been regarded as Americanization of Brazilian music, culture, and identity, whether desired or rejected. In 1960s Brazil, nationalist and cultural debates in the critical discourses about bossa nova and samba jazz in Brazil continued where they had left off from the 1930s, when jazz symbolized American cultural and economic imperialism while samba and *choro* symbolized Brazilian nationalism.[51] Drawing on his participant-observation research in the more recent Brazilian jazz scene of São Paulo, Piedade argues that Brazilian jazz should not be simply interpreted as Brazilians playing their version of North American jazz, but something more categorically consolidated and politically profound. Utilizing Brazilian discourses of nationalism, authenticity, modernism, and cannibalism of foreign cultures, he explains that Brazilian musicians devour North American musical languages, such as bebop, while consciously using music considered Brazilian, such as *choro*, as they create Brazilian expressions of a native-foreign struggle. To excerpt his explanation:

> *Bebopear* [to bebop, as a verb] is the expression of the Brazilian reading of the jazz musicality, yet it is simultaneously both valuable and fearsome [. . .] along with the drive to avoid contamination from the bebop paradigm and to seek an expression that is more rooted in Brazil, there is an absolute cannibalization of the jazz musicality.[52]

Piedade emphasizes that current Brazilian jazz musically plays out tensions between the two nationally associated traditions in a symbolic musical discourse about uneven international relations.

While neither I have seen a critique of Piedade's political explanation nor do I doubt him, the interpretation that musicians are expressing a nationalist critique of US imperialism through Brazilian jazz seems distant from the perspectives I have gleaned in the New York scene. Brazilian immigrant musicians—and musicians of any other nationality—who play Brazilian jazz in New York do not explain their musical activities as expressions of bilateral tensions or anxieties about Americanization of Brazilian culture. I have never heard anything close to this from the musicians. Nor has a musician told me that they were subversively resisting mainstream jazz by championing Brazilian jazz from within the system. Instead I heard quite the opposite from immigrant musicians, that they revel in combining traditions and take great pride in their results. They have loved US jazz most of their lives and wanted to move to New York and the United States to pursue jazz at its source. They seek or sought green cards to work permanently, gain US citizenship, and continue living in the United States. Some may strive for incorporation into US culture, whether through assimilated or hyphenated identities.[53] Jazz helps them integrate into US society, as it has for numerous immigrant musicians—Italians, European Jews, and Latin Americans—though also a sense of double identities may attract some Brazilians as it has attracted Asian Americans to African American music.[54] The perspectives of US-born musicians not of Brazilian descent will be addressed in other chapters, but neither do they explain their music as expressing tensions between Brazilian nationalism and US imperialism.

Hence, the cultural meanings of Brazilian jazz appear different in the New York context, and perhaps more generally in the United States, than they do in Brazil. This conclusion is unsurprising, since myriad studies have shown that migrant musicians and music that circulates far from home often develop and accumulate new cultural meanings, uses, and functions in their new settings.[55] These distant locations would reasonably influence the ways that musicians, audiences, and critics interpret Brazilian jazz through the lenses of bilateral relations and nationalism.

Political anxieties about jazz fusions in Brazil are echoed in case studies from around the world, as the edited volumes *Jazz Planet* and *Jazz Worlds/World Jazz* illustrate.[56] Some musicians and listeners outside the United States may associate jazz positively with a modern or cosmopolitan identity, while others may view jazz suspiciously as a symbol or agent of US might and capitalist global exploitation. By contrast, the most common outlook of Brazilian jazz in New York, a center of American jazz, reaffirms jazz's positive standing in the world, embraced as a sign of flattery or multiculturalism. Musicologists Goffredo Plastino and Philip Vilas Bohlman underscored this contrast when comparing multiple scenarios: "When at home, jazz aspires to the world, welcoming the cross-fertilization of fusion, not as an intrusion of otherness but rather a proliferation of selfness. When in the world, jazz musicians feel the pull toward home, their home, in which jazz sounds musical and ideological dialects that they speak only with those closest to them.

World jazz does not retreat from the tension between home and the world; rather, it realizes the tension and its consequences."[57]

Regardless of differing bilateral political meanings that musicians and audiences might interpret with Brazilian jazz in the United States and Brazil, in both countries the music is correlated with whiter racial demographics. On the other hand, audience members and musicians likely interpret various associations even when attending the same shows in New York. As Chapter 1 will explain, American musicians with many ancestries have been involved with Brazilian-jazz fusions in New York, usually in collaboration with Brazilian musicians, who comprise around half the musicians in the scene. White American musicians with jazz backgrounds are the largest demographic of non-Brazilians playing Brazilian jazz in New York. Similarly in Brazil, instrumental music is played mostly by musicians considered white or whiter according to Brazilian racial discourse.[58] Paula Botelho argues, in her analysis of music criticism about Brazilian music in the *New York Times* during the 2000s, that Brazilian genres most similar to jazz—bossa nova, samba jazz, and Brazilian jazz—enjoyed the highest levels of acceptance in the United States because these genres are considered closest to high culture, Euro-American musical aesthetics, and whiteness. By contrast, Brazilian genres that suggest more African heritage are treated by critics with less respect, considered lower on the cultural hierarchies.[59]

Bossa nova and cool jazz, which are both musically and socio-historically related, were closely associated with white musicians and audiences, even though interracial circles of musicians developed these styles in both countries. Jazz historians have argued that from the late 1940s through the 1950s, cool jazz was an interracial collaborative development that drew significantly on African American precedents along with Euro-American aesthetics; yet, when contrasted to bebop, its emergence offered white American audiences to watch white performers play a more accessible style and thus a comfortable distance from African American culture.[60] In 1960s Brazil, bossa nova was criticized as too white, politically aloof, and overly influenced by North American jazz, thus distanced from genres consider originally Afro-Brazilian or nationalistically Brazilian, notably samba.[61] Musicologist K. E. Goldschmitt connects these situations because bossa nova spread internationally via cool jazz and US jazz critics received both genres similarly as stylistically bland (compared to bebop, hard bop, and free jazz), politically disengaged (compared to the civil rights movement), demographically white and upper-middle class (compared to African American jazz musicians), and commercially too successful.[62]

Despite these strong associations with whiteness in Brazil and the United States, Brazilian jazz in the United States exists in the margins of the mainstream jazz market and is generally associated with Brazil and Latin America. Its Latin identity provides an alternative identity to binary simplifications of white or Black in the United States, what anthropologist Deborah Pacini Hernandez describes as Latin music's "unstable location within an industry" in the United States focused on "unambiguous racial and ethnic categories."[63] This Latin identity partially qualifies the prevalence of white and mixed-race Latin American musicians who perform in New York. Hence, even if historically informed observers associate Brazilian jazz with whiter demographics, US audiences may interpret the music as Brazilian or Latin American and may perceive the musicians primarily as foreign, exotic, Brazilian, Latinx, or of mixed heritage. As well, since whiteness studies have argued that self-identified whites are less likely to notice or note whiteness compared to other racialized groups, white audiences may not perceive Brazilian jazz as white.[64] I did not survey audiences about this topic either.

Brazilian jazz in New York has different contextualized meanings and relationships to US genres than it has in Brazil. First, musicians seem more interested in fitting into the existing jazz scene and creating cross-cultural connections and fusions than expressing musically tensions between US cultural imperialism and Brazilian nationalism. If antagonism is palpable in São Paulo to Piedade, then cooperation appears an overall musical goal in New York. Part of this difference may be due to the dynamics that half the musician experts of Brazilian jazz in New York are not Brazilian. The New York setting of samba jazz discourse also differs from that in Brazil in ways that seem both musically and professionally advantageous for musicians. Botelho's findings that Brazilian jazz connects with high culture in New York suggest that musicians may market their music as samba jazz and bossa nova in New York partially in order to attract the appreciation and patronage from higher-paying audiences than they would by calling it samba or Brazilian popular music alone. At the same time, distinguishing the uniqueness of their fusion from mainstream jazz also emphasizes their specializations in a niche style, which could also generate more work.

The value of Brazilian jazz in New York's jazz scene, and possibly everywhere in US jazz scenes, is largely to provide stylistic diversity, whether or not the musicians have expertise performing Brazilian jazz. Brazilian-jazz fusions contribute positively to jazz shows by entertaining audiences whose tastes may be wider than straight-ahead jazz, or casual listeners who might become bored with less variety. Stylistic diversity helps jazz musicians and venues appeal to broader audiences and thereby stay financially solvent. These points are discussed in Chapter 3, with respect to bossa nova, and Chapter 5, regarding professionals and markets.

For mainstream jazz venues in New York to include Brazilian jazz shows allows them to exhibit openness to diversity within a broadly inclusive jazz umbrella that includes global-jazz fusions. Because these fusions are non-threatening assets for mainstream jazz in New York, the world-jazz fusions also serve to celebrate jazz at home as an international genre, a worldwide success story. If jazz has contributed to US cultural imperialism abroad, then in New York the allegorical colonial subjects are presenting their nationalized interpretations at the jazz masters' headquarters. The presence of fusions in the jazz Mecca also reinforces the authenticity of straight-ahead jazz styles; in other words, the explicitly mixed styles, especially if considered inauthentic, bolster the classical, traditional, and canonical jazz.[65]

Chapter Summaries

This book is not a chronological history, but instead it examines different interrelated topics in each chapter. Following this Introduction, Chapter 1, "'Paying Dues' and 'Carrying Flags': Demographic Diversity and Inequities among Musicians," analyzes a dataset I compiled of 173 musicians who were actively performing Brazilian jazz in New York between the years 2000 and 2020. To explain the distribution of musicians by social categories (nationality, race, and gender) in relation to social dynamics and inequities, I draw on the musicians' perspectives, sociodemographic scholarship, and published data about Brazilian immigrants in the United States and jazz musicians in New York. Approximately half of the musicians are from Brazil, while another quarter are US-born Americans; and around 70 percent of musicians are male. Despite the strong African-diasporic roots of samba and jazz and their histories in racial politics, Brazilian jazz in New York (and in Brazil) is primarily played and listened to by white people of European descent, whether or not they are also Latin American or US Latinx. A minority of musicians and audiences are descendants of Black Africans, East or South Asians, of mixed race, or otherwise considered people of color.

The chapter introduces racial categories, ideologies, and inequities in Brazil compared to the United States, and their impact on transnational migrants. The most significant forces that shaped the demographic imbalances of musicians appear to be societal structures and institutions, historic and current, that have been racist, sexist, and classist. These unfair systems have impeded Brazilian immigrants, people of African descent, and women from working in this scene. These forces seem to have caused greater obstacles than interpersonal discrimination among musicians, who tend to act on their progressive values. Lastly, I consider critiques of exploitative cultural appropriation in this heterogeneous scene of musicians who play transnational hybrid music.

Chapter 2, "SamBop, Brazuca, and Transnational Polymusicalities," presents the book's umbrella framework to interpret the musicians and their music: transnational polymusicalities. This combines the social science theory of transnationalism and the ethnomusicology theory of bimusicality, more broadly conceived as polymusicality. The musicians in this book have developed affinities and identifications with at least two countries, Brazil and the United States, through their prolonged study and practice of music. While learning musical skills and repertoire, people usually gain other cultural competencies—with language, customs, and interpersonal relations. As musicians co-develop musical and intercultural competencies associated with the United States and Brazil, their own self-identities expand to include affinities with two countries. However, when people perform music associated with countries and cultures other than their own, the potential critiques of inauthenticity and appropriation loom large, regardless of musical competency or the music's hybridity. And although the musicians in this book expertly combine multiple music traditions, their shortcomings in a second tradition are the subject of a discourse among musicians about musical accents, akin to spoken accents. Spoken and musical accents also relate to their abilities to assimilate. Analytical frameworks related to transnationalism—diaspora, the Afro-Atlantic, cosmopolitanism, and postnationalism—provide alternative and overlapping insights about the situation. The theoretical explanations are interspersed with profiles of musicians who exemplify transnational polymusicalities: Dom Salvador (continued in Chapter 4), Eliane Elias, Romero Lubambo, Anat Cohen, Miho Nobuzane, and Richard Boukas. The chapter opens with explanations of "SamBop" and "Brazuca," neologisms coined by Brazilians that encapsulate dual identifications with Brazil and the United States through music and life experiences, respectively. As a fusion of samba and bebop that evokes transnational polymusicalities, SamBop aptly helps to title this book.

The next two chapters focus on music as well as the musicians' perspectives in relation to cultural and commercial issues. Chapter 3, "'Bossa Nova York': Popularity, Singers, and Anxieties," delves into several topics concerning the most famous type of Brazilian-jazz fusion in New York City and around the world. A comparison of several renditions of the song "Dindi" by Antônio Carlos Jobim and Aloysio de Oliveira illustrates distinctive musical interpretations as well as nuances of musical notation. Portraits of three prominent singers of bossa nova—Maúcha Adnet, Luciana Souza, and Vinícius Cantuária—highlight their connections to jazz practices of interpretation, improvisation, and experimentation. Turning to North American stereotypes of Brazil, bossa nova provides alternative impressions about femininity and romantic intimacy than the prevailing image abroad of dancing, mixed-race women in Carnival samba parades and hypersexuality. Lastly, musicians hold differing opinions about the ubiquity of bossa nova in New York's jazz industry, which has caused anxieties for those who try to perform other approaches to Brazilian-jazz fusions.

While bossa nova is the best-known and commercially most successful way that samba and jazz have been combined, the label "samba jazz" denotes a historically related approach from 1960s Brazil that features instrumentalists, brisker tempos, and more improvisation. Chapter 4, "Samba Jazz at Carnegie Hall: Genre Fusion in Instrumental Music," explains how musicians in Brazil and New York have drawn on aspects of both progenitor genres to shape and perform this hybrid. After considering theories of musical fusion as its own genre in addition to a combination of stylistic ingredients, the chapter details the practices and compositions of influential New Yorkers. The instrumentation and harmony of jazz is prevalent in samba jazz. Drummers transferred the rhythms, timbres, and roles of samba percussion to the drum set in ways that align with conventional practices of jazz drumming. Musicians commingle swing feels (patterned uneven microdurations of notes) of samba and jazz, whether alternating, overlapping, or adjusting them to blend. Works that exemplify ingenuity and conventions begin with Dom Salvador's "Gafieira" along with the drumming accompaniment of Eduardo "Duduka" Da Fonseca and Maurício Zottarelli. Also examined are Eliane Elias's compositions and arrangement of Jobim's "Desafinado," and Cidinho Teixeira's "Magali," along with biographical portraits of Salvador and Teixeira. In addition to using interviews, secondary sources, and music analysis, the chapter utilizes instructional method books written by several musicians in New York's Brazilian jazz scene, including Teixeira and Da Fonseca.

Chapter 5, "From CDs to Covid-19: Professional Agency in Volatile Industries," focuses on changing business practices that have affected Brazilian jazz in New York. Scholars in popular music studies, musicology, and business currently view music, culture, institutions, and capitalist industries as a holistic system. This framework emphasizes the agency and strategies of musicians, record producers, and live-event presenters, in contrast to Adorno and Horkheimer's "culture industry" critique of top-down control. People work in the local market that supports Brazilian jazz primarily because of their passion for the music, yet they must exercise business savvy to survive, let alone to accomplish their ambitious goals. The performance engagements, recordings, and marketing of the long-standing ensemble Trio da Paz—Lubambo, Da Fonseca, and Nilson Matta—provide a central case study, in particular their annual shows at the upscale Dizzy's Club, the nightclub within Jazz at Lincoln Center. Although they promote bossa nova to attract broad audiences, they perform wide-ranging Brazilian-jazz fusions. The chapter then explains changing business practices for live and recorded Brazilian jazz during the 2010s in contrast to each of the preceding two decades. To illustrate these shifts and individual agency are perspectives from presenter-trumpeter Mark Morganelli, curator-guitarist Billy Newman, and record producer François Zalacain. Starting in 2020, the vast and sudden impacts of the Covid-19 pandemic on local musicians mark the final era in the chapter's chronology. The experiences of musicians and presenters during the pandemic show contrasting ways of adopting new technologies and pivoting business practices.

I selected these subjects, issues, and relevant theories based on combinations of my observations at performances and interviews; analyses of recorded music and musicianship skills; and disciplinary training, topical interests, and secondary sources. The book is not comprehensive in coverage, musicians, subjects, and theories. There are many possible views of the elephant that is Brazilian jazz in New York City.

Research Methods and Subjectivity

I had five main reasons to research Brazilian jazz fusions in New York during the 2010s, all of which have influenced my perspectives and explanations: I like the music, play jazz, already had research experience with Brazilian music, moved to the New York City region in 2010 to teach at Ramapo College of New Jersey, and found that Brazilian jazz in the United States was understudied. I have been playing jazz since childhood in Berkeley, California, primarily as a bassist with some piano, percussion, and saxophone training and experience. My earliest exposure to Brazilian-jazz fusions was as a teenager playing bossa novas from *The Real Book* of jazz standards and listening to jazz-fusion ensembles with Brazilian musicians and influences, which contributed to Brazilian-jazz history: notably Chick Corea's Return to Forever with Airto Moreira and Flora Purim, the Pat Metheny Group with Naná Vasconcelos and Armando Marçal, and Steps Ahead with Eliane Elias. As an adult I developed tastes for Brazilian popular music and then a research specialty in Brazilian music—in Brazil during the 2000s and in the Northeastern United States into the 2010s.[66] After moving from Boston to northern New Jersey in 2010, I regularly watched live jazz, Brazilian music, and Brazilian-jazz fusions in New York City. I also befriended amateur jazz and rock musicians to play with, and continued to play Brazilian music occasionally while teaching undergraduate students. However, I did not pursue performing on the professional level that the musicians in this book do, mainly because their levels of talent, skills, dedication, time investment, and interest in performance are well beyond mine; secondarily, my work and family responsibilities kept me busy.

My focus on Brazilian jazz was also a strategic decision, for it has been studied less than other types of Brazilian music that are played in New York and North America in general.[67] After surveying Brazilian music scenes in New York when I first arrived and while completing research about Brazilian and Portuguese Catholic music in Newark, I gradually designed the scope of this study to supplement the existing and current studies of Brazilian music in New York. These have often focused on single genres—bossa nova, samba, *choro, forró,* and *maracatu*—and the representation of Brazil in music criticism.[68] The most similar project to mine is Eduardo Lis's 1996 master's thesis in ethnomusicology about Brazilian jazz in the United States and Canada, which includes interviews with expert musicians.[69] This book also contributes a new-millennium perspective to scholarship about jazz in New York City.[70] The project complements research on immigrant musicians in New York by studying a scene whose participants include US-born citizens and immigrants from different countries.

My position in relation to the subject and the musicians reveals my biases and preferences, advantages and disadvantages in selecting, documenting, and analyzing materials. My identities during the research were as a trained ethnomusicologist, educator at a local college, occasional presenter and thus possible employer, and amateur musician familiar with the genres that musicians played and combined. I have studied the histories and debates about Brazilian music and jazz, and I regularly teach courses about Latin American and North American music, which informed my conversations with musicians. I also teach courses that incorporate the changing business and technological forces in music industries, which informed my interviews with musicians, presenters, and record producers about their business strategies. I have hired local musicians to teach workshops and present performances to my students or the college's regional community, based on their particular expertise and our curricular needs. Co-producing concerts for the public with my college's performing arts center expanded my knowledge about presenting live music, particularly in the New York area, which has informed this study. Some of the musicians I studied supplement their careers by teaching in local colleges as adjunct instructors (Richard Boukas, Richard Miller, and Adriano Santos), which overlaps with my role as a college teacher and as a coordinator of adjunct faculty. Other musicians studied ethnomusicology as undergraduates (Susan Pereira and Leslie Macedo) or in graduate school (Philip Galinsky and Rubens de la Corte), though they work primarily outside of academia. Learning about their situations expanded my sensitivity to dilemmas of conditional workers in academia; it eventually also influenced my decision not to study the adjunct instructors at Ramapo College who perform, compose, and record Brazilian jazz (Richard Sorce and Marc Sganga) because my unequal power relationship with them would heavily bias our interviews and my analyses. The exception is Amarildo "Popo" Costa, who directs the Brazilian Latin Percussion Ensemble that we cofounded and whom I did interview.

My identity status as a steadily employed, US-born, white, cisgender male in my forties affected my research, a positionality with biases I sought to mitigate. As a full-time college professor, I had the time and financial resources, including research grants, to pay for attending many concerts in Manhattan, to commute to shows and interviews, and to pay student assistants for transcribing interviews and other tasks. I did not feel intimidated to attend shows in nightclubs nor late at night, nor to travel by train at night, which is a privileged position.[71] I made a point to interview males and females of different ethno-racial identities, national backgrounds, ages, instruments, and musical specialties both to sample representatively from the social diversity within the scene and also to diminish my implicit biases. Treating musicians as musical artists, first and foremost, I began my conversations and interviews with questions about their creative work, musical background, career trajectory, and collaborations.[72] Thereafter I inquired about their experiences and perspectives living in New York City, the local music scene and industry for Brazilian jazz, and the diversity of demographics and musical backgrounds among musicians in the scene. Because Brazilian jazz is characterized by a fusion of two countries' music traditions, nationalities were the primary focus of diversity conversations with respect to the music, and they feature more prominently than ethnicity/race, gender, class, and age throughout the book.

I used several conventional research methods of ethnomusicology, with the exception of systematically learning to play the music myself and with the addition of creating a database of musicians. The original research data consist of formal interviews, notes from casual conversations, performance observations, music analysis, and secondary-source research, accumulated during the latter half of the 2010s. I conducted most of the in-depth interviews between 2014 and 2021, with musicians, presenters, and producers, all of whom gave consent through a form approved by the Institutional Review Board of Ramapo College. Not everyone I approached responded or made themselves available for interview; hence the absence of a few key musicians, producers, and presenters. In the wake of the Covid-19 pandemic, starting in 2020, I began communicating with interviewees about their situations and interviewed several about the pandemic in particular (see List of Interviews).

Throughout the research, I compiled a highly useful spreadsheet database of musicians and industry professionals that includes demographic, networking, and musically relevant information. It currently has 234 people, 173 of whom are professional musicians who were playing Brazilian-jazz fusions in New York during the 2000s and/or 2010s. During many interviews I shared this evolving list, which triggered memories of collaborations, commentary, corrections, and suggested additions. This expanding data helped me to analyze demographic trends and to ensure that I was interviewing a proportional representation of demographic categories in the scene. Table I.1 shows the number of musicians I interviewed in various categories relevant to this study, and the percentages of the interviews compared to the total numbers of musicians in those categories. I interviewed 30 percent of all the musicians whom I counted and between a quarter and a third of each demographic category that I documented. A major disclaimer, discussed

Table I.1 Numbers and percentages of musicians I interviewed, by selected categories

Interviews by Category	Total in Category	% of Category
All interviewees	52	30%
Males	37	29%
Females	15	32%
Whites	37	30%
Blacks	7	35%
Mixed	4	31%
Japanese	4	36%
Brazilians	34	36%
Non-Brazilians	18	23%

in Chapter 1, is that I assigned the racial categories in the database (they are not self-identifications) based on my perceptions and presumptions about how individuals likely experience US racial politics based on their appearance. I treat these numbers cautiously as rough, subjective, US-centric, and of limited utility—although they are not useless. I also interviewed more Brazilians and Japanese than other nationalities because they overlapped with my related research projects. The data are analyzed in Chapter 1.

In addition to publishing this book and academic articles, I am gradually placing information on a freely accessible website for the broader public; it is currently available at http://www.newyorkbrazilianjazz.com. While the book and articles foreground specific musicians momentarily through anecdotes and quotes as evidence to support my larger arguments, the website will provide equal attention to all the musicians I interviewed and counted. The website aims to fulfill two moral obligations as an ethnographer to subjects and future researchers: help subjects to present their work to a large audience and deposit original data in a publicly-accessible archive.

Notes

1. Amanda Ruzza, interview with author, August 26, 2015.
2. Ruzza identifies as female in her public biography, http://www.amandaruzza.com/info/bio. html, accessed May 31, 2023. Galvão presents as male in his online photos, e.g., https://www. facebook.com/sergiogalvaosax/, accessed May 31, 2023.
3. See Leni Stern's biography on her website, https://www.lenistern.com/bio, accessed June 8, 2023.

4. Race concepts are explained in Chapter 1, including different racial categories and ideologies between the United States and Brazil, despite the similar racial hierarchies and histories of oppression in both countries. By "white" I mean, generally speaking, people with lighter skin tone who appear to be of European descent and who benefit from white privilege, notwithstanding changing definitions of whiteness; and by "Black" I mean people with dark skin tones who appear to be of African descent. Capitalization follows current trends, notwithstanding debates about capitalizing "white" among musicologists of jazz and Brazilian music (e.g., Packman 2021, 250; Snyder 2022, 247; Klotz 2023, 2). "Female" and "male" refer to categories of gender identity rather than sexual identity.

5. I do not italicize "samba" and "bossa nova" because they are well known by English readers, while other Brazilian genres are italicized.

6. I counted 173 musicians by 2020, but given the frequency that I learned about musicians, I estimate that there have been over 200 musicians in this scene between the years 2000 and 2020.

7. Throughout this book, I use "scene" in the loosely vernacular sense, rather than solely the academic concept, to refer to the general collectivity of musicians in New York City who perform professionally Brazilian jazz; and sometimes I use "scene" to include musicians, audiences, and intermediary music professionals, as the scholarly usage has meant, though without DIY and countercultural implications (Jackson 2012, 55–57; Bennett and Peterson 2004, 1, 5, 12n1; Lena 2012, 33–41; Greenland 2016). This book does not discuss the robust literature about other, relevant types of musical collectivities such as professional network, community, and art/music world.

8. Amanda Ruzza, interview with author, February 10, 2021, and personal communications since.

9. The meaning of culture that best fits this book's scenario encompasses several aspects in dialogue: (1) shared behaviors, practices, products, beliefs, and values, such as musical activities and aesthetics; (2) a non-elitist/non-moralistic notion of cultivation, edification, and education, including self-improvement; and (3) the practices and products of such cultivation, communal and individualized, notably music as art and performance (Middleton 2012, 5ff.; Kuper 1999, 227; "culture, n.," *OED Online*, Oxford University Press, December 2019, www.oed.com/view/Entry/45746, accessed February 4, 2020). Ethnomusicologist Thomas Turino called attention to dialectic relationships within cultures between individuals and "their physical and social surroundings" through the concepts of identity, culture, and society (Turino 2008, 94–95). Literary scholar William Ray's "logic of culture" emphasizes dialectic relationships between the individual and communal perspectives, cultivation, and shared customs. Tracing the culture concept from eighteenth through twentieth centuries, Ray wrote, "the cultural way of thinking imagines the social in terms of a permanent dialectic between autonomy and community, the coherence of the group and the self-realization of its members" (Ray 2001, 8). Within anthropology, there has been a minority opinion that has elevated individual agency in dialogue with shared aspects (Kuper 1999, 64, 67, 68, 237).

10. For chronological histories of "instrumental music" in Brazil, which includes Brazilian jazz but also *choro* and funk-fusions, see Connell 2002, 39–124; Piedade 2003, 2005; Giller 2018.

11. On the early history of jazz in Brazil, see Piedade 2003; Giller 2018.

12. Connell 2002, 39; Piedade 2003, 43.

13. Seigel 2009, Chapters 2 and 3.

14. Connell 2002; Piedade 2003; Piedade and Bastos 2007; Giller 2018.

15. On the blues in 1950s Brazil, see McCann 2007.

16. Piedade 2003, 55; McCann 2007.

17. Connell 2002, 77ff.; Piedade 2003, 46–47; Saraiva 2007; Gomes 2010; Giller 2018.

18. Dom Salvador, second interview with author, April 1, 2020; Cidinho Teixeira, interview with author, September 27, 2019.

19. Piedade 2003, 47.

20. Goldschmitt 2020, 71–74.

21. Connell 2002, Chapter 5; Piedade 2003, 48–50; Giller 2018.

22. Lis 1996, Chapter 5; Roberts 1999, 156–159, 200; Connell 2002, 99–100, 191ff.; Goldschmitt 2020, Chapter 3.

23. Piedade 2003, 45. For a detailed study of *choro*, including its music, history, and revival, see Livingston-Isenhour and Garcia 2005. On "transregional" *choro* in the current United States that includes some musicians in this book, see Stanyek 2011.

24. Connell 2002, 9.

25. Piedade 2003.

26. Connell 2002, 77; Piedade 2003, 46.
27. Pellegrinelli 2005, 2008.
28. Washburne 2020.
29. Roberts 1999; Washburne 2020.
30. "Bridges" episode in *Latin Music USA* (video documentary), PBS, WBGH, BBC, 2009.
31. "Phantom Fish," *CD Baby*, https://store.cdbaby.com/cd/sergiogalvao, accessed December 3, 2019.
32. Díaz 2014, 106.
33. Connell 2002; Mateus 2014, 13–15; Giller 2018.
34. Piedade 2003.
35. See K. E. Goldschmitt's excellent book for a history of bossa nova in Anglophone markets (Goldschmitt 2020). See Ruy Castro's book for detailed history of bossa nova's early years (Castro 2000, 2017). See also Treece 2013; McCann 2019; Freeman 2019.
36. Gerard 1998; DeVeaux and Giddins 2019, 8, 74. On the ongoing historical dialectic between the African American and American identities of jazz, see Evans 2000.
37. On "racialization," see Chapter 1 in this book.
38. B. Johnson 2002, 41ff.; Atkins 2003, xiv–xvi; Bohlman and Plastino 2016, 14; Shipton 2001, 358.
39. Stowe 1994, 125; DeVeaux 1997, 146–156; Levine 1998; Clark 2001, 193–196; Shipton 2001, 378–381; Monson 2007, Chapter 2.
40. Bruce Johnson explained feminine associations with jazz in the 1920s (B. Johnson 2022). On masculinity in jazz and in jazz historiography, see Monson 1995; Pellegrinelli 2008; A. J. Johnson 2022; Karns 2022, and other chapters in Reddan, Herzig, and Kahr 2022.
41. Resler 2022; see also Tucker 2008.
42. Monson 1995; DeVeaux and Giddins 2019, 76.
43. Harris 2000; Nicholson 2002, 242.
44. Tucker 2000, 21, 27–29; Pellegrinelli 2008; Provost 2022; also see essays in these volumes: Rustin and Tucker 2008; Reddan, Herzig, and Kahr 2022.
45. DeVeaux 1998; Levine 1998. This historical trajectory is presented through primary sources in Walser 1999.
46. See the contemporary case studies in these edited volumes: Rustin and Tucker 2008; Reddan, Herzig, and Kahr 2022.
47. See case studies in Atkins 2001; Bohlman and Plastino 2016.
48. Plastino and Bohlman 2016, 6, 8, 18, 21–22.
49. Monson 1996; Bares 2009; Jackson 2012.
50. On anti-American sentiments that jazz evoked in Brazil, see Connell 2002, 60–63; Piedade 2003, 44, 47; Borge 2018, Chapter 3; Goldschmitt 2020, 12–13. On samba and national identity in Brazil, which fomented in the 1930s, see Vianna 1999; McCann 2004, Chapter 4; Murphy 2006, Chapter 1; Avelar and Dunn 2011, 12–17.
51. Béhague 1973, 211; Saraiva 2007; Gomes 2010; Treece 2013; Borge 2018, 114–127; see also Seigel 2009.
52. Piedade 2003, 53, see also 44.
53. Alexander 2006, Chapter 17. Alexander discussed the differences between assimilated and hyphenated identities in the United States for immigrants, as well as anti-Black racial barriers to integration.
54. Fernández 2003; Zheng 2010, 159; Plastino and Bohlman 2016, 31; Plastino 2016, 314f.; Hersch 2017.
55. Musicological and anthropological studies of transnational and diasporic music and musicians often focus on recontextualized meanings in new national settings as music traditions follow migrating populations (Baily and Collyer 2006; Bohlman 2011; Krüger and Trandafoiu 2014). In the new settings, music often supports migrants' burgeoning sense of their transnational or diasporic identity, often theorized by scholars as self-reflexive "diasporic consciousness" (Vertovec 2009, 6; Slobin 2012, 99–100; Solomon 2015, 206 ff.). Different types and circumstances of migrants have been shown to affect the social statuses and recontextualized musical meanings in new settings, such that the musicians in my study have more privileged conditions in comparison to refugees, involuntary, and low-skilled migrant laborers.
56. Atkins 2001; Bohlman and Plastino 2016.
57. Plastino and Bohlman 2016, 35–36.
58. Connell 2002, 66, 87–88, 105.

59. Botelho 2008.
60. On the historical critiques of cool jazz as white and discussions of whiteness in cool jazz, see Meadows 2003, Chapter 11; Gerard 1998, 6, 25; Klotz 2023.
61. Hertzman 2013, 229, 238.
62. Goldschmitt 2020, 34–37, 50.
63. Pacini Hernandez 2010, 13.
64. Lund 2022, 4–8.
65. This is a theme in related literature; for instance, in a study of Indo-jazz, the presence of fusion reasserts the classical status of Indian court/classical music (Higgins 2016, 349).
66. Gidal 2016b, 2016a, 2018.
67. Excluding bossa nova, Brazilian jazz in the United States has been studied by Lis 1996; Roberts 1999; McCann forthcoming.
68. Castro 2000; Lopes 2008; Botelho 2008; Gevers 2010; Stanyek 2011; Coimbra 2015; Stanyek and Moehn forthcoming.
69. Lis 1996. Lis interviewed by telephone JoAnne Brackeen, Duduka Da Fonseca, Peter Erskine, Clare Fischer, Danny Gotlieb, Herbie Mann, Airto Moreira, Claudio Roditi, Paul Sokolow, and others. His thesis and this book overlap the most in my Chapter 4.
70. Stewart 2007; Jackson 2012; Barzel 2015; Greenland 2016; Reynolds 2017; Washburne 2020.
71. On this privileged position for conducting fieldwork, see Appert and Lawrence 2020, 233.
72. Treating musicians primarily as musicians respects them more professionally than prioritizing their involuntary social identities; at the same time, addressing the ways that identity issues inevitably influence musicians' lives and careers can challenge normative hegemony. Jazz scholars Sherrie Tucker and Ingrid Monson advised similarly when studying female jazz musicians (Monson 2004, xii). Tucker concluded with a twofold approach: to foreground their careers and offer a critical analysis of gender in music, drawing on Norma Coates's work on women in rock music (Tucker 2004, 255). Similarly, Monika Herzig gathered the stated preferences of female jazz musicians to treat gender identities secondarily, though she warns that this stance might hinder feminist activism in the jazz industry (Herzig 2022, 470–471).

1

"Paying Dues" and "Carrying Flags"

Demographic Diversity and Inequities among Musicians

Vanderlei Pereira had a gig, but needed a band. The drummer/percussionist from Rio de Janeiro faced a dilemma when Alex Kaye, the owner of the Zinc Bar, at which he was playing regularly with pianist Cidinho Teixeira, offered him to headline a show. Vanderlei recalled telling Kaye in 2006, "Look, I'm thinking about putting a band together." Kaye said, "Oh, then you got a place to play."[1] The dilemma was not so much logistical, since he knew many excellent musicians he could assemble to play Brazilian jazz, but more artistic and collaborative: he asked himself what kind of music he would want to perform and what kind of band he would want to create. He recalled a process of elimination and differentiation, that is, he wanted to distinguish himself from what was already happening in New York. "I'm trying to see if I can come up with something that people are not doing these days."[2] He thought about the prominent bands in New York's Brazilian jazz scene since the 1980s, bands led by Dom Salvador, Tania Maria, Teixeira, Portinho, and Duduka Da Fonseca. He had been playing with Teixeira and guitarist Paul Meyers and wanted to "accept the challenge of having piano and guitar, and make them work well together," because this was a common combination in jazz and Brazilian music. He loves bossa nova but wanted to play something different since it was played so often in New York. He wanted to experiment with Brazilian rhythms and grooves but in a way different from other experimentations while still having music based on grooves. "I'm trying to have a conception where the groove, where the rhythm would be the main focus. And on top of that, I want to have a good soloist. I do want a record where people, in a jazz way, play the head, then solo, and then head out with a coda and that's it. I want something more from old records, where the groove, where the ensemble sounds almost like a percussion section, like what I saw on a James Brown movie." He described a balance between everyone playing their parts with discipline and freedom to improvise variations.

SamBop NYC. Marc Gidal, Oxford University Press. © Oxford University Press 2024.
DOI: 10.1093/oso/9780197619049.003.0002

Pereira grew up in a musical family, studied classical music, performed classical percussion, and became involved in Rio's jazz scene. He decided to move to New York in 1988, motivated by three draws: his urge to continue developing as a jazz musician; encouragement from guitarist Romero Lubambo, his good friend and fellow jazz musician from Rio; and his love for the musician Susan Davis, whom he met when she was exploring Rio's music scenes. Once in New York, he began to substitute for Brazilian drummers, eventually meeting Teixeira, who added Pereira to his band Terra Brasil.

For his new project, in addition to developing an artistic approach, Pereira also deliberated about his band's personnel. "I want a mixed band. You know, Blindfold Test is like that. Three Brazilians and three Americans, including women in the band. But I don't want people that are just good. I want people who paid some dues with Brazilian music. [. . .] I don't want to be the boys' band or the girls' band." Pereira wanted to create a band distinguished by its instrumentation, repertoire, style, and the demographic diversity of its musicians. He wanted the music to be based in different rhythmic grooves, a mixture of jazz and Brazilian styles; and he wanted to include musicians of different nationalities and genders. Although age and ethno-racial diversity were not on his mind,[3] the resulting ensemble's demographic diversity represented the heterogeneity of the Brazilian jazz scene in New York. Because nationality, race, and gender are analyzed in this book, I am foregrounding these identity categories while describing the ensemble. Vanderlei Pereira is an Afro-Brazilian man with medium-dark skin married to a white American woman of European descent, Susan Pereira (née Davis), who has expertise singing and playing Brazilian music on piano and percussion. She "paid her dues," as the two tend to say, long before she met Vanderlei, as an active member of the samba percussion scene in New York during the 1980s, singing and playing samba drums and hand percussion. She formed her own Brazilian jazz ensemble, Sabor Brasil, in which she sings and plays percussion or piano. Vanderlei Pereira's sextet, renamed Blindfold Test a few years later, would include three Brazilians and three US-born Americans, two females and four males, four white musicians and two musicians of color: Susan, white American guitarist Paul Meyers, Brazilian woodwindist Jorge Continentino of mixed European-Amerindian ancestry, white American pianist Deanna Witkowski, and, depending on their availability, white male bassists Gustavo Amarante (Brazilian), Itaiguara Brandão (Brazilian), or Leo Traversa (American) (see Figure 1.1).

Figure 1.1. Vanderlei Pereira's ensemble Blindfold Test. Left to right: Jorge Continentino (woodwinds), Susan Pereira (voice and percussion), Vanderlei Pereira (drums), Paul Meyers (guitar), Gustavo Amarante (bass), and Deanna Witkowski (piano). Photo by Janis Wilkins, reproduced courtesy of Vanderlei Pereira.

Witkowski appreciates the mixture of nationalities in Blindfold Test: "It's a model of what other musical situations would be like, or even goes against this whole idea that only Brazilian people can play Brazilian music. [...] I like the idea that there's a willingness to let people who aren't from your culture play your music. Now, I don't know how that always works. I think there are gradations of things."[4] She also pointed out the age range in the band, concluding, "It's very New York; it's cool that way." She then noted the importance placed on combining their diverse musical backgrounds. "Vanderlei is specific in what he wants us to play a lot of times, but there's also the sense that he wants us to bring what we bring. So yeah, it feels like a band of people who are from different backgrounds," in a broad sense. Continentino and Meyers spoke in similarly positive ways about the ensemble to me, as did Brandão about intercultural collaboration in New York. Continentino complimented many non-Brazilian musicians in New York's Brazilian jazz scene for "carrying the flag," meaning the Brazilian flag, by playing and presenting the music well.[5]

Although demographic diversity and the resulting musical contributions were part of Pereira's goals, the non-Brazilians and women were hardly tokens or surprising additions, for they all have been active professionals in the New York Brazilian music scene with musical experiences and cultural immersions in Brazil. They all learned to speak Portuguese well, too. Vanderlei and Susan contrast these selections with musicians who make a Brazilian-themed recording or performance with little competency playing Brazilian music or understanding of Brazilian culture. Vanderlei explained:

> I don't want to have a new Stan Getz. He loves Brazilian music but he didn't pay his dues learning percussion, and learning deeply about Brazil as a whole country. Not bossa nova. In Brazilian music, that's just one little style within the whole of Brazil. So, I want a musician who has some experience of Brazilian rhythms. And whatever is missing, I'm there to add, too. Because, you see so many records where people are playing, "Now I'll play a Brazilian record," and you just hire a Brazilian drummer and then you blow.[6]

Blindfold Test, the name Vanderlei gave his ensemble, suggested by Susan, came a few years after its formation and addresses another type of diversity within the band, that of blindness/sightedness. Because Vanderlei is blind—his vision deteriorated as an adult—he has his bandmates wear blindfolds to give them a taste of his regular experience and force them to use their memories and ears when playing together. Another impetus for having the musicians wear blindfolds came during a rehearsal when they were struggling to play a complicated section of his music. He told the audience this version at one show I attended and after they played the piece wearing blindfolds. He asked the audience if they sounded better with them on, to which the audience cheered. Talking about his blindness with the audience also seemed to foster a sense of intimacy, judging by their attentiveness and whoops of support.

In other situations, blindfold tests in music have asked a listener to identify recorded music without knowing who is playing or what they are playing—also called a "drop the needle" test. In jazz history there is another type of relevant blindfold test: whether listeners of jazz can tell if the performers are African American or not, publicized tests that contributed to colorblind debates in the United States during the 1950s, as ethnomusicologist and jazz scholar Ingrid Monson has discussed.[7] By extension, Pereira's band name implicitly asks listeners to judge whether the musicians are Brazilian or not, or sound Brazilian or not, though this was not Pereira's intention.

This chapter explores the demographic diversity and accompanying identity issues among musicians who played Brazilian jazz in New York during the first decades of the millennium. To support this goal, I analyze interviews and a detailed spreadsheet of 173 musicians that I compiled during my fieldwork, and compare the dataset to data from social science studies of Brazilian immigrants in the United States and jazz musicians in New York. When comparing social categories—nationality, race, gender, and class—as well as instrumentation distributions, demographic imbalances seem striking but are consistent with existing data.

What will emerge from the quantitative data, musicians' perspectives, and my interpretations are a few significant tensions that are pertinent to the entire book. The first tension seems like a paradox at first: white musicians constitute a majority of those who perform professionally a fusion of multiple Afro-diasporic genres, particularly jazz and samba. Lessening this paradox, though, jazz and samba can also be considered Afro-Euro-American fusions that African descendants in the Americas initiated and primarily developed; as well, musicians of European, Asian, and mixed ancestry have contributed to the continuation and developments of these traditions. The second tension is that the demographic mix, which is skewed toward white male musicians, raises the question whether musicians or music-industry professionals have hindered musicians of color and female musicians from working, whether through self-interest, malice, racism, and/or sexism. Indeed, presented in this chapter are female musicians' accounts of sexism in the local scene and other identity-based biases. Given the prevalence of anti-Black racism in the United States and Brazil, on macro-structural and micro-aggression levels, musicians of color have likely experienced racism in this local Brazilian jazz scene, although racist experiences that interviewees told me about happened to them outside this scene and especially in Brazil. A third set of overlapping tensions concern competition for work, power, privilege, cultural authority, audience expectations, industry marketing, and musical competencies; these pertain to critiques of cultural appropriation in the sense of exploitation (discussed in this chapter), perceived authenticity of performers of musical fusion (see Chapter 2), exotification of others and selves (Chapter 3), and the musicians' competencies or polymusicalities (Chapter 2). These tensions will emerge in various forms and combinations in this chapter and subsequent chapters, yet they will raise more interpretive challenges than yield concrete answers. To preview multiple summarizing points: first, musicians of many national, ethno-racial, and gender identities have contributed to all the genres and their fusions, and in different settings. Second, there are multiple types of interactions, exchanges, and appropriations to consider when heterogeneous groups of musicians play musical fusions that draw on other fused traditions. Third, I have no evidence that any of these musicians have been financially exploiting others, yet they all compete for work. Fourth, highly competent musicians inevitably face judgments from the public and other musicians based on their appearances in relation to social identities, judgments about their perceived authenticity and acceptability to play music associated with certain populations, even when playing a transnational musical fusion like Brazilian jazz. Fifth, although strong stereotypes about Brazilians are prevalent in the United States and although some musicians leverage them for professional gain, as audiences become familiar with Brazilian jazz they might appreciate it as a richly nuanced expressive genre and develop alternative associations.

The most significant contributions to the demographic imbalances appear to be societal structures and institutions, historical and current, which have been nationalist, racist, sexist, and classist. In turn, such systemic inequities based on involuntary identity categories have limited which musically talented people have had the resources, support, and confidence to pursue becoming a professional musician in New York City and who have had the interest, drive, and training to play Brazilian jazz at the required expert levels. In my mind, the blame for the resulting imbalances should primarily be directed toward the historically unfair systems that continue to impede immigrants, people of African descent, and women from moving to and working in this music scene in New York. This seems to have been a far greater obstacle than the implicit biases and micro-aggressions within the scene, while certainly those are inexcusable, damaging forces that should change. The musicians and industry professionals should be practicing anti-racist and anti-sexist behavior, but my impression is that many musicians already do this, some more actively than others. This is generally a socially progressive, liberal collection of musicians, many of whom have altruistically leveraged their power to help the less fortunate among them in concrete ways. At the same time, their progressive politics and interpersonal behavior does not entirely vindicate musicians who benefit from white and male

privilege.[8] As transnational polymusical musicians, their prolonged engagement in cross-cultural studies, activities, and relationships may have fostered
these progressive values—and vice versa.

To focus momentarily on the musicians' nationalities, demographic diversity can be found not only within New York's Brazilian jazz scene of musicians
but also within ensembles, as Blindfold Test illustrates. Some ensembles are
comprised solely of Brazilians and sometimes by choice, such as "Monika
Oliveira and the Brazilians." Yet most groups I witnessed, like Blindfold Test
and Amanda Ruzza and Sergio Galvão's *Phantom Fish* project, are mixed by
nationality and sometimes by age. This generally reflects the international
character of music scenes in New York and the positive value placed on
interculturalism, where an open-mindedness to cross-cultural interactions
and creative fusions is part of the general values and practices of professional
musicians in New York. There is so much intercultural fusion in New York
that a Brazilian musician I spoke with longed for a bit more preservation of
musical traditions. As with Pereira and Ruzza, some Brazilians I interviewed,
such as Vinícius Cantuária, Luciana Souza, and Vitor Gonçalves, intentionally collaborated with non-Brazilian musicians in order to forge new sounds,
which is partly why they moved to New York in particular.

Mitigating this value in intercultural musical collaboration, everyone
experiences exclusion to some extent based on their social identities rather
than musical competencies. Regarding nationality, Brazilian immigrants
who considered themselves jazz musicians in Brazil experience exclusion
from New York's jazz scene that prioritizes US American musicians, especially African Americans; consequently, Brazilians play more Brazilian
genres than they had expected. Meanwhile, most non-Brazilian musicians
who wish to play Brazilian-jazz fusions hire Brazilian accompanists to benefit from their expertise, most often Brazilian drummers to create authentic
Brazilian grooves. This approach is so common that it also becomes ridiculed
if a bandleader is not believed to be deeply committed to Brazilian music, as
Vanderlei Pereira said. Some leaders advertise their Brazilian musicians, perhaps to add branding and credibility to their ensemble, like the Dutch-born
female singer Fleurine and her band, the Brazilian Boys. Only a few non-
Brazilians have ensembles without any Brazilians, usually when Brazilian
jazz is only a part of their repertoire. Although bands with only Brazilian
musicians go without comment, Brazilians I spoke with are annoyed when
they encounter acts that play mainly Brazilian music though lack a single
Brazilian musician. Whereas audiences might question such an ensemble's

authenticity, the Brazilian musicians often raise questions of cultural appropriation, charging that the band is profiting from Brazilian music without
employing Brazilian musicians. The Brazilian musicians may also think
that their music is played incorrectly, and easily blame the lack of Brazilian
musicians involved. A common counter-argument is that the Brazilian
musicians are less likely to hire non-Brazilian musicians; partially due to this
exclusion, non-Brazilians form their own groups, play a mix of Brazilian and
non-Brazilian music, and draw on their own circles of musician friends. This
description fits at least three ensembles I encountered. Clearly the situation
is complex with multiple possible ensemble configurations, intentions, and
judgments with respect to authenticity, cultural ownership, appropriation,
and audience expectations, often irrespective of musical competencies. Yet,
these identity politics are not limited to the national origins of the musicians;
examined in this chapter are interrelated dynamics with respect to nationality, race/ethnicity, sex/gender, and instrumentation.

Racialized Identities in Transnational Contexts

Before interpreting the demographic data, the racial terms and issues require
introduction primarily because the United States, Brazil, and other countries
have different racial ideologies yet similar empirical inequities, and resulting
dilemmas can affect the experiences of transnational musicians and their reception by audiences. While introducing current race theories relevant to
Brazil and the United States, this section will establish two main points: first,
there are many terms for describing racial identities, and they can differ by
country and cultural situations within countries; so, to categorize musicians
by racial identity is challenging and dynamic both for observers and themselves. Regarding national racial ideologies, Howard Winant, a historian of
comparative race studies, summarized: "For a long time, the foundation of
all comparative studies of race in the United States and Brazil was the *contrast* between the two countries. In the United States, so the argument went,
a rigid color line divided white and black, and 'hypodescent' or the 'one-
drop rule' made all gradations of racial difference insignificant. In Brazil,
on the other hand, the gradations were of immense importance, since racial categories were organized along a 'racial continuum.'"[9] Furthermore,
the transnational migration of musicians and resulting shifts in people's
identity categories can complicate their experiences and understandings of

racial identities. Before returning to this national comparison, the second main point is that regardless of differences in racial terminology and national ideologies, musicians probably experience either discrimination or privilege in both countries based on their racialized appearance. In this respect, international similarities that current scholars emphasize are tensions between *discrimination* and *inclusion* with respect to racialized identities in the United States, Latin American countries, and elsewhere.[10] In *Racial Formation in the United States*, Michael Omi and Winant conclude that "race and racism [are] continuing encounters between despotism [i.e., discrimination] and democracy [i.e., inclusion], in which individuals and groups, confronted by state power and entrenched privilege but not entirely limited by those obstacles, make choices and locate themselves over and over in the constant racial reconstruction of everyday life."[11] Similarly, sociologist Jeffrey Alexander situates the ethno-racial history of the United States between "[inclusive] civic-ideological and [discriminatory] ethnic-primordial understandings of citizenship" as exemplified in stigmatized restrictions on America's promised assimilation into democratic life.[12] More recently, race scholar Ibram X. Kendi has called the simultaneous progress toward racial equity and justice, and fortifications of inequity and injustice the "dual racial history of two opposing forces" in the United States.[13]

Scholars have noted similar tensions in Latin America and for Latin American immigrants to the United States, who navigate hierarchical racial discrimination in multiple countries while having also internalized national beliefs in racial democracies that celebrate integration and progress. Regarding discrimination, a current social science consensus about race in Latin America—and to an extent in the United States—is that people's skin color and other phenotypical features (rather than ancestry, census categories, or other racial identity labels) in conjunction with contextual factors are the strongest determinants or indicators of their experiences with race-based discrimination or privilege.[14] In other words, people are more likely categorized and treated in public as, for example, a medium-light skinned brunette with European features than as Brazilian of Portuguese-Italian ancestry. Encapsulating the skin-color outlook of society are framing concepts such as "colorism" (discrimination based on skin color) and "pigmentocracies"; the latter term titles a robust multi-country, survey-based, sociodemographic study in Latin America, conducted around 2010. The principal investigator, sociologist Edward Telles, summarized, "*Pigmentocracies* highlights our finding that skin color is a central axis of social stratification in at least several Latin American countries, though it is often ignored."[15] National integrationist ideologies from the early twentieth century, which argue that countries like Brazil draw strength from their racial heterogeneity and mixture, are ingrained in the minds or rhetoric of politicians, citizens, and outside observers; yet, they are inconsistent with the proven existence of racial hierarchies, inequities, and discrimination based on appearance.[16] Therefore, returning to Winant's summarizing quote, on the one hand, the color-spectrum approach to race in Latin America has long been contrasted with the biracial, white-Black dichotomy in the United States, with judgments shifting in favor of one over the other depending on the era. On the other hand, developing understandings about Latin American situations have helped to challenge and change the racial dichotomy based on hypodescent in the United States: Eurocentric colorism significantly affects racism in the United States as experienced by African Americans, Black immigrants, US Latinos, and Asian Americans.[17] Meanwhile, on the integrationist side, anthropologist Ana Y. Ramos-Zayas found that Brazilian and other Latin American immigrants mentally apply their home countries' integrationist concepts of racial democracy to interpret the inter-ethno-racial encounters they experience in the United States.[18] Omi and Winant summarize studies that support this conclusion, offering: "Thus migrants can maintain, adopt, and strategically utilize different concepts of race in transnational space."[19]

These current theories of race and racism as hierarchical pigmentocracies that coexist with ideals of racial democracies and progressive politics begs questions for this book. First, which racial terms should be used to categorize and describe musicians and audiences of Brazilian jazz in New York City? When compiling my dataset of musicians, I loosely categorized musicians' appearances in order to gain a general sense of demographic distribution and to predict how they likely experience race-based biases in the United States. However, this was not a rigorous sociodemographic study and my interviews only included basic questions about demographic diversity among musicians. To decide which terms to use in the book's prose is also challenging. My US bias first led me to prioritize generalized ancestry— Afro-Brazilian, Afro-American, Euro-Brazilian, Euro-American—and the common terms "white" and "Black," capitalized (or not) following current conventions. Yet, as the previously mentioned studies indicate, named ancestry (e.g., Brazilian, European, and African) is not as strong an indicator of experienced racism as are skin color and phenotypical appearance.[20] An alternative approach in social science writings is to describe relational shades of skin tone: whiter, blacker, lighter, darker, medium-toned, medium-light, and so forth. Whereas the US census commingles racial, ethnic, national, and cultural categories,[21] the Brazilian census foregrounds generalized skin-color categories based in its social constructions of race: white, *pardo* (often glossed "brown"), black, yellow (referring to Asians), and, since the 1990s, indigenous.[22] *Pardo*, which has long been part of the Brazilian census, can encompass numerous vernacular categories that evoke racial mixture;[23] those relevant to this book are *pardo/a*, *mestiço/a*, *mulato/a*, and *moreno/a*. These terms appear in the book usually as shorthand for racially mixed Brazilians related to appearance, ancestry, and colonial subjectivity; when relevant, they are explained as social constructs for Brazilian identities.[24] Sociologist Tiffany Joseph points out that if President Barack Obama would have been Brazilian, as a medium skin-toned, mixed-race person, he might have been considered *pardo* in Brazil, although Black in the United States.[25] The musician Vanderlei Pereira, with a phenotypical resemblance to Obama, may have had similar racialized experiences in the two countries. I also write "mixed" as an intentionally generic umbrella that could apply to multiple countries' racial conceptualizations, although it risks reaffirming biological racial categories.[26] If the term "Afro-Brazilian" emphasizes ancestry over appearance, it also has contemporary social-political valence in support of Brazil's Black Consciousness Movement (along with *negro*), as does "African American" in support of civil rights and social justice.[27] Authors use combinations of these many terms they deem appropriate.[28]

A second set of corollary questions concern the perspectives of musicians in this book: how might they understand racial, ethnic, national, and gender identities, both their own and those of others, including those of collaborators within demographically diverse ensembles? These questions are mainly addressed in this chapter with respect to biases in the music marketplace, participation in ensembles, and concerns over cultural authenticity and appropriation.[29] In other words: whose music is being played and by whom? Who is claiming cultural authority over the music? And whom might audiences expect to perform and in what roles? Ancestry-based racial self-identities might support racial-group ownership; that is, a belief that only African descendants have the right to perform Afro-diasporic genres for profit. By contrast, an ideology of racial democracy that Brazilian immigrant musicians might have internalized supports a nationalistic understanding of Brazilian music, which can empower all Brazilian musicians to feel cultural ownership when playing Brazilian music. Musicologist K. E. Goldschmitt makes this point about the prevalence since the mid-twentieth century of white Brazilian musicians abroad: "those white Brazilians often performed a version of Afro-Brazilianness while the discourse of 'racial democracy' and national identity gave them cover from critique."[30]

With regard to the transnational context for musicians, a key finding from studies about international migrants is that the racial systems of different countries can alter their own self-identities.[31] Racialized identities—both self-concepts and categorizations by others—are gendered and can vary by setting and situation.[32] Brazilian migrants might have viewed themselves and experienced life as, for example, white or mixed-race in Brazil only to find themselves perceived and treated as mixed, Black, or Hispanic/Latinx in the United States, which then affects their self-image.[33] Anthropologist Suzana Maia, a self-described *morena* who researched female Brazilian erotic dancers in New York during the 2000s, noted changes in their racialized identifications.[34] Most self-identified as *morenas*, but situationally and with ambivalence: "White, but really Brazilian *morena*," is what a dancer told Maia after she reconsidered her appearance as more racially mixed than dominant notions of white in the United States.[35] Similarly, Joseph interviewed a Brazilian *morena* with light skin, brown eyes, and dark hair, who identified as white in Brazil but whom a US official labeled as Black.[36] In both scenarios, the ingrained belief in hypodescent in the United States shifted categorizations of these immigrants toward Black identities. Joseph's research on Brazilian immigrants to the United States who move back to Brazil shows that they return with altered ideas about their racial identities.[37] The dynamic varieties of identifications can cause confusion, frustration, and sometimes humor for travelers, sojourners, and migrants.[38] Analyzing transnational cultural interactions in Brazil, the United States, and Europe during the 1920s, Micol Seigel argues that these countries' nationalized racial systems also influenced each other's development; and these changes have been shaped not only by intellectuals and national policies but also through the lived experiences of ordinary people such as, potentially, those Joseph studied and the musicians in this book.[39]

Regarding ethno-racial categorizations of the musicians in the United States, although I did not research the topic, I suspect that the whiter Brazilians—as well as whiter Europeans, Israelis, and other Latin Americans—are generally perceived and treated as white in the United States. I do not mean a nineteenth-century sense of Anglo-Saxon Protestant or Nordic white American, but in the more expansive sense of whiteness that over the twentieth century gradually incorporated southern and eastern Europeans, Italians, Poles, European Jews, Turks, and some swaths of West Asians and Latinos.[40] These groups as well as whiter Brazilians currently benefit from white privilege.[41] As well, darker immigrant musicians likely experience public life in the United States as non-whites, Blacks, or people of color without the same opportunity for integration into white privileged society. Meanwhile, musicians with diverse national backgrounds likely perceive themselves through different nation-based racial ideologies and conceptualizations. Their self-identifications probably change as they live in New York, interact with ethno-racially and nationally diverse musicians, and create or perform music that combines already hybrid Afro-Euro-American genres. In sum, the racial terms used in this book are loosely applied and vary by country and settings in subtle ways; however, they likely indicate the musicians' experiences with racial privilege or discrimination in both countries.

Imbalanced Demographic Diversity of Musicians

Approximately half the total musicians in my dataset about this scene are from Brazil, while US-born Americans make up another quarter, and the remaining musicians come from Japan, Israel, Canada, several European countries, and elsewhere in South America (see Table 1.1). Despite the strong African-diasporic roots and connected histories of samba and jazz, Brazilian jazz in New York is primarily played and listened to by whiter people, whether or not they are also Latin American or Latinx. A minority of musicians and audiences are Black, East or South Asian, mixed, or otherwise people of color. Around three-quarters of the musicians present as male, such that out of 173 musicians whom I have counted in this scene, only two appear to be female Black Brazilians—singer Ana Fernandez and percussionist Nêgah Santos—both of whom occasionally play Brazilian jazz (see Table 1.2).[42] Studying a similar paucity of female African American instrumentalists in the jazz scene, Yoko Suzuki concluded, "a longstanding notion of double burden in the context of the white-driven music industry might discourage black women to choose a jazz musician as a career."[43] Nevertheless, my figure seems astonishing low at first glance. Were my counting methods skewed toward male and non-Black musicians? Is there

Table 1.1 National origins and genders of the musicians in this study

National Origin	Total #	% of Total	Males	% of Males	Females	% of Females
Brazil	94	54.3%	68	54.0%	26	55.3%
USA	38	22.0%	27	21.4%	11	23.4%
Japan	11	6.4%	5	4.0%	6	12.8%
Israel	6	3.5%	4	3.2%	2	4.3%
Germany	2	1.2%	2	1.6%	0	0.0%
Russia	2	1.2%	2	1.6%	0	0.0%
Argentina	1	0.6%	1	0.8%	0	0.0%
Australia	1	0.6%	1	0.8%	0	0.0%
Canada	1	0.6%	1	0.8%	0	0.0%
Chile	1	0.6%	1	0.8%	0	0.0%
Colombia	1	0.6%	1	0.8%	0	0.0%
Cuba	1	0.6%	1	0.8%	0	0.0%
Holland	1	0.6%	0	0.0%	1	2.1%
Italy	1	0.6%	0	0.0%	1	2.1%
Panama	1	0.6%	1	0.8%	0	0.0%
unknown	11	6.4%				

Table 1.2 Gender categorizations of musicians in this study

Gender	Total #	% of Total
Male	118	71%
Female	49	29%
Total	167	

something particular about the ratios of racial and gender identities among musicians in New York who play Brazilian jazz? Does the category "Brazilian jazz" exclude female Black Brazilians, who might be more likely to play different genres? Upon reflection, the reasons for these dramatic imbalances were slightly skewed by my research subject and fieldwork practices, as I will explain, but primarily they strongly resemble the intersecting demographics of Brazilian immigrants and jazz musicians in the New York City area. These demographic imbalances are related to layers of white privilege and male dominance, aligned with class hierarchies, in particular with regard to the Brazilian immigrants in this scene and the jazz industry. On a subtle level, however, immigrants who are professional musicians have a slightly different situation from that of other professional categories of Brazilian immigrants.

I counted eleven Japanese (6.4% of the total), nearly even numbers of males and females, among the musicians who were playing Brazilian jazz professionally in New York during the 2000s and 2010s (see Table 1.1). This was the largest nationality other than Brazilians and native-born US Americans, none of whom in my study was of Japanese descent; the next largest nationalities were six Israelis, two Germans, and two Russians. Example musicians include pianist Ryuichi Sakamoto, whose collaborations with guitarist-singer Vinícius Cantuária are discussed in Chapter 3; guitarist Masa Shimizu, who routinely recorded and toured with singer Bebel Gilberto in the 2000s and 2010s; pianists Miho Nobuzane, featured in Chapter 2, and Mamiko Watanabe, quoted in this chapter; and percussionist-drummer Keita Ogawa, who regularly performed, toured, and recorded with pianist-singer Clarice Assad during the 2010s before touring the world with singer-composer Cécile McLorin Salvant (see Figure 1.2). Japan, Brazil, and the United States are far from a random trio of countries for musical circulation, as situations throughout the book will exemplify. Relatively high numbers of citizens and their descendants have moved between these countries, according to estimates from around 2010. Among the more than 3 million Brazilians living abroad, nearly half—between 800,000 and 1.5 million—live in the United States and 230,000 in Japan; and 70 percent of Brazilians abroad live in the United States, Japan, or Paraguay.[44] Meanwhile, Brazil

Figure 1.2. Clarice Assad (voice and piano) and Keita Ogawa (drums) at Subculture, May 4, 2018. Photo by author.

boasts the largest Japanese population outside of Japan, with approximately 1.5 million Japanese and their descendants.[45] Among the 1 million Japanese citizens living abroad for three months or longer, at least 170,000 (17%) live in seven cities in the United States and 14,000 in São Paulo, Brazil.[46] Waves of Japanese, Brazilians, and others have immigrated to the United States after official quotas were lifted by the US Immigration and Nationality Act of 1965 and successive legislation.[47] "Cultural migrants" is how Yuiko Fujita, who studied Japanese media professionals in New York, described young Japanese who move abroad to develop their skills and careers in music, visual arts, and fashion, whether or not they return to Japan.[48] This trend has increased threefold since the 1980s for Japanese, who have primarily moved to the United States and secondarily to countries such as Brazil; among the top twenty cities they have chosen, New York City ranks first and São Paulo eleventh.[49] In terms of their changing racialized identification in a transnational context, "diasporic racialization" is how anthropologist Nobuko Adachi generalizes a persistent outsider status that people of Japanese descent experience in Brazil and the United States, and that Japanese Brazilians experience in Japan, as they are often treated according to each country's hegemonic racial identities.[50] Fujita found that professional Japanese artists in New York tend to revise their national self-identities based on US stereotypes, sometimes adopting seemingly positive stereotypes as hardworking, punctual, caring, and assimilating, even if they run counter to their experiences.[51]

Because I did not survey the musicians in my dataset, but instead documented them from afar, Table 1.3 shows racialized identities that are my subjective categorizations of the musicians based on their appearance. As

Table 1.3 Racialized identities of all musicians in this study and of the Brazilian nationals

Racialized identities	Total #	% of Total	Brazilians	% of Brazilians
white	122	70.5%	67	71.3%
Black	20	11.6%	16	17.0%
mix	13	7.5%	8	8.5%
unknown	5	2.9%	3	3.2%
Japanese	11	6.4%		
South Asian	2	1.2%		

explained, I use "mix" as an umbrella category for anyone whose darkness of skin tone or phenotypical characteristics might cause them to experience life in the United States as a person of color other than Black. "White" Brazilians includes anyone who likely experiences white privilege in the United States due to their looks. These classifications are highly subjective, ambiguous, and debatable. I therefore interpret these numbers as approximations and of limited usefulness. But they are not entirely useless, either; indeed, the sociodemographic study of racial identification in Brazil in *Pigmentocracies*, which accounted for both people's appearance and census categories, "confirm[s] previous findings that [self-]identification and categorization by others largely overlap."[52] Nevertheless, I point out the subjectivity of my labels in the tables and analyses.

Musician Demographics Compared to Brazilian Immigrants in the United States

Brazilian immigrants in the United States tend to be from Brazil's middle and upper-middle classes in order to have the financial resources, access to information, and connections to emigrate.[53] Because class and racial segmentation are closely aligned in Brazil, upper- and middle-class Brazilians tend to have lighter skin and European features such that they are publicly perceived as white or whiter in Brazil and the United States.[54] As well, Black and brown Brazilians tend to be working-class and poor, a point underscored in recent ethnographies about Black poverty and performing artists in Bahia, Brazil, which would significantly impede professional musicians who might want to tour internationally or emigrate.[55] In fact, most Black male percussionists whom I interviewed moved to the United States without parental wealth but instead with assistance of wealthy sponsors, US American individuals or institutions (e.g., Berklee College of Music), and/or through their work with celebrity musicians. Percussionist Edson "Café" Aparecido da Silva, for example, had been performing with the Brazilian pop star Djavan and then toured with American jazz singer Roberta Flack before settling in the United States.[56] In the 1980s, more Brazilian men migrated than Brazilian women, an imbalance that has evened out in recent years.[57] These trends explain the high number of white, male Brazilians and low numbers of Black or mixed, female Brazilians in the United States, compared to the demographic distribution in Brazil, in which around half the population are Black or *pardo/mulato*.[58]

Amplifying these imbalances within the Brazilian immigrant population, professional musicians in Brazil who play bossa nova and Brazilian instrumental music (*música instrumental brasileira*)—genres under the umbrella of Brazilian jazz in New York City—are mainly from the middle class and have whiter complexion.[59] Musicians who play these genres are usually from the large cities—such as Rio de Janeiro, São Paulo, Belo Horizonte, Brasília, Porto Alegre, Campinas, Curitiba, and Salvador—which is also where most of the upper-middle-class émigrés originate.[60] Meanwhile, the lower-middle-class émigrés, who have been increasing in recent decades, may originate in smaller towns. Indeed, although immigrants from the state of Minas Gerais have disproportionately dominated the numbers of émigrés to the United States, most Brazilians in my study are from Rio de Janeiro and São Paulo, the historical centers of bossa nova and Brazilian instrumental music; and very few musicians in this scene come to the United States from small towns. Therefore, had my study focused on a more widely popular genre like samba, or on genres popular among the lower middle class or among people from Minas Gerais, like Brazilian country music (*música sertaneja*) in Newark, New Jersey, I would likely have encountered more Brazilian musicians of lower economic classes and of mixed race—although, not many more, given the already skewed demographics of immigrants. When considering these limiting factors, it becomes less surprising that Brazilian immigrants who play Brazilian jazz in New York City are disproportionally white, male, and from the middle-to-upper-middle classes compared to the Brazilian population, despite the prominent Afro-Brazilian origins of the music.

There is a major exception to these constraints that directly relates to the Brazilian music scene: the number of Black male Brazilians in this study is far higher than the trends of Brazilian immigration. This is especially remarkable because before the 1960s, in the segregated United States, Black Brazilian musicians rarely toured or immigrated and, when they did, they encountered discrimination.[61] Although I counted only two Black female Brazilians in the scene, there are fourteen Black male Brazilians, accounting for 21 percent of the male Brazilians. This percentage is much higher than the percentages of Black Brazilians in social science studies of Brazilians in New York City—Maxine Margolis reports 8 percent and Thely Carvalho Lopes reports 4 percent —and even higher than the sum totals of Black and mixed-race Brazilians in those datasets: 16 percent and 19 percent respectively (compare Tables 1.3 and 1.4).[62] Included in my data is one of the most celebrated pianists in this study, Dom Salvador, who, unusually, came from

Figure 1.3. Valtinho Anastásio (voice and percussion), with Vinícius Gomes (guitar), leading weekly Brazilian music in the Zinc Bar's outdoor shed during the Covid-19 pandemic, July 2021. Photo by Maria Traversa, reproduced courtesy of Traversa.

a small city, Rio Claro in São Paulo State (see Figure 4.1 in Chapter 4). Most of the Afro-Brazilian men are drummers/percussionists and from the cities of São Paulo, Rio de Janeiro, and Salvador, Bahia. For example, Valtinho Anastácio is a Black male Brazilian percussionist and singer from São Paulo who moved to New York in 1984 and has been headlining the Zinc Bar's Sunday night Brazilian music shows since the pandemic (see Figure 1.3).[63] In the state of Bahia, a vast majority of the population is of African descent, many Afro-Brazilian genres thrive, and the percussion traditions are famously rich and influential, even while percussion is prominently used in other sending cities in this study. In New York, Black Brazilian percussionists play professionally a variety of Brazilian genres for dancing—varieties of samba, *axé* music of Bahia, and *forró* from Brazil's northeast; some also practice *capoeira*, sing, and compose music. Had the present study focused on these genres, the percentages of Black and mixed-race Brazilian musicians would have been higher and the study would have included a few more Black

Table 1.4 Race categories of Brazilians in New York City from studies by Thely Carvalho Lopes and Maxine Margolis

Data from Lopes, 2009	
Category	**% of Category**
white	68%
Black	4%
pardo & *moreno*	15%
no answer	13%
Data from Margolis, 2009	
Category	**% of Category**
white	83%
Black	8%
mulatto	8%

women. In this respect, the choice of musical genre for study influenced the demographic makeup of the musicians.

Despite the subjective ambiguity of my data about musicians who appear as mixed race, comparing them to published studies of Brazilians in New York suggests similarities among total numbers, although half the percentage of Brazilian restaurant customers. In Table 1.4, which compares datasets about Brazilians' race categories in New York City, the first rows show the self-identified racial makeup of Brazilian customers of Brazilian restaurants in the city, studied by Lopes in 2004 and 2006.[64] The bottom rows show the racial makeup of local Brazilians whom Margolis studied in the early 1990s and 2000.[65] It is unclear whether Margolis's numbers are self-reported or her estimations. Lopes and Margolis use the Brazilian terms "*pardo* and *morerno*" and "*mulatto* and light *mulatto*" in their respective studies; my term "mix" encompasses *pardo/a* and *mulato/a*, so they are compared here.[66] In all three of our studies, the percentages of mixed-raced Brazilians—*pardos, mulatos,* and *morenos*—are much lower than percentages of Brazilians who self-identified in open-ended questions as such in the *Pigmentocracies* survey conducted by Graziella Moraes Silva and Marcelo Paixão around 2010: 11 percent as *moreno* and 25 percent as *pardo*.[67] In short, Brazilians who have migrated to New York City are a whiter subset of the Brazilian population, whether or not they play Brazilian jazz.

In addition to these quantitative demographic differences between the Brazilian musicians in the Brazilian jazz scene of New York City and Brazilian immigrants in the metropolitan region in general, there appear to be qualitative differences between how Brazilians can position themselves and are positioned with respect to social-identity categories in the United States. Instead of using categories supplied in the US census, Brazilians in the United States often prefer to identify themselves as "Brazilian," which they write on forms instead of checking a box; alternatively, they may self-identify as "white" or "Latino" rather than as "non-white," "Black," or "Hispanic."[68] These and other acts of self-identification in their lives are partly strategic: as many strive for upward mobility, they avoid associating themselves with Hispanics and Blacks because those groups are discriminated against in the United States.[69] For the same reason, scholars report that Brazilian immigrants may embrace and perform stereotypes of Brazilians as exotic, tropical, sexy, and erotic—however demeaning—if it helps to distance themselves from Hispanics, Latinos, and Blacks, notwithstanding overlapping stereotypes among these ethnic groups (see Chapter 3).[70]

Such attitudes contrast somewhat with those of Brazilians playing Brazilian jazz in New York. While musicians use their Brazilian distinctiveness to their advantage, they do not seem to be distancing themselves from African American and Latinx music or musicians. If anything, possibly the opposite: they work within the jazz industry in which African Americans hold the most prestige and authenticity; Latinx musicians of Hispanic-Caribbean heritage also hold significant authority, especially regarding Afro-Hispanic-Caribbean Latin jazz, which is a far more prominent and prevalent jazz style in New York than Brazilian jazz. This effects perceptions of authenticity within the United States as well as in Europe, thereby influencing who is hired to perform in clubs, concerts, and festivals.[71] The Brazilian musicians pursue niche markets for bossa nova and Brazilian jazz while also striving to participate in the larger jazz scene, which may be biased toward African American and Latin music if not necessarily musicians. Indeed, Brazilians often gravitate to play Brazilian music because they are rarely accepted in the mainstream jazz scene. It is in this context that the white Brazilian percussionist Sergio Krakowski recalled being impressed when he saw Continentino playing straight-ahead jazz with American musicians in a New York nightclub, remarking that Continentino had achieved a level of success by transcending the niche of Brazilian music.[72] It is possible that no greater compliment could be paid a Brazilian musician than if hired by successful bandleaders, which of course includes African American and Latinx musicians. These situations are some of the Brazilians' greatest success stories: Joe Henderson and Yo-Yo Ma hired Nilson Matta, Kenny Barron hired Trio da Paz, Dianne Reeves hired Romero Lubambo, Rufus Reid hired Duduka Da Fonseca, Danilo Perez hired Rogério Boccato, Arturo O'Farrill hired Lívio Almeida, John Patitucci hired Rogério Boccato, and Paquito D'Rivera hired Paulo Braga, Lubambo, Zottarelli, and others. The most celebrated and influential of these collaborations, though outside of New York City, was when Chick Corea hired Flora Purim and Airto Moreira to form his group Return to Forever in the early 1970s; similarly, Pat Metheny hired Naná Vasconselos. This happens beyond the jazz scene, too: Björk hired Eumir Deodato, Paul Simon hired Cyro Baptista, Steve Winwood hired Edson "Café" Aparecido da Silva, Angelique Kidjo hired Rubens de la Corte and Itaiguara Brandão, the Platters hired Vanessa Falabella, and David Byrne hired Mauro Refosco. African American bandleaders have also hired Afro-Brazilian musicians, such as Harry Belafonte who hired Dom Salvador and later da Silva, who previously toured with Roberta Flack; and, more recently, Brianna Thomas hired Fernando Saci. These stories parallel earlier stories of Brazilians hired by non-Hispanic white Americans—Stan Getz and João Gilberto, Frank Sinatra and Antônio Carlos Jobim—though they also clearly differ with respect to the US ethno-racial hierarchies at issue. These generalizations are undoubtedly broad and paint an incomplete picture, yet they contrast with the identity politics that Brazilian immigrants in the United States typically navigate and the strategies typically used, as reported in the social science literature. Regardless of how the musicians navigate ethno-racial and nationality categories in their daily lives, which is beyond the scope of this study, within their careers, they operate within different identity hierarchies. All the more reason it is to situate the musicians demographically within the jazz scene and industry.

Musician Demographics in Jazz Compared to Brazilian Jazz

The demographic breakdown of the 173 musicians of Brazilian jazz in New York in comparison to published data about jazz musicians in the New York metropolitan area shows that the Brazilian jazz scene has more female musicians yet fewer Black musicians than the larger jazz scene. A 2003 study by the National Endowment of the Arts surveyed two groups: union members of the American Federation of Musicians (AFM) who play jazz, and jazz musicians contacted through snowball method (chain-referral sampling method) that utilized networks of jazz musicians for referrals. These studies produced remarkably different numbers.[73] The first study cast a very wide net by surveying any musician who answered affirmatively to the question, "Do you ever play or sing jazz music?"[74] The report estimated that there are 33,000 musicians who play jazz in the New York area, although only 7,000 in the AFM union.[75] Ethnomusicologist and jazz scholar Travis Jackson cites the latter number from this report, though he dismisses several attempts to count musicians as inaccurate.[76] Caveats notwithstanding, comparing my data to the NEA study shows, first, that Brazilian jazz musicians constitute a half-percent of the estimated 33,000 jazz musicians and 2.4 percent of the 7,000 union members. Second, a higher percentage of musicians in the Brazilian jazz scene present as female (30%) than self-identified women musicians who "ever play or sing jazz" (either 15.6% or 26%, depending on the dataset).[77] By contrast, the Brazilian jazz scene appears to have a lower percentage of Black musicians (11%) or people of color (19%) than self-identified Black jazz musicians in the NEA study (17.3% or 32.8%, depending on the dataset).[78]

A Privileged Class of Immigrant Professionals

The immigrant musicians in this book—Brazilians and people from other countries—are relatively privileged thanks to their musical talents, skills, often their socioeconomic class backgrounds, and professional networks. This was also the case for Brazilian musicians in the 1930s through 1950s.[79] Many recent immigrant musicians hold O-1 visas for "Individuals with Extraordinary Ability or Achievement," because they have proved themselves to be talented professionals who can contribute positively to the US culture and economy.[80] Those who receive this legal status can work in the United States and travel abroad, which enables touring, with certain rules and requirements for renewal that vary by country. (Brazilians have more restrictions than Israelis, for instance.) The O-1 visa carries financial and logistical burdens, too. Nevertheless, this work visa elevates the musicians to a privileged status that allows them to accumulate international experiences and transnational identities. Some musicians are consciously grateful for the US immigration policies that allow them to migrate and try to earn a living in music, which would not be possible in other countries that are similarly desirable for their occupations. Not all the musicians who play in New York's Brazilian music scene have this immigration status; most are US citizens (by birth, parentage, marriage, or due process), permanent residents, student-visa holders, and green card holders, while some are un-documented residents and thus do not have the same level of mobility, which limits their career growth. Among Brazilian migrants, this undocumented status usually results from entering the United States on tourist visas and overstaying its time limits. Apparently, in the 1980s and 1990s this could be rectified, transformed into legal permanent residency. But in the aftermath of September 11, 2001, according to Margolis, immigration policies and en-forcement practices changed such that overstaying time limits on tourist visas would prevent Brazilians from entering the United States legally in the future. To receive a tourist visa, Brazilians now need to show proof of enough financial resources and convince officers that they will return to Brazil.[81]

US-Born Musicians and Nationality Biases

To continue the introductory discussion of nationality biases, almost all the 38 US-born American musicians I counted in the Brazilian jazz scene (22% of the total) appear as white and of European descent. White privi-lege compounded by their home-turf advantage have likely bolstered the Americans' access to higher education, capital, and career opportunities. Generally a socially conscious and progressively minded group, some American musicians have used their citizenship status and capital to support Brazilian musicians wishing to travel, study, or migrate to the United States, such as sponsoring their visas, providing lodging and contacts, organizing shows and tours for the visitors, and so on. The same can be said of Brazilian musicians after becoming American citizens. Some of the non-Brazilian musicians have married Brazilians, which of course influences their actions on behalf of Brazilian in-laws and other relatives.

Despite these advantages of white privilege and navigating US society in general, some of the Americans I interviewed have felt passed over in favor of Brazilians for performance opportunities. This was not voiced as a major complaint, but noted as a common bias in the industry and yet an-other reason to be proactively entrepreneurial. The nationality-bias espe-cially irks the US-born musicians when they feel they play Brazilian music better than some Brazilians who started playing professionally after arriving in New York in order to gain work. Presenter Jane Stein, who regularly books the Brazilians Maúcha Adnet and Trio da Paz for university stages, acknowledged that usually musicians from the culture are hired to represent their culture.[82] Musician-curator Billy Newman has encountered this bias when seeking gigs for himself, too. "Of course, totally, if you're Brazilian, someone's going to be much more interested in you."[83] On the other hand, in their roles as presenters, Newman and Mark Morganelli regularly book non-Brazilians to play Brazilian music. Newman explicitly described his curatorial vision for the Brazilian series at Cornelia St. Café as for non-Brazilians who play Brazilian music and, conversely, Brazilians who play jazz or experimentations with other music.

The musicians experience nationality prejudices related to instrumentation. US-born pianist Deanna Witkowski and percussionist Scott Kettner face additional hurdles of playing rhythm section instruments, because bandleaders commonly hire Brazilians for those roles regardless of who plays the other parts.[84] Brazilian musicians, perhaps especially percussionists, can empathize as they struggle to be hired to play anything other than Brazilian music in the United States, despite their interests and competencies in American genres.[85] Vanderlei Pereira could more easily find work in New York playing Brazilian jazz and jazz with Brazilians than he could playing jazz in American-led ensembles.[86] Such competition among musicians seems more based on national origins than racialized identities, nor was race/ethnicity mentioned by the musicians regarding this topic; although, with so few people of African descent in the scene, this intersectional tension is hard to discern.

Instrumentation

The distribution of instrumentation among Brazilian jazz musicians is distinguishable from trends in mainstream jazz, which also connects to gender relations, discussed next (see Table 1.5). The most prominent instruments, irrespective of identity categories, are, in descending order, voice, percussion, piano, guitar, bass, and drum set; woodwinds and brass form distant next places along with some specialty instruments. In the jazz scene, saxophone is far more popular (12.5% in the NEA study), and percussion trails much further behind in numbers (1.5%).[87] The popularity of the voice

Table 1.5 Instruments played by musicians, totals and by gender. Some musicians play multiple instruments.

Instrument	Total #	% of Total	Males	% of Males	Females	% of Females
voice	45	26.0%	11	8.7%	34	72.3%
percussion	35	20.2%	30	23.8%	5	10.6%
piano	30	17.3%	22	17.5%	8	17.0%
guitar	26	15.0%	26	20.6%	0	0.0%
bass	18	10.4%	17	13.5%	1	2.1%
drum set	22	12.7%	22	17.5%	0	0.0%
flute	7	4.0%	4	3.2%	3	6.4%
saxophone	7	4.0%	6	4.8%	1	2.1%
trombone	4	2.3%	4	3.2%	0	0.0%
accordion	3	1.7%	3	2.4%	0	0.0%
woodwinds	3	1.7%	2	1.6%	1	2.1%
pandeiro	2	1.2%	2	1.6%	0	0.0%
trumpet	2	1.2%	2	1.6%	0	0.0%
vibraphone	2	1.2%	2	1.6%	0	0.0%
clarinet	1	0.6%	0	0.0%	1	2.1%
harmonica	1	0.6%	1	0.8%	0	0.0%

certainly distinguishes the Brazilian jazz scene (28%) from the overall jazz scene (14.4%). Its popularity among female musicians in my data (75%) likely contributes to the higher percentage of women than in the jazz scene. Compared to most Brazilian genres, the piano is more prominent in Brazilian jazz; in fact, one way that people compare samba jazz to bossa nova is through the use of the piano instead of the guitar. Pianos are far less popular in Brazil than they have been in the United States and are still hard to find in performance venues, according to Eliane Elias.[88]

Female Musicians

There are quantitative disproportions and discriminatory relations between female and male musicians in the Brazilian jazz scene, which are mostly consistent with the broader jazz world. With musicians who present as female constituting 30 percent of the musicians I counted, the Brazilian jazz scene has a higher percentage of females than the larger jazz scene, though still quite imbalanced. Most jazz scenes have historically marginalized female musicians, as well as queer musicians, despite exceptions and efforts to effect change. As jazz historian Sarah Caissie Provost recently summarized the situation, "all people who do not fit into this straight cisgender group of men experienced exclusion from jazz."[89] Historians have documented female jazz musicians throughout the twentieth century, though jazz histories, including textbooks, have sidelined them by privileging men, instrumentalists, and a selection of star performers.[90] Ethnomusicologist and jazz scholar Lara Pellegrinelli surveyed this trend and concluded, "Jazz historiography effectively cements the marginalized status of women early in a tradition of representation as well as musical chronologies."[91] The resulting male-dominated professional marketplace and educational settings for jazz became normalized as heterosexual masculine domains that discourage female participation. Girls, young women, and female adults encounter myriad disincentivizing practices: gender-based assumptions and negative stereotypes, sexist remarks and behavior, lower expectations yet higher measures of achievement than their male counterparts, and so on.[92] All-women's jazz programs, festivals, and bands have provided a double-edged sword alternative: although reinforcing gender segregation, they provide comradery and mentorship, build competencies and confidence, and open professional doors. As jazz pianist-scholar Monika Herzig assessed: "as long as we don't have equal parity in participation, opportunities, and pay rate for women in jazz, all-women bands continue to provide the safe, nurturing, and inspiring environment that supports self-efficacy, high levels of performance, and role models. Furthermore, the presentation on prominent stages eliminates perceptual barriers and counteracts lingering instrument stigmas. Once such parity is achieved, the music will represent the democratic principles of creating jazz in true fashion."[93]

Among the female musicians of Brazilian jazz in New York whom I interviewed, some feel that men do not take them as seriously as the male musicians, which is consistent with women's experiences in jazz.[94] They describe an uphill battle, though not unsurpassable. Pianist Mamiko Watanabe, a Japanese female, reflected, "always [when] working with guys, it's not easy, but they listen [to] and respect me."[95] Instrumentation here is largely gender-segregated such that usually females are vocalists and pianists while usually males are instrumentalists. This gendered influence on instrument choices, or sex-stereotyping, is consistent with historic trends in jazz and Western art music.[96] Nationality compounds gender biases in various ways: non-Brazilian female musicians may feel greater discrimination in the Brazilian music scene. On the other hand, white American female musicians benefit from white privilege and American citizenship; meanwhile, female Brazilians benefit from perceived authenticity and authority—and for singers, language fluency. Non-Brazilian and non-American female musicians navigate these stereotypes and others; for example, the Japanese females likely encounter orientalist stereotypes and issues related to general Japanese Brazilian and Japanese American histories and identities.

Witkowski suspects that being a female instrumentalist in a male-dominated field has reduced the chances that male bandleaders will hire her and has negatively affected her interactions with male bandmates.[97] In fact, one male Brazilian bandleader I spoke with hired Witkowski as a substitute after being unable to hire two male Brazilian pianists. Then, when playing in that ensemble, Witkowski felt a subtle condescending attitude from male bandmates: "sometimes more with some male musicians—I mean it can happen with women too—but there's just a dismissal . . . or maybe if even knowing I can play, there's never going to be an acknowledgment. And I felt that, but it would be very hard to point it out exactly."[98] She contrasted this situation with the welcome she felt when playing in female-led ensembles, such as Sherrie Maricle's all-women's DIVA Jazz Orchestra and Annette A. Aguilar's mixed-gender ensemble, the StringBeans. About Aguilar's group, which plays Brazilian jazz and Afro-Hispanic-Caribbean Latin jazz, Witkowski said:

> She definitely has women in her bands and that's always something I've liked about her groups. So, it just has a different feel, even just socially or just playing . . . she respects the music and she knows the history, and she plays the stuff, but it's not about being faster or louder. . . . There's not that drive, that purpose that that is it. It's more like, "We're here to make music, to make people feel good, and have fun."

The result is, "It's like you feel a little more like a community; that's different than some other groups I have played in."

Make no mistake, percussionist Aguilar views herself as a strict bandleader with high expectations for musicianship, knowledge of repertoire, work ethic, and professionalism.[99] For Aguilar, these aspects are interrelated with her approaches to leadership, entrepreneurship, and facing down sexism. When we spoke, she singled out her work creating and presenting a "Women in Latin Jazz Festival" as a recent career highlight: she curates and promotes shows in New York City that feature female musicians and composers, though they include male musicians and composers, too.[100] "It's very difficult to be a bandleader and to do what I'm doing. I think I learned a lot from my mom and my grandmother, them coming from Nicaragua and women raising us basically, and what they did, what our grandparents, what hell they had to go through." Aguilar segued from reflecting on the challenges of bandleading, including logistical and physical, to the sexism she has had to dismiss as a drummer and percussionist: "When I was a kid, if somebody would've told me, 'Girls don't play drums,' which they told me, I didn't listen to them. [Her response:] 'Well then, fathers don't leave mothers with six kids. Who are you? No, I know what I'm doing.'"

Susan Pereira faced gender discrimination when playing percussion that she had to work overly hard to overcome.[101] The samba scene in the 1980s was even more gender-segregated than it is today, she commented. She was allowed to play the small *tamborim* frame-drum but was not allowed to play *surdos*, the largest bass drums. The male teacher/leader, she recalled, "didn't believe that I could do it because I'm small and I am a woman. And then I had to prove to him that I could do it. So, I did in this class. It was like this big moment. And then I became the *surdo* [player]. But I could only play second [*surdo* . . .] the answer part." A glass ceiling remained. Over the decades she has noticed more women playing samba percussion, both in Brazil and in New York.

Woodwindist Anat Cohen, a white female Israeli, avoids sexist men when she can, though has noticed fewer among musicians than in the greater population. "Of course there are some people that still symbolize the machoism, but I don't hang out with people like that. I like cool people. If I get any sense or bizarre vibe, I smell it a mile away and I'm like, 'I'm out of here.'"[102]

These female instrumentalists and the other women in this book tend to lead their own ensembles, which in part helps them to control their performance opportunities and dynamics within their ensembles, and attempt to bypass sexist musicians and microaggressions in the scene. When women are bandleaders they seem to hire more women in their ensembles.[103] To speculate, because there are more female musicians in the Brazilian jazz scene compared to the overall jazz scene, it is possible that there are more female-led ensembles that also include additional women than there are in the larger jazz scene.

Exploitative Appropriation or Systemic Inequity?

With so many non-Brazilians performing Brazilian music, so many non-US-born musicians playing jazz, and so many non-Black musicians of various nationalities performing Afro-diasporic traditions (jazz, samba, etc.), suspicions of cultural appropriation loom large. Appropriation means that a person or entity is making something one's own, taking ownership, or making private property;[104] and the phrase "cultural appropriation" commonly extends the appropriated object to the practices of less-powerful peoples with little or no attribution or compensation. Hence, an accusation of cultural appropriation implies that musicians are playing music from demographic groups other than their own for commercial gain and without compensating heritage musicians or composers enough, or in a disrespectful or misrepresentational way.[105] To reel back the accusations momentarily, musicians in this book have indeed incorporated into their professional lives Brazilian jazz as a cross-cultural musical fusion. If the sole question is whether non-Brazilians are playing Brazilian music with respect and an understanding of the music, then those in this book easily pass muster according to their Brazilian colleagues. The non-Brazilians who play Brazilian genres at expert levels of competence have developed deep commitments to long-term study and performance, in contrast to musicians who occasionally play a couple Brazilian songs or make a sole Brazilian-themed album. Likewise, most of the Brazilian musicians were so committed to playing jazz that they considered themselves jazz musicians in Brazil before moving to the United States, only to find themselves treated as outsiders. The expert musicians tend to accuse dilettante musicians of profiteering, which is the exploitative critique that the phrase "cultural appropriation" has come to encompass. This section raises alternatives to critiques of cultural appropriation, instead of presuming exploitative practices by musicians from privileged identity categories, while also acknowledging that all musicians have agency to practice anti-racist and anti-sexist behavior. As discussed already, unfair institutional systems in society are largely responsible for causing the imbalanced demographic diversity within New York's Brazilian jazz scene.

Georgina Born and David Hesmondhalgh, in an influential publication from 2000, argued that appropriation should primarily concern ownership and profit, regardless of intentions or other criteria.[106] For a well-known example, some scholars have admonished Paul Simon for profiting from copyright ownership, despite his well-meaning intentions toward Black

South African musicians with whom he created the smash album *Graceland* (Warner Bros., 1986).[107] White-Black interactions in music, which feature prominently in Born and Hesmondhalgh's survey of musical appropriation, have been variously interpreted: neutrally as cross-cultural borrowing; positively as intercultural dialogue that have produced fusions, such as, collaborations of white and Black jazz musicians; and negatively as exotification of African descendants, dilutions of the Black music into bland mainstream music, and race-based discrimination and exploitation.[108] The expression "white appropriation of Black music" foregrounds a racially unequal music industry that has produced, for example, white swing bands who achieved greater financial success in the 1930s than Black bands, and white covers of rhythm and blues songs by Black musicians that did not compensate performers, improvisors, and arrangers in the 1940s; the latter was due to a limitation of copyright law until the 1970s.[109] Before judging instances that may seem to constitute white exploitation of Black music around the world, Born and Hesmondhalgh advised avoiding two common pitfalls: not to essentialize the music or people and instead take stock of particularities, that is, judge specific situations instead of generalizing; and not to over-celebrate cross-cultural musical exchanges and fusions as necessarily overcoming racial or socioeconomic power inequities or indicating achievements of progressive politics.[110]

Cultural appropriation can also include middle-ground scenarios other than the extremes of either benign adoption or exploitation. Useful here, anthropologist Richard A. Rogers distinguishes exploitative appropriation from other cross-cultural artistic encounters, based on his studies of Native American ethnographic arts in the southwestern United States.[111] In addition to situations of "cultural exchange," "cultural dominance," and "cultural exploitation" —the last of which he defines as "the appropriation of elements of a subordinated culture by a dominant culture without substantive reciprocity, permission, and/or compensation"—he discusses in detail "transculturation." If transculturation sounds as utopic as an even exchange, he emphasizes that systemic power inequalities help to "structure" its "dynamics," with which Born and Hesmondhalgh might agree.[112] Ethnomusicologist Bruno Deschênes connects transculturation in cross-cultural music practice to "transpropriation," an alternative to appropriation that emphasizes mutual exchange while acknowledging shared loss and gains. "For transculturality to occur, there must be transpropriation, since there must be an awareness that everyone is forging a common identity through giving and sharing, not only taking and appropriating unilaterally without consideration of who gives us what is being appropriated."[113] These concepts of creative cultural exchange contextualized in systemic power dynamics provide alternatives to appropriation (or alternative readings thereof) as an overly critical and generically applied critique. A common point about judgments of appropriation, made by the musicians in my study and by scholars cited in this chapter, is the importance to co-consider hybridity and anti-essentialism, notions embedded in transculturation. If a model of appropriation assumes the prior existence of an original static form, the model is essentializing a population group and ignoring the continual processes of hybridity; Marwan M. Kraidy calls this process "cycles of hybridity," a concept utilized by other scholars.[114] These theoretical discussions reinforce the general point that there is room for middle-ground understandings of "appropriation" as non-exploitative and respectful musical borrowing with cautious consideration of historical and structural power inequalities.

The musicians in this book tend to argue that to delve into someone else's musical culture to the extent that they have is a respectful and laudable endeavor. At least two white American musicians with whom I discussed this issue, Richard Boukas and Deanna Witkowski, explained a similar point that Brazilians Vanderei Pereira and Jorge Continentino made about "paying dues" and "carrying the flag" through the prolonged and committed processes of developing musical and cultural competencies. They state that if someone from outside a musical culture makes a concerted effort to learn how to play a music with respect to the culture, including learning other cultural aspects such as the language and aspects of the music's meaning and social-historical significance, it is likely that they are neither exploiting nor using inappropriately the music. They did not discuss fair financial compensation beyond employing Brazilian musicians for accompaniment or collaborations, however. Most musicians in this study have spent decades studying, practicing, and performing these music traditions and their combinations—Brazilian-jazz fusions—with considerable attention to learning the cultural and historical contexts of the music, including language acquisition.

My current opinion—though recognizably biased to support this book's musicians and from the perspective of a white jazz musician and ethnomusicologist—is that critiques of cultural appropriation (a) should be considered situationally and (b) can help educate musicians and institutions about potential exploitative situations and pitfalls, as a form of advocacy; however, they (c) should not be used loosely to blame musicians in social positions of greater privilege for historical systematic repression and for the minimal presence of Afro-descendent musicians in New York's Brazilian jazz scene. It would be unfair to blame the white and non-Black musicians of any nationality in the scene en masse; and at the same time, it is indeed morally critical to point out how few Black musicians are involved in performing these Afro-diasporic traditions that their communal decedants pioneered through centuries of tremendous suffering. Instead, the pool of musicians working in the scene should be widened to encourage and include more Afro-descendants and persons of color, despite competition for work. The US and Brazilian institutions that created and continue to maintain this situation should be critiqued and reformed, while also striving to change biases and microaggressions about authenticity and discriminatory beliefs and practices. Why have not more people of color been able to create careers as professionals and to migrate to the United States if they wanted to do so? Sources that provide historical answers are cited in this chapter, answers that rest largely in generations of unequal access to power, money, education, and work opportunities that compound family wealth, which determines musicians' unequal access to professional and migratory paths. If the main hurdle is currently financial, then how can Afro-Brazilian musicians receive funds and other resources to pay for the visas, travel, relocation, and initial support in New York while developing a viable career?

Summary

This chapter presented and interpreted the imbalanced demographic diversity among professional musicians who played Brazilian jazz in New York City between 2000 and 2020. Among the musicians playing Brazilian jazz, approximately 70 percent are male and 70 percent are white; half are Brazilians, a quarter are US-born Americans, and the rest immigrated from Japan, Israel, Canada, Europe, and elsewhere in South America. Regarding these imbalances, I placed most of the blame on historical and systemic racism, sexism, and classism in the United States and Brazil, while calling attention to discriminatory practices among musicians and within the music industry. An original dataset of 173 musicians, their instruments, and social categories (nationality, race, and gender) shows similar demographic imbalances when compared to published data about Brazilian immigrants in the United

States and jazz musicians in New York, with differences in the percentages of female musicians and Black Brazilian musicians. A comparison of racial categories, ideologies, and inequities in Brazil and the United States, as well as their impact on transnational migrants, informs the use of racial terms in the book; the comparison also suggests that Brazilian and US American racial ideologies might influence differently the interpretations of Brazilian jazz in New York. I also discussed class advantages for immigrants and the experiences of female musicians, while Chapter 3 presents stereotypes of Brazilian femininity. Given the demographic diversity and hybrid music, potential critiques of exploitative cultural appropriation are considered with caution.

Notes

1. Vanderlei Pereira, interview with author, August 8, 2015.
2. Pereira, interview.
3. Vanderlei Pereira, email communication, July 27, 2023.
4. Deanna Witkowski, interview with author, March 19, 2019.
5. Jorge Continentino, interview with author, August 24, 2015.
6. Pereira, interview. Ethnomusicologist Eduardo Lis heard similar complaints from North American experts in Brazilian jazz during the 1990s, that many musicians only knew bossa nova and had not listened closely to or studied Brazilian music (e.g., Lis 1996, 132–133).
7. Monson 2007, 78–80.
8. Jazz scholar Kelsey Klotz explored the tension between progressive social activism and white privilege in American jazz with respect to Dave Brubeck (Klotz 2023).
9. Winant 1999, 98, italics in original. Winant's chapter concerns critiques and nuanced attitudes toward contrasts between Brazil and the United States, through the 1990s. Legal scholar Dorothy Roberts explains how the colonial Black-white racial classification in US racial ideology related to policing interracial sex, privileging white male slaveholders, and enforcing rules of matrilineal descent for the enslaved: "if a mother was Black and enslaved, so was her child" (Roberts 2021, 48).
10. "Racialization" can mean "the extension of racial meaning to a previously racially unclassified relationship, social practice, or group" (Omi and Winant 2015, 111) and, more specifically, according to scholars of race politics in Latin America, "the ways in which the codification of racial categories and hierarchies assigns values based on skin color and phenotype resulting in negative differential treatment in the political economy, labor markets, education, health care and the administration of justice" (Dixon and Johnson 2018, n.p.).
11. Omi and Winant 2015, 266; see also 138–140.
12. Alexander 2006, 425–426.
13. Kendi 2021, 425.
14. Anthropologist Jennifer Roth-Gordon, for instance, argued that Brazilians in Rio de Janeiro make judgments concerning degrees of whiteness and blackness both with respect to people's appearance and their etiquette, behavior, and speech (Roth-Gordon 2016).
15. Telles 2014, 3.
16. Historian Barbara Weinstein and anthropologists Roth-Gordon and Peter Wade reiterated this prevalent dichotomy between inclusive ideology and discriminatory practices in Brazil (Weinstein 2011, 224; Roth-Gordon 2016, Chapter 1; Wade 2017, 477).
17. Monk 2013, 2021. On challenges to the bi-racial classification in the United States, see also Skidmore 1993; Seigel 2009, 283 n.3.
18. Ramos-Zayas 2012, 19–24, 123.
19. Omi and Winant 2015, 126.
20. For example, in the *Pigmentocracies* survey of Brazil, only one person out of a thousand wrote "Afro-Brazilian" in an open-ended question about self-identity (Silva and Paixão 2014, 191).
21. Omi and Winant 2015, 122.

22. Silva and Paixão 2014, 184–188.
23. Brazilian Institute of Geography and Statistics 1999; Silva and Paixão 2014, 187. Historian George Reid Andrews clarified that, in Latin American societies, the term *pardo* was intended to distinguish anyone with African ancestry from white elites (Andrews 2004, 6).
24. Micol Seigel cautioned that to embrace these commonly used terms uncritically risks reinforcing outdated colonialist terms with their power inequities (Seigel 2009, xvii). Although "mulatto" is an English word that some authors cited here use, I only use the Portuguese spelling of *mulato* in the book because it only appears in reference to Brazilian racial constructions and the term *mulato* may not match the use of mulatto in US racial history.
25. Joseph 2015, 184. Joseph found herself classified as either *parda* or *morena* in Brazil (10). Similarly, when Henry Louis Gates Jr. asked people in Brazil how he would be classified there, he received seven categories as answers. He commented on the ideology of inclusion and the discriminatory reality: "Many people wanted me to be one of Brazil's seemingly endless shades of brown, not black, and to assure me that I was brown, too. Were these categories, these many names for degrees of blackness, a shield against blackness? [...] these many shades of black and brown clearly weren't equal" (Gates 2011, 39).
26. On problems with "mixed race" discourse and its integration into the US census, see Omi and Winant 2015, 109, 124.
27. Baran 2007; Seigel 2009, xvii; Silva and Paixão 2014, 191. Social contexts in Brazil also influence racial self-identifications, such as identifying as *negro* or *moreno* (Silva and Paixão 2014, 201).
28. For example, after wrestling with these nomenclature dilemmas, Seigel used a combination of terms for his study of racialized cultural encounters between the United States and Brazil: "whiter" rather than "white," and "black," "Afro-Brazilian," "Afro-descendent," "African American," and "Afro-American" (Seigel 2009, xvii–xviii). Ethnomusicologist Andrew Snyder, studying street Carnival scenes in Rio de Janeiro, used "Whiter" and "Blacker" multi-purposely to avoid binaries, to account for diversity within mostly white or mostly Black music scenes, and "to emphasize the relational element of racial formation in critical race studies" (Snyder 2022, 17).
29. Wade identified this type of focus—on discrimination based on race and gender in a labor market—as an example of research on race and gender, rather than on race and sex (Wade 2017, 10–11).
30. Goldschmitt 2020, 18. Goldschmitt also noted that samba music and dance have long encapsulated Brazil's brand internationally as racial mixture through a comparative racial lens: "The durability of samba and mixture as metonyms for Brazil's brand is indelibly tied to perceptions that the country is better than most at race relations" (17). Anthropologist Hermano Vianna explained how samba became a symbol of Brazilian national identity connected to its ideology of racial democracy (Vianna 1999).
31. Wade surveyed scholarship about Latin American migrant identifications in the United States that support the pigmentocracy inequities as well as show myriad strategies to navigate combinations of biracial and gender norms in the United States, home-country identity politics, and local contexts (Wade 2009, 232–236).
32. Joseph explained how the self-identifications of Brazilian migrants in the United States were influenced by ways that others perceived them, the perspectives of Americans about them, and how social settings and social relations influence how they thought they were perceived. External classifications shaped their self-categorizations. Their skin color and hair as well as social factors were more influential on identifications than ancestry (Joseph 2015, 40–41).
33. McDonnell and de Lourenço 2008, 153, 167; Joseph 2015, 35, 37–39. Similarly, Hispanic/Latinx people might be received as white or Black in the United States based on skin tone (Monk 2013, 2–3), though they may also reject these biracial categorizations (Wade 2009, 232–238).
34. While *Pigmentocracies* glosses *moreno* in Brazil as "dark" (Silva and Paixão 2014, 191), Maia defined *morena* as a "Europeanized mixture that became nationalized and 'improved' in the Brazilian tropics," pointing out that *morenas* represented Spanish mixture with Moors in pre-conquest Iberian Peninsula. She described *morena* identity as a flexible approach to national identities that whiter middle-class Brazilian women have adopted since Brazil's industrialization in the mid-twentieth century (Maia 2012, 50; see also 49).
35. Maia 2012, 51–52.
36. Joseph 2015, 31.

37. Joseph 2015, 32.
38. Maia 2012, 51–52; Joseph 2015, 32.
39. Seigel 2009, 4.
40. For oft-cited histories of European immigrant integration into American white society and expansions of whiteness, see Jacobson 1999; Roediger 2005. The assimilation of European immigrants in the United States is the heart of ethnicity theories that Omi and Winant criticized for not addressing racial exclusion of Blacks, Mexican Americans, Asian Americans, and other people of color (Omi and Winant 2015, Chapter 1). Alexander also distinguished assimilation and hyphenated identities apart from racial exclusion, while recounting the history of European immigration (Alexander 2006, Chapter 17). An analogous, though also contrasting, situation happened in Brazilian history when racial ideologies and immigrant policies coalesced in attempts to "whiten" Brazil's population by encouraging European immigration (Lesser 2013, 11–14).
41. I might be convinced otherwise if studies show that African Americans perceive whiter Brazilians in the United States as Black and feel that their discrimination in the United States is comparable.
42. Fernandez was working mainly as a samba singer in New York, though she also performed bossa nova and other Brazilian genres and had been developing her jazz skills with help from Cidinho Teixeira and her husband, trumpeter Spencer MacLeish (Ana Fernandez, interview with author, May 28, 2021). Nêgah Santos mainly works as a percussionist in the house band for the *Late Show with Stephen Colbert* ("About," Nêgah Santos website, https://www.negahsantos.com/about, accessed August 23, 2023). I did not collect data about gender self-identifications and sexual preferences, mainly because I did not survey musicians but collected data about them from afar. To conduct a rigorous sociodemographic survey was not part of my interview practice.
43. Suzuki 2011, 158.
44. Margolis 2013, 5, 76, 122.
45. Margolis 2013, 122.
46. Fujita 2009, 30.
47. Lobo and Salvo 2013, 36–37.
48. Fujita 2009.
49. Fujita 2009, 29–30.
50. Adachi 2004, 71; 2014.
51. Fujita 2009, 83–86.
52. Silva and Paixão 2014, 192–193.
53. Jouët-Pastré and Braga 2008, 5; Lopes 2009, 54; Margolis 2009, 25–30.
54. Davis 1997, 11; Margolis 2009, 26, 99.
55. In his ethnomusicological study of professional musicians in Bahia, Brazil, Jeff Packman emphasized the poverty of the city relative to Brazilian cities, the close mapping of race and class lines, and the enduring hard work that musicians must invest in order to gain work (Packman 2021, 14–23). Anthropologist Christen Smith also painted a bleak picture of racist and impoverished Bahia, Brazil, in which theater artist-activists struggle to protest anti-Black state violence (Smith 2016).
56. Edson "Café" Aparecido da Silva, interview with author, January 24, 2020.
57. Margolis 2009, 35.
58. Andrews reported that 45 percent of Brazil's population in 2000 were Black or mulatto, and less than 1 percent were indigenous (Andrews 2004, 156). In *Pigmentocracies*, Silva and Peixão's survey in 2010 found that 54.9 percent of their 1,000 participants were Black or *pardo* combined, compared to 50.7 percent in Brazil's 2010 census (Silva and Paixão 2014, 191).
59. Connell 2002, 66, 87–88, 105. For more about Brazil's white/whiter middle class, see Owensby 1999, and in connection to music scenes in Rio de Janeiro, see Moehn 2012, 13–17, passim; Snyder 2022, 15ff.
60. Margolis 2009, 31.
61. Davis 2008, 43–47.
62. Lopes 2009; Margolis 2009.
63. "Biography," Valtinho Anastácio's website, https://valtinho.net/biography/, accessed August 2, 2023.
64. Lopes 2009, 68.
65. Margolis 2009, 26.

66. Maia 2012, 49–50.
67. Silva and Paixão 2014, 191.
68. Davis 1997; Margolis 2008, 343; 2009, 96; McDonnell and de Lourenço 2008, 153, 167; Ramos-Zayas 2012, 284; Chen et al. 2018, 605–606.
69. Davis 1997, 11; Lopes 2009, 69; Ramos-Zayas 2012, 179.
70. Davis 1997, 2008; Beserra 2008; McDonnell and de Lourenço 2008; Ramos-Zayas 2012.
71. See studies about the French jazz scene and concerts (Picaud 2016) and the experiences and reception of women jazz saxophonists in the United States, whom the public compares to African American men and masculinity in their sound and appearance (Suzuki 2011). On nationality and ethno-racial biases regarding jazz musicians in European concerts and festivals, see Bares 2009 and McGee 2022.
72. Sergio Krakowski, interview with author, January 12, 2016.
73. Jeffri 2003.
74. Jeffri 2003, 6.
75. Jeffri 2003, 16.
76. Jackson 2012, 71.
77. Jeffri 2003, 7. Jazz scholar Thomas Greenland used the 15.6 percent figure, which is nationwide (Greenland 2016, 14).
78. Jeffri 2003, 8.
79. Davis 2008, 32.
80. US Citizenship and Immigration Services, "O-1 Visa: Individuals with Extraordinary Ability or Achievement," USCIS.gov, last updated Jan 21, 2022, accessed March 19, 2022, https://www.uscis.gov/working-in-the-united-states/temporary-workers/o-1-visa-individuals-with-extraordinary-ability-or-achievement.
81. Margolis 2008, 357.
82. Jane Stein, interview with author, June 15, 2017.
83. Billy Newman, interview with author, January 26, 2018.
84. Deanna Witkowski, interview with author, March 19, 2019; Scott Kettner, interview with author, September 18, 2019.
85. Susan Pereira, interview with author, August 8, 2015; Leslie Malmed Macedo, interview with author, October 10, 2013. The two were speaking about experiences of male Black Brazilian percussionist-drummers.
86. Vanderlei Pereira, interview.
87. Jeffri 2003, Vol. III, 41–42.
88. Judy Cantor-Navas, "Eliane Elias on Returning to Her Home Country for 'Made in Brazil,' Being Blond & Female in Jazz," Bilboard.com, March 30, 2015.
89. Provost 2022, 423.
90. For an overview about the historiography of research on jazz and gender, see Rustin and Tucker 2008b. Although this research field began earlier than these publications, see Tucker 2000, 21, 27–29; 2004, 2008; Pellegrinelli 2008. See essays on wide-ranging sub-topics in these volumes: Rustin and Tucker 2008a; Reddan, Herzig, and Kahr 2022.
91. Pellegrinelli 2008, 44.
92. See Boeyink 2022; Castaneda and Quinlan 2022; and other essays in Reddan, Herzig, and Kahr 2022.
93. Herzig 2022, 476. On successes and failures in promoting women-in-jazz themed events, see Zola 2022, and Tucker's research approach mentioned in my Introduction, note 72.
94. Negative attitudes toward women who study and perform jazz is a recurring theme that Natalie Boeyink discusses in the context of higher education (Boeyink 2022).
95. Mamiko Watanabe, interview with author, August 10, 2015.
96. On gendered instrumentation as a force that limits female participation in jazz, see Tucker 2000, 6, 11; DeCoste 2017; Provost 2022, 430–431; Castaneda and Quinlan 2022, 272–273. For a general overview of gender and instruments, see Doubleday 2008.
97. Witkowski, interview.
98. Witkowski, interview.
99. Annette A. Aguilar, interview with author, July 11, 2019.
100. For a comparative critique of "women in jazz" festivals in New York City, see Zola 2022.
101. Susan Pereira, interview.
102. Anat Cohen, interview with author, June 14, 2017.
103. On women-led jazz ensembles in recent years, see Pellegrinelli et al. 2021.

104. "appropriation, n.," *Oxford English Dictionary* (online), last updated 2021.
105. Feld 1996; Young 2011.
106. Born and Hesmondhalgh 2000.
107. Born and Hesmondhalgh 2000, 26.
108. Born and Hesmondhalgh 2000, 22–23.
109. Among the many examples discussed in music scholarship, see Jones 1963, 163–164; Monson 2007, 29–30; Starr and Waterman 2010, 203–204; Maultsby 2017.
110. Born and Hesmondhalgh 2000, 22.
111. Rogers 2006.
112. Rogers 2006, 493.
113. Deschênes 2018, 279.
114. Kraidy 2002; see Rogers 2006; Weiss 2014.

2

SamBop, Brazuca, and
Transnational Polymusicalities

Pianist Dom Salvador, an icon of Brazilian jazz who moved to New York City from São Paulo state in 1975, composed "East River" in 1981. Named after the borough-dividing waterway, this brisk instrumental piece in a twelve-bar-blues form alternates between samba and jazz-swing grooves during the solo section. A Black Brazilian male, Salvador explained to me his motivation to mix the two genres using a term ripe with significance relevant to this book: "Because I have a lot of influence from Thelonious Monk and of course Charlie Parker, I tried to do something that I could put together the samba rhythms, the samba with bebop, like it's sambop."[1] The neologism "sambop" has multiple transnational connections, beyond the styles that Dom Salvador sought to combine. "Sambop" is also the title of several Brazilian-jazz compositions, the best known of which is by Maurício Einhorn and Durval Ferreira, from 1958, which Dom Salvador was likely referencing. It was famously recorded by the female Brazilian singer Leny Andrade and the male African American saxophonist Cannonball Adderley in the early 1960s, and analyzed by American and Brazilian scholars in English and Portuguese publications.[2] Other composer-performers of Brazilian jazz have recorded works bearing this title, including Randy Brecker in the United States and Paulo Morello in Germany.[3] Historian Bryan McCann explains how the original "Sambop" and Einhorn, its co-composer, epitomize musical "hybridity": this vehicle for up-tempo improvisation in an AABA song form with a samba groove was an unconscious amalgamation from the musical passions and autodidactic idiosyncrasies of a Brazilian harmonicist-composer in Rio de Janeiro, the son of Polish Jewish immigrants, obsessed with US jazz.[4] Enhancing the combinatory nature of "Sambop" were the improvised scat singing of its Brazilian singers, a hallmark of US jazz that was atypical for Brazilian performance practices.[5]

When titling my book, I took creative license to capitalize "SamBop" with a capital S and capital B in order to emphasize visually the combinatory nature

SamBop NYC. Marc Gidal, Oxford University Press. © Oxford University Press 2024.
DOI: 10.1093/oso/9780197619049.003.0003

of Brazilian jazz and make the book's subject quickly understood. However, a strength of the lowercase "b" in sambop is that it implies a bridging and blurring of boundaries between samba and bebop through their shared middle "b." This symbolic overlapping of styles appealed to Dom Salvador and is an argument I make in this book about Brazilian-jazz fusions. I have therefore retained conventional capitalization practices for the song and album titles "Sambop" and for the concept "sambop" in the book's prose.

Like sambop, Brazilian immigrants in the United States often experience expanding self-concepts of dual identities, denoted in the term Brazuca. "Brazuca" is slang for Brazilians living in the United States and elsewhere outside of Brazil, and has been used by journalists and social scientists to explain their experiences and the process of developing this transnational or binational identification.[6] Brazilians who have lived in the United States not only start thinking of themselves differently while abroad, but also notice their expanding identity when they visit or return to Brazil, as sociologist Tiffany Joseph has explained.[7] Some scholars ask if the term should be spelled "Brasuca" with an "s" to mirror the Portuguese spelling of Brasil rather than the English spelling, Brazil: the middle letter joins both countries and languages, but the "z" emphasizes the US side of people's experience.[8] The "b" in sambop bridges samba and bebop, irrespective of the languages used by musicians in Brazil, the United States, and, in the aforementioned example, Germany. Similar are compound song titles by musicians in this book, such as "Samblues" by Cesar Camargo Mariano, "Bluezilian" by Clarice Assad, and "Bluesbão" by Lívio Almeida.

The terms sambop and Brazuca suggest comparisons between the creation of music that combines the nationally associated genres and the self-identification of Brazilians living in the United States. While "Brazilian jazz" juxtaposes two categorical labels, implying that one qualifies the other, a compound word such as sambop implies something new or different, forged from two contributing genres. The situation that these terms symbolize is not solely about emerging immigrant identities, however, somewhere between hyphenated and assimilated incorporation into a host country's culture.[9] Brazilian-jazz fusions, like the various tunes titled "Sambop," were composed, performed, and recorded inside as well as outside of Brazil, aided as much by recordings and radio as through in-person collaborations. Mariano composed "Samblues" in Brazil, released in 1966, well before moving to the United States in 1994. So, sambop neither requires nor is solely the by-product of mobile people, but is primarily mobile music. Nevertheless, the international experiences that produce sentiments of being Brazuca should also affect a musician's ability to create, record, produce, and perform a sambop composition. If composing sambop in Brazil through the process of studying recordings—in addition to hearing occasional touring musicians and studying with teachers—is based on a certain understanding and competency with jazz from the United States, then musicians would presumably gain much more by playing and listening to jazz while living in the United States. Dom Salvador made this claim, that his education in jazz improved tremendously by listening to jazz musicians in New York's nightclubs and playing with American musicians since the 1970s, at a time when traveling between the countries was much less common than it is today.[10] For non-Brazilians, playing and collaborating with Brazilians has served as a key element of their education in Brazilian music and Brazilian-jazz fusion. Brazuca clearly addresses a process of forming a transnational identity from a Brazilian perspective. Since the Brazilian-jazz scene in New York includes non-Brazilians, learning to play jazz, Brazilian music, and Brazilian-jazz fusions—and play them well—also helps them to develop dual affinities with multiple nationally associated genres, affinities that can grow into more significant self-identifications.

I have found it most productive to consider the musicians in this study, their artistic work, their life experiences, and commonalities among their musical self-identities through two intersecting theoretical frameworks: the interdisciplinary theory of transnationalism and the ethnomusicology theory of bimusicality or, more broadly conceived, polymusicality. Combining these concepts yields *transnational polymusicalities*, which I have returned to repeatedly over the past several years when contemplating my study. Not entirely novel, my framework compares to interpretations by other ethnomusicologists who studied Brazilian jazz. Most relevant, Acácio Tadeu de Camargo Piedade advanced the concept of "friction of musicalities" to explain Brazilian jazz, especially in Brazil: "there is constant reference in Brazilian jazz to North American jazz, mainly in the realm of improvisations, and that these references mark the tense encounter between Brazilian and North American musicalities, a founding characteristic of this music."[11] Eduardo Lis, who studied Brazilian jazz in North America during the 1990s, highlighted the music's transnational quality, while using ethnomusicologists' theories of transculturation: transformative intercultural exchange.[12] Related to these interpretations are Jason Stanyek's notion of transregional *choro*, Natasha Pravaz's "diasporic musicscape," and

K. E. Goldschmitt's transnational bossa nova.[13] The musicians in my study are transnational in that they have developed affinities and identifications with at least two countries, Brazil and the United States, through their engaged study and practice of music along with other cultural aspects. This pertains to musicians of any original nationality or ethno-racial category, even though Brazilian jazz combines Afro-Euro-American fusions from Brazil and the United States. Bimusicality means competencies in multiple musical traditions, usually those that are significantly different and distanced from each other. In the process of developing musical skills, musicians usually develop related competencies with language, customs, and historical knowledge. Just as bimusical scholars have explained transformations in their self-identities through years of studying a second music and culture, so have many musicians. The musicians' polymusicality, meaning advanced skills in Brazilian genres, jazz, and Brazilian jazz, connects and overlaps with their transnational identities, meaning the intercultural competencies, expanded self-identities, and affinities with two nationally based musical cultures that they co-developed with music skills. This chapter introduces several musicians with respect to their transnational polymusicalities: Dom Salvador, Eliane Elias, Romero Lubambo, Anat Cohen, Miho Nobuzane, and Richard Boukas. Interspersed between these portraits are discussions of relevant concepts and issues: transnationalism and bimusicality/polymusicality, authenticity, musical accents and assimilation, and changing self-identities. Subsequent chapters introduce more musicians with respect to other topics, while continuing to imply the lens of transnational polymusicalities.

Eliane Elias

Pianist-singer Eliane Elias provides a second introductory example musician before further explaining the theories. A white Brazilian female of European descent from São Paulo and a New York resident since 1981, Elias plays annually at the major local nightclubs like Birdland, Iridium, and City Winery when she is not touring internationally and recording. A special event that speaks to this chapter's theme was her 2017 concert in Jazz at Lincoln Center's 1,200-seat Rose Theater and livestreamed/webcasted at jazz.org; it was among the largest concerts of Brazilian jazz in New York City during the 2010s. Titled "From Bill Evans to Brazil," the show encapsulated her fluencies in jazz and Brazilian genres, at the highest competency levels of transnational polymusicality in this book. Her first set featured pieces dedicated to one of her jazz idols, as she used to transcribe solos by Evans when she was from age eleven through fifteen, along with those of virtuosi Art Tatum, Bud Powell, Oscar Peterson, and Keith Jarrett.[14] This alone is an extraordinary feat. Their influences can be seen in her piano-trio format and heard in her jazz-oriented playing, stylistically comparable in my ears to Herbie Hancock and Chick Corea, with whom she has dueted. In the second set, Elias played sambas and bossa novas. Her grand finale was a ten-plus minute rendition of Antônio Carlos Jobim's classic "Desafinado" (Off-key) in an arrangement she has been developing for decades that combines singing and virtuosic piano improvising, expressing different aspects of her changing musical and personal identity. Her rendition moves seamlessly between grooves of bossa nova, samba, jazz swing, and rhythm and blues; the structure is explained in Chapter 4.

Elias developed her polymusicality in classical, jazz, and Brazilian genres from an early age. Her mother was a piano teacher who loved classical music and jazz. Elias grew up in São Paulo during the 1960s and 1970s with bossa nova and samba jazz around her, as well as rock and pop music.[15] As a child prodigy, Elias is a unique example in this book and an unfair benchmark to compare to other musicians who developed expertise in multiple genres over decades, often after they moved to or sojourned in another country. Nevertheless, even the wunderkind of this book gradually expanded her tastes, competencies, and approaches with her life experiences while living in the United States.

Elias's professional career began in Brazil and then took off in the United States. Starting at age seventeen, around 1977 in Brazil, she toured for three years with guitarist Toquinho and singer-lyricist Vinícius de Moraes, during which time she also met Jobim and Carlos Lyra. She moved to New York City in 1981 at age twenty-one to pursue a career in jazz and study classical piano at Juilliard. She attended jazz jam sessions and soon rose to prominence in the successful jazz ensemble Steps Ahead, with founding vibraphonist Michael Mainieri, saxophonist Michael Brecker, bassist Eddie Gomez, and drummer Peter Erskine. She also played and toured with the Charles Mingus tribute ensemble, Mingus Dynasty, and recorded with trumpeter and first husband Randy Brecker. Soon she began leading her own piano trios, signed with Blue Note Records, and produced best-selling/charting records on multiple continents; she made many of these records with her second husband, bassist Marc Johnson, who had played with Bill Evans.[16]

As her solo career developed, she began to sing professionally in addition to playing piano. She explained in 2009 how singing became part of her dynamic musical self-identity:

> To describe myself as an artist, I guess I could use the word chameleon, you know, changing colors. I have different sides. There is the side of the pianist. And then there is the side of the singer. And then there is the Brazilian music that I do. A composer too. All of those different things that are part of me are *true*. [...] All of those sides are different sides of me. They are all real. (Emphasis hers)[17]

She summarized her evolving interests in a 2013 interview, noting how each recording project documents a different phase:

> There are different sides of my music. Being born in Brazil, the Brazilian music is very strong. But I'm really a jazz pianist and I grew up with jazz, I've done classical work, I love R&B. There are so many things I love in music. And each project that I complete and release demonstrates a time of my life, what's been happening. And this last seven, eight years, I started singing a lot more.[18]

This trajectory of including more singing and shorter improvisations is not simply linear, though, perhaps due to her wide-ranging talents, musical interests, and audiences. Her live performances—more than her studio albums—combine both approaches that vary from show to show. I compared ten of her performances of "Desafinado" over thirty years, 1989 to 2018, and found that over the years they have included more singing and less avant-garde piano playing while her arrangements have also extended longer because she delineates more discrete sections. In a sense, her renditions have moved from lengthy improvisations to a segmented, stylistically diverse arrangement that creates a "a journey into a song that launched the bossa nova in 1958," as she prefaced her performance for the audience at that "From Bill Evans to Brazil" concert. Although the concert was bifurcated between American jazz and Brazilian song, her complex rendition of "Desafinado," as a Brazilian-jazz fusion, a work of sambop, encapsulates her polymusicality, developing interests, and expanding, perhaps Brazuca, self-identity.

Bimusicality/Polymusicality

In order to create and perform Dom Salvador's composition "East River," Elias's multi-groove arrangement of "Desafinado," and other Brazilian-jazz fusions, and to do them well, many musicians need high levels of competency with multiple music traditions, for instance samba, bossa nova, and bebop. They may also need competency with the conventional ways that Brazilian-jazz fusions are typically played. Musicians in New York's Brazilian jazz scene have myriad levels of competency playing jazz and Brazilian genres. A majority of musicians have considerable competencies in jazz and samba, if not also other Brazilian and US genres, especially *choro*, *baião*, *maracatu*, blues, rock, and funk. They have also developed expertise in common ways to combine them, which can be generalized as a competency in Brazilian jazz.

These musicians strive to achieve bimusicality, a term akin to bilingualism that ethnomusicologists use to describe their own learning process for research purposes. I will be drawing on bimusicality in this book, rather than simply speaking of competencies, because it helps connect several concepts relevant to the musicians' practices, experiences, and identities. In company with other scholars, I utilize bimusicality as a lens to understand the professional musicians I am studying. My focus is not the initial stages of learning an unfamiliar music, which is what most ethnomusicologists do during fieldwork research, as I also did when conducting research on Afro-Brazilian religious music in Brazil during 2007 and 2008.[19] Instead, the application is to analyze musicians who have already developed advanced skills and even expertise in Brazilian genres and jazz as well as conventions for combining them in Brazilian jazz.

Ethnomusicologists have expanded Mantle Hood's concept of "bimusicality" beyond his straightforward argument that learning to perform an unfamiliar music with deliberation and commitment, in addition to one's primary music (i.e., the music with which one is most familiar and competent), should be part of any music research.[20] Surveys of this intellectual history have noted the prominent position of bimusicality among ethnomusicological research methods as well as expanding theories of bimusicality.[21] Scholars have suggested a range of alternative terms over the years: polymusicality, multimusicality, intermusability, bimusicalism, and transmusicality.[22] Some prefer musicianship over musicality, and even Hood initially suggested to call this situation simply "musicality" because of the quantity of traditions a student could learn to perform.[23] Scholars have foregrounded composition as a bimusical practice related to performance and noted that many competencies can exist within a single music tradition.[24] Though Hood was a pioneer advocate of performance-based studies, musicians had already been developing multiple competencies well before ethnomusicology began to distinguish itself with this research practice.[25] More than "a way of expressing musical competence in disparate styles," as Stephen Cottrell says, most scholars point out the cultural insights gained from the experiential processes of learning to make music and making music with others, hence its utility as an ethnographic research method.[26] Bimusical ethnomusicologists have shared that these processes of accumulating musical and cultural competencies have also changed their self-conceptions from observers to participants and then subjects, a point that will be applied to discuss the changing self-identities of musicians.[27]

Bimusicality is aspirational, not necessarily an achieved or static state that the phrase "bimusical musicians" suggests. Musicians have wide-ranging and ever-developing skills playing and composing in multiple genres and their combinations. Ensembles may intentionally include members without competency in one or another style for various strategic purposes, including the artistic goal of creating something new or, for marketability, including a musician who will attract audiences. Bimusicality is not the only criterion for success in New York's Brazilian jazz scene, just as musical ability is not the only prerequisite for success in the music industry, which is not a meritocracy based on musicianship alone. However, bimusicality among many musicians does contribute to the creation and performance of Brazilian-jazz fusions, just as it does to music fusions around the world. The process of developing bimusicality, striving toward musical fluency in multiple traditions and their combinations, while accepting inevitable shortcomings, has expanded musicians' cross-cultural competencies and shaped their self-identities along the way.

Many musicians in this study are similar to ethnomusicologists in their commitment to developing bimusicality and reaping its extra-musical rewards such as self-cultivation and increasing their intercultural perspectives. In fact, there are also trained ethnomusicologists among the musicians in the local music scene: Philip Galinsky earned a doctorate in ethnomusicology before starting a professional samba ensemble; Susan Pereira, Scott Kettner, and Amanda Ruzza studied ethnomusicology in college; several musicians earned master's degrees in music that entailed musicological theses, notably Abelita Mateus; and, at the time of writing this book, Rubens de la Corte was a doctoral student in ethnomusicology, Deanna Witkowski in a jazz studies doctoral program that likely includes ethnomusicological training, and Lívio Almeida was conducting practice-based music research for a doctoral program. Their advanced levels of bimusicality will undoubtedly influence their research experiences differently than most ethnomusicologists, as Liza Flood has shared reflexively.[28] For the musicians in this study, bimusicality has shaped in individualized ways their professional opportunities, the Brazilian-jazz fusions they have created, their cross-cultural understanding, and their transcultural identities. What ethnomusicologists have elucidated about their own gradual learning processes into musical cultures that differ significantly from their original traditions seems to fit many professional musicians in this study who spent a decade or decades of study and performance experiences as they gained advanced skills with multiple genres and also created musical fusions. Contrasting lengths of time constitute a major difference between scholars and performers, with exceptions. If most ethnomusicologists dedicate around a year conducting fieldwork that includes basic studies in performance but still provides them valuable insights into musical and cultural nuances, how much more insight would professional musicians gain during decades of continuous study, performance engagements, participation in intercultural collaborations, and the achievement of expert levels of musical competency? To be sure, many ethnomusicologists spend decades improving their performance skills in the tradition of their scholarship.

Cottrell made a similar leap to what I am doing here by using bimusicality as a framework to interpret aspects of professional, classically trained, freelance musicians in London who must play multiple styles of Western music: art music, musical theater, jazz, and rock. Acknowledging similarities among these genres, Cottrell delimited his topic as "local bimusicality" and analogized these to "dialects rather than languages, when the genres are similar enough."[29] Likewise, the musical distance between samba and jazz as cousin Afro-Euro-American traditions contrasts my research with studies of bimusicality that consider distinct traditions, such as European art music and Indonesian gamelan.[30] Similar to the musicians in my study, Cottrell's professionals in London have to play many types of music in order to build a sustainable career for themselves.

In fact, bimusicality may be a more important goal for some musicians, while creating original art may be a secondary concern, because their livelihood depends on playing existing repertoire and they may not be able to compose impressive new works. It stands to reason that there is more at stake in learning to play the second music well for these musicians than there is for ethnomusicologists, because the musicians are judged mainly on their abilities to play music whereas scholars are evaluated on their publications, collegiate teaching, and service to their institutions. Instead of writing scholarship to explain musical traditions, the musicians' professional goals are to perform, collaborate, compose, and create new music variously influenced by both countries' traditions.

Bimusicality denotes competencies with two musical traditions, yet many musicians in the Brazilian jazz scene of New York have assimilated more than two; hence, polymusicality is a more suitable expression. Common third genres are Western art music and various popular music such that their artistic works reveal influences of classical, jazz, rock, funk, Caribbean traditions, and Brazilian genres, including its popular music. Religious music is a less-common area of influence, usually Christian worship music or Afro-Brazilian religions. Some musicians also have significant competencies in folk music related to their ethnic heritage or national backgrounds, which have influenced their careers and original music: Japanese folk songs and festival music for Miho Nobuzane; Greek and Balkan music for Richard Boukas; various Latin American genres for Annette A. Aguilar and Memo Acevedo; Klezmer, Jewish music, and some Middle Eastern music for Anat Cohen; and a range of regional Brazilian folk traditions for the Brazilian musicians, especially from Northeastern Brazil.

To develop bimusicality in the United States can be an unexpected outcome for migrant musicians who originally sought to play jazz in its homeland. Once in New York, many Brazilians who had considered themselves jazz musicians found it challenging to break into the jazz scene. By contrast, they found opportunities to play Brazilian music and sometimes delve more deeply or broadly into Brazilian music once abroad, due to feeling distant from and nostalgic for their home culture. Cyro Baptista, a successful white Brazilian male percussionist who has lived in New York and New Jersey since the 1980s, spoke humorously, as he does, about this common phenomenon as he has experienced and witnessed it:

It's so funny because the people who are out of Brazil—this not only happen with me, it happened with many other players—because you go out of Brazil, you miss so much Brazil, you have this face that [seems to say], "Oh, Brazil, Brazil, Brazil," and you are not there. Then you start to be more Brazilian than the Brazilians. It's something that happens. It doesn't happen anymore with me because I'm old now.[31]

As Brazilian immigrants continue to pursue jazz and play Brazilian music simultaneously, they may combine their musical interests. But given the high demand for bossa nova in the jazz scene that they are exploring, they inevitably play bossa nova more than they had expected.

By comparison, the Japanese and Israelis who move to New York to develop their jazz careers eventually also develop their skills playing other genres whether due to the genres' prominence, personal interests, networks, or happenstance. These often include various Latin music, especially salsa and Brazilian genres. And again, given the presence of bossa nova in the jazz scene, they learn bossa nova to play jazz gigs. Some, but not all, of them had some exposure to Brazilian music in their home countries, though they developed their competencies in the United States, learning from musicians active in the local scene. A byproduct of this scenario is that immigrant musicians develop competencies playing bossa nova and other Brazilian styles and repertories well enough to perform in Brazil. Some musicians reside in Brazil to develop their skills, while others learn the music solely in New York. When some tour to Brazil, Brazilians comment in surprise at how impressively they play. Furthermore, their collaborations with other international artists in New York have taken them to other countries to play Brazilian music and jazz.

Given the presence of eclecticism, it may seem prudent to describe the new music as more generally cosmopolitan, postnational, or uniquely idiosyncratic to each musician rather than focus on the binational/bicultural fusions that bimusicality implies. However, most examples in this book are rather conventional Brazilian-jazz fusions and definitely show fusions of two main progenitors: US-originated jazz and Brazilian genres, especially samba. Worldly eclecticism, general cosmopolitanism, and idiosyncratic approaches are better suited to describe the more experimental creations I witnessed, which I do not delve into in this book other than passing mention.

Critiques of Authenticity

If pursuits of bimusicality sound solely meritocratic and democratic, bimusical musicians are commonly suspected of cultural inauthenticity and exploitative appropriation, depending on their privileges in social hierarchies. Since appropriation received attention in the previous chapter, authenticity is introduced here, though both issues are relevant throughout the book. Ethnomusicologist Bonnie Wade explained authenticity with respect to musicology by first tracing the concept's roots to nationalist constructions of collective identity based in language and folk music. She then observed: "Authenticity is also thought of as residing in a person who has acquired the knowledge that permits him or her to perform authentically or to evaluate 'authentically' as a critic. Here, 'authenticity' resembles 'authority.'"[32] She pointed out that a "lively debate persists" whether a bimusical musician can be accepted as representing music not from their own cultural background or historical era. Within this debate, ethnomusicologist Ricardo Trimillos discussed power implications: "The non-native who attempts to perform another's culture immediately confronts issues of entitlement and reception, as well as suspicions of 'going native' or 'playing ethnic.' For the outsider, performing another culture is almost always the result of conscious code switching. If one decides to do this, the challenges is to switch without appearing exploitative, condescending, or colonial."[33] Trimillos was remarking on the participation of cultural outsiders and insiders in traditional music ensembles on college campuses; therefore, the dilemmas differ for those playing a hybrid music like Brazilian jazz, which is played globally: to various extents, all the bimusical musicians involved have insider and outsider status, so everyone is non-native and native. Yet, perceptions of authenticity by audiences and industry personnel who market the music tend to reduce this nuanced perspective to stereotypes regardless of musical skills: the Brazilians tend to be perceived as authentic performers of any Brazilian genre, even Brazilian jazz; African Americans are accepted as the most authentic jazz musicians; Latinx musicians of Hispanic Caribbean ancestry are considered authentic performers of Latin jazz; and so on. As demographic tensions discussed in Chapter 1 emphasized, bimusical musicians in the Brazilian jazz scene face perception biases as authentic/inauthentic musicians based on their social identity categories, and sometimes despite their expert levels of musical and cultural competencies in multiple traditions.

Ethnomusicologist Aleysia Whitmore, who studied musicians, industry professionals, and audiences with respect to fusions of West African and Cuban music that is performed in Europe and the United States, made several points about authenticity relevant here. Although she found the concept of authenticity too nebulous to pinpoint,[34] she envisioned "axes of authenticity" with intersecting and dynamic spans between the dyads pure-hybrid, traditional-modern, original-copy, close-distant, local-global, live-mediated, and altruistic-commercial. "Finding the places where these axes collide, merge, and coexist helps us understand not only the values at play here (how authenticity is simultaneously traditional, modern, pure, and hybrid), but also how values change as industry actors choose various points along these axes and bring them together in different ways."[35] Drawing on music scholars Simon Frith, Timothy Taylor, and Sarah Weiss, Whitmore foregrounded a wide range of audience expectations about authentic performances, and a general flexibility, which means they are willing to embrace explicitly hybrid music as authentic. Audience subjectivities are also contextual: "The ways these consumers define authenticity and codify the real depend on individuals' subject positions and expectations, which are shaped by each person's culture, society, and politics, and the larger music and ethnicity industries."[36] By extension, polymusical musicians who perform Brazilian jazz in New York likely face judgments about their authenticity, right to perform, and suspicions about cultural appropriation; this pertains to musicians of any national, ethno-racial, and gender background, but unequal power hierarchies affect musicians' receptions differently. There are likely tremendous variations in definitions and evaluations of authenticity, with many influencing factors.

Transnational Polymusicalities

Given the international scope of the musicians who circulate in this scene and the binational nature of Brazilian-jazz fusions, transnational polymusicalities offers a suitable umbrella for the process of assimilating musical competencies associated with national cultures across cultural and nation-state lines. If this book's focus were solely on cross-cultural competencies, then intercultural or transcultural polymusicalities would be an appropriate framework; but the topic at hand is musical exchange between nationalized cultures of different countries, whose societal structures influence mobility and interpersonal interactions as well as cultural practices, values, customs, and aesthetics. Here "national" includes and implies cultural, societal, and political characteristics, not only nation-state polities. Culture often figures prominently in late-twentieth-century theories of nation and nationalism in history and the present, as political scientist Umut Ozkirimli has surveyed.[37] While theorists of nationalism have addressed culture as societal systems stemming from religion and dynasty or state-sponsored political symbols like flags and anthems, theorists also include vernacular language, literature, arts, and music in nationalist public cultural.[38] In this light, jazz in the U.S. and samba in Brazil symbolize nations and national identities within public cultures, as the Introduction discusses.

"Transnationalism" generally means, following anthropologist Steven Vertovec's extensive literature review, "sustained cross-border relationships, patterns of exchange, affiliations and social formations spanning nation states" by non-state actors.[39] Anthropologist Aihwa Ong and historian Micol Seigel use transnationalism to analyze ways that people can transform not only themselves, but also international relations through cultural practices.[40] In a volume of essays that critiques dichotomous border studies and reinterprets the US-Mexican border region via music, musicologist Alejandro Madrid and contributing scholars apply transnationalism to examine multiple aspects of musical expressions: the music, people, identifications, social dynamics, region, and the border. Madrid summarized, "The transnational musical bodies discussed in these essays occupy the border space and its imaginary through performance and the creation of expressive culture, and thus reterritorialize it into a transnational representative space."[41] A corollary suggestion that, through Brazilian jazz, people might transform international relations and regional spaces is intriguing; yet this book's project is narrower in focus than studies by Ong, Seigel, and Madrid, et al., by focusing on the experiences, expressions, and self-identities of transnational musicians and their music. I consider many musicians in this study to have developed transnational identities and the music they create and play to have transnational qualities. The music can be transnational not merely because it is played in multiple countries, but when it can contribute to, support, or express transnational experiences or identities.[42] Developing polymusicality is a process of transnationalization, both for musicians and for their music, with respect to musical practices, creations, interactions, and values. Various levels of access to international mobility have affected career trajectories and personal well-being; and career trajectories and aesthetic influences have coincided with musicians' expanded experiences, skills, and musical creations. Meanwhile, despite musicians' expanding interests, conservative tendencies of the music industry have encouraged certain types of music to flourish over others.

Transnationalism Compared to Related
Analytical Frameworks

I have found that transnationalism is overall more applicable to this project than several related frameworks for analysis: diaspora, the Afro-Atlantic, cosmopolitanism, and postnationalism. However, these concepts have not only informed each other and this book in specific situations and subtle ways, but their overlapping definitions and usages can at times render them synonymous. Although distinctions between diaspora and transnationalism can be elusive, transnationalism, first of all, includes experiences and perspectives of the non-Brazilian and non-immigrant musicians who develop close affinities with the United States and Brazil through bimusicality. Second, Brazilian jazz as a musical fusion combines characteristics and repertoires from genres closely associated with different countries.[43] While immigrants in this book may develop "diasporic consciousness," as many scholars have reported in other situations, non-migrant musicians may also cultivate levels of transnational consciousness. The multiple identifications that transnationalism conveys emerge when Brazilians adopt US customs and musical aesthetics, when Americans adopt Brazilian musical practices and aesthetics, and also when musicians from Japan, Israel, Germany, Russia, Colombia, and other countries develop affinities and competencies in American and Brazilian genres. Music scholars use both "transnational" and "diasporic" to describe people's movement between nations, experiences that continually shape the musicians and allow them to contribute in multiple countries. "This reflexive diasporic condition" develops during several stages of mobility, Simone Krüger and Ruxandra Trandafoiu summarize, including "the return/s to the homeland that help the circulation of the acquired transnational capital and reapplied diasporic reflexivity."[44] Transnational migrants maintain different levels of contact with home countries, which mass media has increased.[45] Studies of transnational and diasporic music and musicians have highlighted recontextualized meanings in new national settings as music traditions follow migrating populations.[46] To be sure, the conceptual distinction may be partially semantic, for some scholars extend diaspora to include non-migrants; for example, anthropologist Natasha Pravaz's notion of "diasporic musicscapes" includes Brazilian and other Latin American migrants as well as Canadian-born Canadians, all of whom identify strongly with each other and the music through participation in Toronto's Brazilian percussion groups.[47] However, those Toronto ensembles primarily play

Brazilian genres rather than a binational hybrid; also, the Canadian-born participants rarely travel to Brazil and appear more as allied participants in a diasporic musical community than do the musicians who create Brazilian-jazz fusions in New York.

An Afro-Atlantic, Afro-diasporic, or Pan-African interpretive framework is also appropriate, because the US American and Brazilian genres that are typically combined in Brazilian-jazz fusions—jazz, blues, funk, samba, *baião, afoxé, maracatu*—are Afro-diasporic with comparable roots, musical characteristics and aesthetics, and social-cultural significances for people of African descent.[48] In *The Black Atlantic*, Paul Gilroy noted the overlaps among approaches mentioned in this section in contrast to definitions of identity bound to essentialized notions of African-descended peoples and cultures: "In opposition to both of these nationalist or ethnically absolute approaches, I want to develop the suggestion that cultural historians could take the Atlantic as one single, complex unit of analysis in their discussions of the modern world and use it to produce an explicitly transnational and intercultural perspective."[49] The Afro-Atlantic has been a productive frame for scholars interpreting similar musical traits among genres and interna-tional collaborations among African descendants and/or Africans, which could extend to musicians in New York in some instances.[50] However, the ethno-racial heterogeneity of musicians in New York's Brazilian jazz scene, the strong European musical influences in Brazilian jazz, and variety in the local discourse render a solely Afro-Atlantic perspective as limited for an umbrella framework. The local discourse does not help matters, though this should not be the sole determinant. During my fieldwork, musicians and presenters rarely portrayed Brazilian jazz in New York as an Afrocentric project, with notable exceptions: a collaboration in 2015 between Arturo O'Farrill, Letieres Leite, and their large ensembles explicitly emphasized Afro-Atlantic connections.[51] The Black male Brazilian musicians Dom Salvador, Cidinho Teixeira, and Edison "Café" Aparecido da Silva created the ensemble Folia de Reis, the album *Ancestors* (1999), and live performances that emphasized Afro-Brazilian culture. Several musicians I interviewed—Brazilians, US-born Americans, and Japanese—spoke explicitly about African roots and diasporic connections of the music and its significance. These included Black Brazilians—da Silva, Amarildo Costa, Jailton "Dendê" Macedo, Ana Fernandez, and Fernando Saci—who noted or emphasized such personal resonances.[52] Regarding local discourse, it is possible that the sizable numbers of non-Black musicians and audiences has reinforced a

colorblind bias in the local discourse that fails to recognize, let alone emphasize Afro-descendent origins, innovators, and cultural ownership inherent in
Brazilian jazz.[53] Clearly, for Brazilian jazz in the Americas, transnationalism
and polymusicality are interrelated to the Afro-Atlantic content and context.
Although not the umbrella theory for this book, Afro-diasporic relationships
are discussed in particular with respect to samba-jazz fusions in Chapter 4.

Compared to "cosmopolitanism" and "postnationalism," in the ways I am
using these terms, "transnationalism" better describes most of the committed
musicians in New York's Brazilian jazz scene, primarily because transnationalism retains a focus on specific nation-states while emphasizing dual
affinities and trans-state relations. Among the multiple meanings of cosmopolitanism, I apply it to describe as a general empathetic openness to combining local and global trends, styles, and moral values, with or without
deeper cultural identifications and commitments; this can produce stylistically eclectic music or describe globally circulating aesthetics (including jazz
and Brazilian genres).[54] Authors have used "cosmopolitanism" variously to
interpret international circulations of fashionable ideas, products, aesthetics;
urban European (and then also American) influences abroad; proclivities toward global elite culture; or fusions of these with local culture.[55] Yet, cosmopolitanism is rarely as bi-directional as I employ transnationalism here.
In this book, cosmopolitanism is most apparent when musicians eclectically embrace globally circulating music, practices, or tastes in combination
with established or local music; meanwhile, a transnational interpretation
foregrounds cultural connections between particular nations, whether
Brazil-US identifications and musical fusions or trinational relationships.
Most musicians in this book are more binationally or trinationally focused
in their cultural affinities than generally eclectic, globally omnivorous, or
Eurocentric elitist. Similarly, anthropologist Deborah Pacini Hernandez applied "transnationalism" and "cosmopolitanism" differently to help explain
hybridity, her primary framework, in popular genres associated with US
Latinx populations: she advocated for "a multilateral transnational model"
to explain the ascendance of Mexican regional music in the United States,
where it has increasingly been produced, while distributed by multinational
record conglomerates; and she noted "the extent to which 'here and there'
patterns of transnational life and identity formation have added additional
layers to the already complex hybridity of U.S. Latino musical practices."[56]
By contrast, she described the circulation of Colombian *cumbia* music
through Mexico to the United States, "into cosmopolitan and cosmopolatino

dance-oriented settings around the globe," which she describes as globally omnivorous scenes of bicultural urban youth.[57] Nonetheless, there may exist movement and overlaps among these positionalities as the musicians' increasing polymusicalities affect transnational or cosmopolitan aspects of their practices, values, or identities. It is also possible that their location in the United States and looking toward making bilateral connections with Brazilian culture differentiate them from musicians in Brazil looking generally abroad for musical competencies to absorb, notably classical, jazz, rock, hip-hop, electronic dance music. For instance, both Piedade and Connell interpreted Brazilians learning jazz in Brazil as a cosmopolitan strategy to the extent that musicians sought a globalized musical language through which to dialogue and eventually travel internationally.[58] Whether or not cosmopolitanism inspired the musicians in this book, from any country of origin, I focus on their deep engagement with binational musical connections and affinities that transnationalism describes slightly better.[59]

Postnationalism offers another informative framework to interpret the musicians in this book, yet transnationalism may better capture their dependence on state institutions, immigration policies, and cultures. With "postnational music scholarship," Ignacio Corona and Madrid proposed an approach to look beyond limiting aspects of nation-state frames and normalize transnational experiences and influences, thereby sequestering the nation-state to one of many forces. As they write, "recognizing the contingency of the essentialist discourses about nationalist meaning would allow us to better understand the continuous processes of identity negotiation that permit citizens of a given nation-State to establish effective transregional and transnational relations."[60] Introducing the book *Jazz Planet*, E. Taylor Atkins points out that jazz has been "both a national and postnational music" since the early twentieth century, but only the national history in the United States has received attention, whereas the postnational history would reveal jazz's role in globalization.[61] I agree with these authors, if a postnational frame can credit significant power to nation-state policies, enforcement, and structures in shaping opportunities and experiences for musicians with international careers. Seigel made a related point about the emphasis on nations in his transnational method for historical inquiry: "Transnational subjects overflow and challenge national borders not in blithe disregard for those borders but because nation-states so profoundly, even violently, constrain them."[62] Similar to cosmopolitanism, postnationalism risks under-emphasizing the national settings in which the musicians in this book encounter, learn, and assimilate music and other cultural aspects. Ong points out: "Transnationality induced by accelerated flows of capital, people, cultures, and knowledge does not simply reduce state power, as many have claimed, but also stimulates a new, more flexible and complex relationship between capital and governments."[63] The abilities of non-American musicians to obtain visas and residency status in the United States directly influence their opportunities to tour internationally, therefore to be hired by major artists, and thus to advance their international careers. Even with these statuses, international movement is not seamless.

Socioeconomic class status is a prominent variable in studies of globalization theories such as transnationalism and cosmopolitanism.[64] Most musicians in this book are middle-class professionals, neither socioeconomic elites nor lower-working class. They are neither transnationals "from above" nor "from below," as scholars commonly distinguish among migrants.[65] The immigrant musicians playing Brazilian jazz have access to international living and travel through cultural talents more than through financial wealth. Nevertheless, the musicians must have access to a certain level of wealth or sponsorship to afford migration, whether through family or patrons. Because race and class lines overlap considerably in Brazil and the United States, though more in Brazil, this wealth threshold has limited Black migrant musicians to the United States and therefore has directly impacted the racial demographics of musicians in New York, as discussed in Chapter 1. Although I chose to focus primarily on transnationalism, these related frameworks clearly overlap and inform each other as well as my understanding of the situation, and therefore this book.

Romero Lubambo

A rich example of a transnational polymusical musician is Brazilian-American guitarist Romero Lubambo, who has had well-above-average success playing and recording Brazilian jazz internationally while based in New York and New Jersey, and currently in Nevada (see Figure 2.1). A white male, he moved to the United States as an adult, after studying mechanical engineering and classical guitar in Brazil, and after working as a musician in São Paulo. Lubambo is a virtuosic finger-picking guitarist best known for his acoustic playing, while he also plays electric guitar professionally. Fast bebop-style runs and blues-inflected pentatonic riffs abound in his precise

Figure 2.1. Romero Lubambo. Photo by Chris Drukker, reproduced courtesy of Drukker.

solos during up-tempo pieces. Lubambo is equally capable of emotionally rich lyrical playing on ballads, and he occasionally inserts interludes of baroque guitar. He is often hired to play sparse, quiet, and tasteful accompaniments for other people's projects. With a successful career in the United States, he remains connected to musicians in Brazil and has reached the Japanese market for Brazilian jazz.

Lubambo has built a major part of his career as an accompanist and occasional collaborator. When he first moved to the United States, in 1985, Astrud Gilberto—easily the most famous female Brazilian singer in the United States at the time—became his main employer for four years. She also helped him secure a work visa that allowed him to stay in the United States and tour internationally with her.[66] He met Gilberto through drummer Duduka Da Fonseca, who was already playing in her band. Lubambo, Da Fonseca, and bassist Nilson Matta formed their long-standing Trio da Paz in 1985, in Manhattan. While in Gilberto's band, Lubambo met the American keyboardist Gil Goldstein. Their collaboration, *Infinite Love* (Big World Music, 1993), is a favorite project of Lubambo and his wife, the US-born singer Paula Driggs. Shortly after arriving in the United States, he also started playing regularly in the group of Herbie Mann, an American jazz musician at the vanguard of championing bossa nova internationally. Lubambo wound up playing with Mann "for the last seventeen years of his life," adding affectionately: "He became my American father. I was his Brazilian son." In recent years, Lubambo has primarily been accompanying Dianne Reeves, a famous African American jazz singer, in whose band he plays acoustic and electric guitar. He tours the world most of the time with her, playing her repertoire and occasionally Brazilian music. Meanwhile, over the years, many female Brazilian singers have hired Lubambo to play duet projects, notably Leny Andrade, Gal Costa, Luciana Souza, and Claudia Villela, whether on recordings or for concerts and tours. In the mid-1990s, a decade after moving to the United States and collaborating on record projects with Trio da Paz and many other musicians, Lubambo began to make albums as a bandleader, totaling ten by 2021 and released on different labels in the United States and Japan.[67]

Lubambo views his self-identity as having evolved in transnational ways:

When I was very young, I used to be really crazy about the United States because of the cars and technology. [. . .] I grew up with Brazilian music, but American music was big in my house with my mother listening to American music, all the orchestras, all the jazz guys. And my uncles playing music, and they loved jazz, they loved American music. So, I always had this crazy thing about American music and American engineering![68]

Working as a musician playing jazz and Brazilian music, Lubambo became disappointed with the lack of opportunities to play instrumental music and did not enjoy the commercial music on Brazilian radio and television; other Brazilians told me similar reasons for emigrating. "I wanted to do more serious work. I wanted to go deeper in music," Lubambo said. "It would be very hard for me to do my music, instrumental music, and play jazz. [. . .] I left to come here and do something more serious."[69] I interviewed Lubambo in 2018, thirty-three years after he moved to the United States, and he reflected on his changed personality.

When I came here I very quickly became—I felt at home here in the States. I felt at home here because the way people live, the way people think, and the way people work here is much more the way I am. So, this made me feel very comfortable here, you know. So, a lot of times I feel very American. But of course, when I open my mouth, I start talking and there is always

an accent that's not. I'm not going to even ever speak like an American native. But, I'll always have an accent. So, I'm not totally American. But, when
I go to Brazil now, I see that I'm not totally Brazilian also, because I have
so much influence from living here for such a long time. So, basically, I'm
nothing [laughs]. I'm not totally American; I'm not totally Brazilian. But,
I like a lot of both cultures. That's the important thing for me. I like a lot
American culture and like a lot of the Brazilian culture, and I try to combine that the best way possible and I think is very good for me to have both
cultures, you know, together.

Lubambo's dual identifications with the cultures of two countries is a
key feature of transnational identity. Although his Brazilian accent when
speaking remains a reminder of his upbringing, and signals his foreignness to American audiences, his polymusical fluencies at playing Brazilian
and American genres have supported a successful career accompanying top
singers in both countries' music. He plays the genres without a musical accent, a notion explained next. Lubambo's transnational life experiences and
self-concept relate to and inform his polymusicality and the Brazilian-jazz
fusions he plays and creates exceptionally well. Lubambo will return as an
example in several chapters.

Anat Cohen and the Discourse of Musical Accents

Many Brazilian musicians in New York I spoke with praised the woodwindist
Anat Cohen for playing Brazilian music "without an accent," which is
a typical way to compliment a musician for playing a style fluently and
authentically—or even approaching fluency. I asked Cohen what she thought
of this expression. "I take it as a compliment because not having an accent is a
matter of dedication and of choice."[70] She reflected on her process of learning
new music styles: "I think the idea is to be able to learn to play with the existing vocabulary offered, yet still to search for my individuality. That's really
the game." She explained her intentions: "to really get the way the music feels
and then add my own spices. But first I want to try—I like to assimilate."

The Israeli-born clarinetist and saxophonist has become one of the most
successful musicians in New York's Brazilian jazz scene, though her international acclaim first came from playing mainstream jazz. As of this writing,
she had earned ten *Down Beat* awards for Best Clarinetist and three Grammy

nominations; some of these recordings include or combine jazz, Brazilian music, and other influences. In fact, she may have brought Brazilian genres to large audiences because of her notoriety in the jazz world, such as performing *choro* with Wynton Marsalis, Paquito D'Rivera, and her own *choro* groups in major jazz venues and jazz festivals internationally, such as Choro Aventuroso with New York–based Brazilian musicians (see Figure 2.2). Growing up in Israel and speaking Hebrew, she has managed to master music traditions from two foreign countries as well as learning to speak English and Portuguese, although certainly the United States has had close ties with Israel, where English and American culture are common, and where jazz and Brazilian music have long been popular. Cohen also shared insights about her process of learning, or "assimilating," foreign music styles, as she says, and teaching them to others, while developing her own individual "style" or "voice" as a musician, terms related to "accent." These terms interrelate with the development of multiple competencies, whether in music or in other aspects of culture and identity.

Figure 2.2. Anat Cohen and Choro Aventuroso, 2014. Left to right: Vitor Gonçalves (accordion), Cohen (clarinet), Sergio Krakowski (pandeiro), and Cesar Garabini (guitar). Photo by Fran Kaufman, reproduced courtesy of Cohen and Kaufman.

I asked Cohen, "Is there a tension between this drive to have your own individual voice and this drive to learn the music from within and assimilate the tradition? Do you try to do that first and then bring in your individual voice?" She answered:

Exactly. I don't think there is tension. I think it's a process. My process is first to learn to assimilate and to learn to be part, and to not sound like a foreigner. And then say, "Okay, I'm comfortable enough that I can start finding who I am inside this music." Of course, now that I've been doing that for many years, the process is almost happening at the same time because I have a little more experience doing that. So, I'm okay, I'm more confident with who I am when I play the clarinet. So, it's becoming who I am no matter what I play. [. . .] First try to imitate—the same thing as trying to imitate Benny Goodman. Try to transcribe a solo, get his time feel, get his articulation, get the right sounds. And then say, "Okay, it's been done." There are all these people that are doing that. There's only one Benny Goodman. [. . .] Now let me find who I am, but still learn from the way it feels. So, you learn to get a swing feel the same as you try to get a Brazilian music feel. It's not different as far as a foreigner for all of those styles.

Regarding how she technically plays the music with an accurate musical accent, Cohen understands what she has learned to do in part based on "articulation," articulating notes and phrases correctly. She connects articulation with speaking languages without accents, too.

In general, really it all comes down to articulation and that's also talking about an accent. The way I look at it is like most American people—I would say 90 percent of the people around me call me Anette, and that's not my name. My name is Anat. But they can't conceive of the N-A-T as "nat" [she pronounces with a short a] and say "not" [with a short o]. They call me Anette [with a short e]. I don't correct them anymore because I'm not going to correct everybody. Friends have called me this for twenty years: Annette. And I'm like, "alright." Some people call me Anat [properly] and I know they're making an effort to try to imitate the accent and the way to use my name. It's the same kind of a concept of trying to make the language sound different. It's the same thing of using articulation. Articulation is very rooted. And jazz articulation is very soft, in a way. It depends what style you're playing, but for the most part, when you play swing music or more modern jazz it's "zzzah, zzah."

She sang a short melodic line with this articulation. "You can make an attack, but the swing," she sang a short melody, "is 'dah' and 'thah.' In choro it is 'tah' [with a hard t]. And you can't swing with 'tah.' You don't play," she sang a jazz melody with a hard t, stumbling to illustrate its awkwardness. "It's how you produce a note and how you say a word. How you can say 'Brasiu' [pronouncing the country's name as Brazilians do] or 'Brazil' [as Americans do] or 'Brazeel.' Or, you know, 'choro' or 'shoro.' Most American people say 'choro' [with a hard ch as in cheese]. They can't even realize they are saying 'choro' [with a hard ch]."

To play music "with an accent," *sotaque* in Portuguese, a musical foreign accent, is a common expression among professional musicians in the Brazilian jazz scene of New York as well as in Brazilian music scenes elsewhere in the United States. Spoken accents concern language while musical accents concern music, although musicians speak of linguistic accents when discussing singers as well as musical accents of instrumentalists. Accents differ from idiosyncratic styles by referencing conventional ways that a primary music tradition can be heard when musicians play a second tradition. Stanyek found a similar discourse of musical accents among non-Brazilian *choro* musicians in the United States, which he connected to the "stretching" of *choro*'s stylistic conventions in a "transregional" and "intercultural" setting. He also noted their interpretive significance: "But an accent is also something that is heard and which prompts various responses: epistemological ones of coding, hermeneutic ones of decoding and imaginative ones of recoding."[71] In New York's Brazilian jazz scene, the accent discourse resonates with musicians' intentions to bridge and combine two or more traditions when collaborating. The musical accent discourse therefore concerns aspirations toward bimusicality/polymusicality. As "bimusical" is analogous to "bilingual," musical accents reveal musicians' native traditions and also indicate shortcomings in achieving complete fluency in a second (or third) musical language. Although a "heavy accent" in this discourse indicates beginning and intermediate levels, the advanced professionals usually mentioned accents when accounting for the subtle differences between musicians approaching expert-level competencies in multiple traditions and musicians with native musical fluency.

The accent metaphor usually emerged during my interviews after I asked musicians about diversity of musical backgrounds and nationalities within the scene, with many non-Brazilians playing Brazilian styles and many non-Americans playing jazz. Musicians often responded that they, too, are still somewhat outsiders to other people's music, and that everyone may play with a bit of an accent that reveals their musical origins. They usually expressed comfort with such heterogeneity and desires for acceptance. Brazilian pianist-accordionist Vitor Gonçalves rephrased my question about playing with non-Brazilians to comment on authenticity with respect to bimusicality, reinforcing musicians' common goal to achieve fluency playing genres originating in both countries: "Can someone play authentically Brazilian? And I think the other way goes, can a Brazilian authentically play as American? A lot of times I think it's really hard; but a few times, for instance the pandeiro player, Ranjan."[72] US-born Ranjan Ramchandani and Gonçalves played together in the *choro* ensemble Regional de NY. "I think it's amazing. He plays like a Brazilian. Actually, I think he plays better than a lot of Brazilians. [. . .] Anat is another." Gonçalves has played in Anat Cohen's Choro Aventuroso, Tentet, and Quartetinho ensembles. "It's something that I search for myself and feel like myself doing it. I think she plays so authentically and at the same time, so much her."[73]

Though most musicians in this study strive toward bimusical fluency, they acknowledge the inevitability of falling short of that goal and playing with musical accents, usually saying something along the lines of this: "They play with an accent but I probably play with an accent, too." Pianist-singer-composer Clarice Assad spoke humbly of musical accents: "Sometimes I can hear an accent when people play *chorinho*, especially string players who play *chorinho*. For some reason I can hear. 'Ah, these are not Brazilian players.' I can hear it. It doesn't bother me. I think it's fantastic that they're—it's like me playing jazz, I think. I feel the same way."[74] She specifically recalled hearing mandolinists play with a melodic phrasing closer to American bluegrass than to Brazilian *chorinho*.

A musician's attitude toward musical accents seems to correspond with their attitude toward intercultural musical collaborations and professional acceptance. For example, the Brazilian bassist Itaiguara Brandão connected these topics:

If they're good musicians, a musical conversation with someone not well-versed in the style can still be pleasurable, and the audience can still gain

access to valuable artistry. In a larger picture, it's great that Americans
or anybody from other cultures take interest in Brazilian music. It raises
awareness about the Brazilian culture, which is better for us than being
ignored and forgotten. It's like language: if a super smart and interesting
person wants to talk to you, you're not going to be focusing on and judging
his or her accent. I'm sure I play American music with a Brazilian accent
too, but I still love it and get hired often to play it in New York City.[75]

Singer-percussionist-guitarist Nanny Assis views similarly his open-
mindedness to musical accents and other musical differences as a personality trait that has helped him develop a career outside Brazil.[76] All these
musicians exercise a flexible attitude that may minimize their judgments
about musical accents, foster intercultural collaborations, and possibly
create new fusions.

The local discourse of musical accents indicates a common goal toward
bimusical fluency while acknowledging inevitable shortcomings; it hints at a
second goal for musical and cultural assimilation while supporting musical
individuality. These musicians' objective to minimize their own musical accent speaks to their dedication toward mastering a second musical tradition,
while their humble admission of having an accent from their primary music
traditions—presumably small but noticeable—acknowledges the enor-
mity of this aspiration. In turn, this humility among experts relates to their
openness to the diversity of their collaborators' musical backgrounds and
bimusical strivings. This accent discourse therefore also concerns musical
interactions and collaborations among musicians with different musical
backgrounds, particularly those from different countries. Because accents
are part of polymusicality, they inform how musicians view their changing
self-identities as they develop polymusical and cross-cultural competencies.

Transnational Polymusicality and Changing
Self-Identities

Musicians evoke assimilation when describing the process of learning
new music traditions as well as language and other cultural aspects.
Here, "assimilation" refers to integrating these skills, practices, and
values into conceptions of themselves: self-concepts, self-identities.
Assimilation speaks to people's changing identifications that result from

developing bimusical, bilingual, and bicultural competencies; assimilation suggests parallel goals and processes of increasingly identifying with the broader culture in which they live—in this case, becoming more of a New Yorker or an American—and identifying with nationally associated music traditions like jazz or samba. Assimilation includes cultural aspects beyond music that the musicians internalize when learning more about Brazil or the United States through travels/sojourns, studies, collaborations, and friendships: in sum, their artistic, professional, and life experiences. Learning to speak Portuguese or English is a major part of assimilation for most musicians in this study, including the benefits of interacting more easily with others, understanding song lyrics, and learning to sing lyrics accurately and convincingly during performance—without spoken accents. Musicians also cite language acquisition as a topic analogous to learning music, and indeed the two forms of communication/expression have functional similarities and possibly evolutionary relationships.[77] Accents may represent the final hurdle of assimilation for musicians, which cause them to feel self-conscious about their foreignness. Musicians' self-narratives may foreground temporal change and therefore highlight the processual nature of their musical and cultural assimilation. In fact, they are expanding their cultural competencies, assimilating to one set while retaining another.[78] Without claiming that everyone achieves near-fluent levels of competency in all domains, at least a spectrum of abilities in multiple languages, music traditions, and cultural understandings can be conceived, along which all the musicians in the scene might locate themselves moving in each domain.

To develop polymusicality at expert levels has shaped the musicians' understanding of previously unfamiliar cultures and also their self-identities. Some ethnomusicologists have discussed these types of changes from their own development of bimusicality. Michelle Kisliuk summarized:

> [T]he deeper our commitment in the field, the more our life stories intersect with our "subject's," until Self-Other boundaries are blurred. The "field" becomes a heightened microcosm of life. When we begin to participate in music and dance our very being merges with the "field" through our bodies and voices, and another Self-Other boundary is dissolved.[79]

Jeff Todd Titon wrote reflexively that bimusicality transforms researchers into objects of their own studies:

Bi-musicality, in my view, when practiced deliberately and reflectively, constantly rubs up against musical difference that becomes a cultural difference. Bi-musicality becomes a strategy in which these differences that are thrust upon us, not simply because we "notice" them as observers close to the action, but because we live them, we "experience" them in our performance of another music.[80]

Titon conceptualized these revelatory and transformative moments as "subject shifts" and "subject breakthroughs."[81] Bruno Deschênes elaborated on Titon's theme in his self-reflection as a non-Japanese performer of *shakuhachi* flute tradition that is connected with Zen Buddhism. He proposed that the word "transmusicality" conveys the process through which an apprentice's self-concept changes when internalizing the technical, aesthetic, cultural, and ideological aspects within a musical practice. "There must be a 'subject shift', as with Titon, but more specifically, and I would even say more crucially, an intentional shift of *identity*, which takes the form of a cultural shift that goes beyond one's self and primary identity."[82]

Two US-born researchers—one white, one Black—reflected on their developing perspectives about Afro-Latin religious music and dance with respect to religious practice and ethical commitment. As Katherine Hagedorn expanded her participation in Afro-Cuban folkloric performance to become initiated in the religion, her perspectives on music and dance about both areas changed, with a new appreciation for intention as a common trait.[83] Yvonne Daniel is an African American dancer and dance teacher from New York City who then researched, as an "observing participant" anthropologist, Afro-Caribbean and Afro-Brazilian religious dance and music. Although she could relate personally with the Afro-diasporic communities that she studied, her self-identity changed as she enhanced her competencies in dance, music, and other cultural aspects. For instance, she noted:

As a result of my spiritual journeys and dance/music performance among many dancing worshipers, I have acquired more assuredness and calm, and over time I have also connected with a powerful sense of cultural integrity, in the same ways that I have witnessed some ritual performers grow. When performers gain an acute sense of individual and community awareness, they behave with social responsibility.[84]

The self-reflections of Michael Tenzer provide further insights into the depth of bimusical identification but also suggest limits deeper than musical accents. A lifelong researcher, performer, composer, and teacher of Balinese gamelan and Western art music, he self-analyzed the extent to which he has "integrated" gamelan into his self-identity as much as he had Western art music, his primary musical background; he questioned whether the two traditions could satisfy him equally during listening experiences. He concluded that the two traditions are unbalanced in his self-identity: "Evidently my decades of immersion in Balinese music have so far not caused me to neutralize my native values."[85]

These reflections by ethnomusicologists/anthropologists engaged in life-long bimusical self-cultivation consistently reinforce a common assertion that an immersive study of a music tradition second to one's primary musical background changes one's subjectivity, identifications, and self-identity. Yet, bimusicality can remain aspirational, even for long-term students. With this in mind, this chapter concludes with illustrative reflections from two non-Brazilian professionals in New York's Brazilian jazz scene who discussed with me relationships between their developing transnational polymusicalities and changing self-identities.

Miho Nobuzane

Pianist-singer Miho Nobuzane learned to play jazz in Japan and worked professionally in nightclubs there before she moved to the United States in the 1990s, where she has expanded her polymusicality and also felt her personality change (see Figure 2.3).

> I chose New York as my home city because I wanted to live in a real jazz city, a city that attracts musical talents from all over the world. Immediately after arriving in New York, I had the opportunity to play with great Brazilian musicians, and after many years of playing among them, I have come to understand and play Brazilian music more deeply than when I was playing in Osaka, Japan. By playing not only Brazilian music and jazz, but also African music, Latin music, etc., with people who came to New York from many different countries, I have come to understand a greater variety of rhythms.[86]

Figure 2.3. Miho Nobuzane. Photo by Samuel Elijah, reproduced courtesy of Elijah and Nobuzane.

While living in New York, she became enamored with Brazilian music, although she had already performed bossa nova during her jazz sets in Japan. She studied by watching Brazilian musicians play Brazilian jazz in the 1990s and 2000s: weekly Saturday shows at the Coffee Shop led by singer Maúcha Adnet, and weekly Sunday shows at the Zinc Bar led by pianist Cidinho Teixeira; these two regular shows influenced many musicians.[87] She began sitting in with the musicians and eventually leading her own Brazilian jazz ensembles. Nobuzane reflected that she started "swinging" and "grooving" more in the United States than she had in Japan by immersing herself in the music and scene. She said:

My professional music experience is much longer here than [my] Japan experience. I was a beginner actually in Japan. So, my musical experience developed here. I started swinging, maybe in Japan, but more here.[88]

Nobuzane noticed a parallel development of her musical skills and personality or identity, partly due to living in the United States rather than improving while remaining in Japan. She described feeling more relaxed in American culture than she did when living in Japan and when she visits Japan. She felt that she has a truer feeling of jazz and Brazilian jazz having lived in the States than she did in Japan. She played competently in Japan, but not with the level of expertise that she developed in the United States.

Nobuzane's original music offers an example of applying transnational polymusicality to create a novel musical fusion. In her arrangement of "Kawachi Ondo," recorded on her album *Simple Words* (2014), she intentionally combined festival music from Japan, the United States, and Brazil (see Figure 2.4 for the melody with her harmony). She explained:

"Kawachi Ondo" [...] is what you play for a summer festival, in Osaka. [...] So, it's a festival and everybody enjoys it. So, I wanted to have that kind feeling plus I wanted to make it funky. And I wanted to have a Brazilian feeling also. So, I used the rhythm of *afoxé*, Brazilian rhythm.[89]

Rhythmically, Nobuzane combined North American funk music and *afoxé* groups, a type of Afro-Bahian Carnival parading ensemble. On her studio recording, the New York–based Brazilian drummer Maurício Zottarelli transferred the *afoxé* percussion rhythms to the drum set: he played the *ijexá* rhythm, which *afoxé* groups play on an *agogô* double-bell, on his hi-hat and ride cymbal; and he played reduced rhythms of the conical drums *rum*,

Figure 2.4. Excerpt from "Kawachi Ondo" by Miho Nobuzane. Reproduced courtesy of Nobuzane.

rumpi, and *lé* on his bass drum.[90] Simultaneously, Bernard Purdie, the second drummer on the recording, improvised in a funk style; Purdie is an African American drummer celebrated for contributing to rhythm and blues, soul, and funk music. In Nobuzane's arrangement, the form begins and sometimes ends with drum set improvisations, before presenting the song's melody and improvisations. She sings a refrain before and after each presentation of the melody and solos: "*A, Enyakorase Dokkoise!,*" a call of encouragement that lacks specific meaning, generally called *hayashi kotoba* in Japan.[91] The harmony she composed to accompany the traditional melody and her keyboard improvisations have strong jazz influences, though too technical to explain here. Clearly even a superficial description of this work by Nobuzane and her collaborators shows combined influences from Japan, Brazil, and the United States. Although anyone could mix musical elements of these traditions into a new work, her creation is part of her prolonged and immersive engagement of developing expertise and her self-identity. Nobuzane's experiences and music underscore a process of simultaneously developing polymusicality, music fusion, and a transnational identity. She combined multiple traditions with which she had gained competencies: Japanese festival music, *afoxé*, funk, and jazz, all in one.[92] Nobuzane understands her own musical development as closely related to her cultural assimilation in the United States.

Richard Boukas

Richard Boukas's self-reflections touch on several topics discussed here and elsewhere in the book—polymusicality, assimilation, fusion, and musical accents—thus providing an apt closer for the chapter. A guitarist, vocalist, composer/arranger, bandleader, and educator, Boukas is a white American male of Greek descent who has brought Brazilians and non-Brazilians together to make music. Boukas is primarily a performer and composer, having incorporated many Brazilian genres into his work for forty-five years. His website catalogs copious original projects, compositions, collaborations, and performance ensembles, with recordings and sheet music.[93]

I will also highlight his work as a college educator, which he was doing during my field research and affected other musicians in this book. Fourteen years after he began to combine Brazilian, American, and European music in his own artistic work, he began teaching at the School of Jazz and Contemporary Music, part of the New School, in Greenwich Village, from

1989 until 2021, stopping because of the pandemic. In the New School's progressive conservatory environment, his performance and educational endeavors overlapped as students performed his compositions and arrangements, performed his transcribed tributes to Brazilian masters, and became part of his professional ensemble. Guitarist-curator Billy Newman said of Boukas's contribution as an educator, "He is really important because of what he does at the New School, which is inspiring people about Brazilian music."[94] His legacy there will certainly include the Brazilian Jazz Ensemble he founded in 1995, the Choro Ensemble he founded in 2008, and a student exchange program with Brazil's Federal University of Minas Gerais that he co-created in 2012 with pianist Cliff Korman. Bassist Amanda Ruzza played in an ensemble and praised Boukas's ability to teach Americans to play Brazilian styles by explaining and demonstrating how they differ from music familiar to them.

Boukas's composition "Chorizinho" from 2008 illustrates how his transnational polymusicality has informed his compositions of Brazilian-jazz fusion and, by implication, his performance of originals. In June 2016, Boukas performed "Chorizinho" in a concert at the New School as the bandleader of his professional ensemble, Quarteto Moderno, with Lucas Pino (woodwinds) and Brazilians Gustavo Amarante (bass) and Maurício Zottarelli (drums) (see Figure 2.5). The concert was co-presented by the New School and an annual music-theory conference of Analytical Approaches to World Music, which the New School was hosting. Because of the academic conference, his program notes described the formal qualities of "Chorizinho" with more technical details than he includes on his website:

> CHORIZINHO is a jazzy AABC choro dedicated to Hermeto Pascoal. Set in an unidiomatic $\frac{3}{4}$ meter (most choros are in $\frac{2}{4}$), this permits the harmonic rhythm to be one, two or three chords per bar. Combined with a motivically economical approach to thematic writing (endemic of traditional choro), abrupt modulatory passages are facilitated which in turn challenge the improviser. Vocal and soprano saxophone solos on the AABC form follow. The restatement of the theme is followed by a four-bar vamp over which both soloists trade improvised lines before the final coda.[95]

Other formal elements that the lead sheet reveals are the voicings and harmonic movements typical of jazz such as chord extensions, slash chords, variants of ii-V-I progressions, and the AABC form. Elements typical of *choro*

Figure 2.5. Richard Boukas and Quarteto Moderno at the New School, 2016. Left to right: Maurício Zottarelli (drums), Gustavo Amarante (bass), Lucas Pino (woodwinds), and Boukas (voice and guitar). Photographer unknown. Reproduced courtesy of Boukas.

include the running sixteenth-note melodic ideas, and *baixarias*; these are swift scalar runs in the bass lines that respond to the melodic instruments, an approach typical of the seven-string guitar in *choro*.[96] Boukas utilizes the five-string electric bass to play bass notes below E (see Figure 2.6).

I asked Boukas about his concern with playing and teaching *choro* music authentically and whether that approach constrains his creative freedom as a performer and composer. When answering, he addressed authenticity while expanding on his approach to fuse different traditions as a performer and composer, too:

Just like I feel Brazilian music saved me as a player, as an improvisor, a rhythm section player, also accompanist, it saved me as a composer. As a composer not only in jazz-related music, but chamber music, choral music,

Chorizinho

Figure 2.6. First nine measures in score of "Chorizinho" by Richard Boukas. Copyright 2008 Richard Boukas / Diatessaron Music Publishing. Reproduced courtesy of Boukas.

solo guitar music, all of it. It has given me horizons and avenues of creativity where the very thing that I am not preoccupied with is whether or not
what I am writing as a composer is authentically Brazilian or not. It can't
be, because Brazilian, in this case, classical music, or let's say contemporary chamber or choral music, is already an amalgam of so many different
styles.[97]

He offered as an example the composer Heitor Villa-Lobos's love for and
integration of the then-popular *choro* music. "If Brazilian music is already
an amalgam of so many diverse influences then what's the problem with you
having your own spin on it?" Not only is hybridity unavoidable, but it is to
be relished, he said: "The thing that is exciting to me as a composer is for all
of these non-Brazilian influences to come together with Brazilian genres."
He highlighted his impressive album of original works, *Amazóna* (Jazz
Essence, 1992):

> *Amazóna* was a perfect example of this. Here's this American guy that's
> gotten really taken by Brazilian music. Do I play Brazilian music with an
> American accent? Probably. Or with a jazz accent? Probably. I spent all
> these years playing all this other music. I'm not going to rid myself of all
> those other unwanted influences in order to play purely Brazilian. And so,
> I don't obsess over it.

By "it" he means playing authentically Brazilian. Bimusicality is an aspirational goal that reduces his uneliminable accents. Boukas immediately added
that he does not let this inevitability stop him from studying with dedication
the Brazilian traditions as meticulously as possible in order to compose and
play within their styles accurately and convincingly.

> But I think that there is a certain specific. It's either there or it's not. There's
> very little grey area whether it's happening or not. And the kind of home-
> work you need to do in terms of really listening to recordings of the real
> deal, that's where the assimilation happens.

Assimilation here is a musical as well as an identity-changing process,
supported by musicians' cultural studies and experiences, despite accepting
that Boukas will always maintain multiple-stylistic consciousnesses,
competencies with musical accents, and other aspects of his self-identity. His

prolonged studies of music traditions and related cultural aspects from two countries have expanded his polymusicality and transnational affinities with the United States and Brazil.

Summary

This chapter introduced the book's umbrella framework of transnational polymusicalities—combining transnationalism with the ethnomusicology theory of bimusicality—to interpret the professional musicians who played Brazilian jazz in New York City between 2000 and 2020. The musicians tend to develop affinities and identifications with Brazil and the United States through their sustained study and practice of music, gaining intercultural competencies with language, customs, historical knowledge, and interpersonal relations. This process compares well to ethnomusicologists' reflexive explanations of bimusicality in their own lives as researchers. When compared to transnationalism, theories of diaspora, the Afro-Atlantic, cosmopolitanism, and postnationalism provide related and overlapping perspectives. Profiles of Dom Salvador (continued in Chapter 4), Eliane Elias, Romero Lubambo, Anat Cohen, Miho Nobuzane, and Richard Boukas illustrated transnational polymusicalities with respect to Brazilian jazz in New York City. Despite expert levels of musical competency among musicians in this book, polymusicality raises potential critiques of inauthenticity, discussed here, and appropriation, treated in Chapter 1. A discourse among musicians about musical accents, akin to spoken accents, concerns shortcomings in their fluencies playing a second music tradition and therefore also in their goals toward bimusicality and assimilation. The rest of the book introduces more musicians who can be described through the lens of transnational polymusicalities. I do not always foreground this interpretation because the remaining chapters concern other topics that the musicians' lives and work illustrate.

Notes

1. Dom Salvador, interview with author, January 4, 2018.
2. Leny Andrade, *A Sensação* (RCA, 1961); Cannonball Adderley with the Bossa Rio Sextet of Brazil [Sérgio Mendes], *Cannonball's Bossa Nova* (Riverside Records, 1963); Nestrovski 2013; McCann 2015.
3. Randy Brecker, *Randy in Brasil* (Mama Records, 2008); Paulo Morello, *Sambop* (In+Out Records, 2021).
4. McCann 2015.
5. Nestrovski 2013; McCann 2015, 174.

6. Jouët-Pastré and Braga 2008, 3; Margolis 2008, 342; 2013, 76. Brazuca may have different or additional meanings in Brazil, however; for example, Piedade uses Brazuca as a category of Brazilian jazz epitomized by Hermeto Pascoal, who was not a Brazilian emigrant (Piedade 2003, 49).

7. Joseph 2015.

8. Jouët-Pastré and Braga 2008, 16–17; T. C. Lopes 2009, 41.

9. Alexander 2006, Chapter 17.

10. Dom Salvador, interview with author, April 1, 2020.

11. Piedade 2003, 41.

12. Lis theorized transculturation, but not transnationalism (Lis 1996, 107, 154).

13. Stanyek 2011; Pravaz 2013; Goldschmitt 2020.

14. "Interview Eliane Elias and Her Husband Marc Johnson" posted to YouTube.com by FaceCulture, June 28, 2011, https://www.youtube.com/watch?v=XzXdgbpTCrE&list=PL22EDC465AE01481A&index=6, accessed November 25, 2019. Claude Thibault and Myreille Bédard, "Eliane Elias Interview from the 30th FIJM—part 1—TVJazz.tv," July 3, 2009, Montreal, https://www.youtube.com/watch?v=XPkcI2VCyek&list=PL22EDC465AE01481A&index=1, accessed November 25, 2019.

15. "Jazz Musician, Brazilian Eliane Elias," *CBS News Transcripts*, November 8, 1992. "Eliane Elias on Returning to Her Home Country for 'Made in Brazil,' Being Blond & Female in Jazz," *billboard.com*, March 30, 2015. Thibault and Bédard, "Eliane Elias Interview from the 30th FIJM."

16. Craig Harris, "Eliane Elias" biography, *Allmusic.com*, https://www.allmusic.com/artist/eliane-elias-mn0000171220/biography, accessed March 15, 2022.

17. "Eliane Elias Bossa Nova Stories EPK," posted to YouTube.com by WLWEW, June 22, 2009, https://www.youtube.com/watch?v=8V9Uj8I5dTs&list=PL22EDC465AE01481A&index=3, accessed November 21, 2019.

18. "Eliane on Pandora 'The Heart,' Legends and Icons series," posted to YouTube.com by WLWEW, Mar 7, 2013, https://www.youtube.com/watch?v=3gkPKiuSMd4, accessed November 21, 2019.

19. Baily 2001; Rice 2003, 67; Cottrell 2007, 87; Gidal 2016b, 17–20.

20. Hood 1960.

21. Silverman 1995; Titon 1995; Baily 2001; Rice 2003; Cottrell 2007; Witzleben 2010; Deschênes 2018; Woolner 2021.

22. Regarding these terms: polymusicality, see Carlson 1968; multimusicality, see Nettl 2005, 55–57; intermusability, see Baily 2008; bimusicalism, see Wong, Roy, and Margulis 2009; Tokita 2014; transmusicality, see Deschênes 2018.

23. Hood 1960; Kingsbury 1988; Cottrell 2007.

24. Perlman 1994; Brinner 1995, 83–84, 106–109; Diamond 1998.

25. Brinner 1995, 82.

26. Cottrell 2007, 101.

27. Titon 1995; Deschênes 2018.

28. Flood 2017.

29. Cottrell 2007, 102, 103.

30. Brinner 1995; Hood 1960; Perlman 1994; Diamond 1998; Tenzer 2011.

31. Cyro Baptista, interview with author, June 7, 2016.

32. Wade 2013, 181.

33. Trimillos 2004, 42.

34. "Authenticity is a prime yet elusive currency. [. . .] Despite its prevalence in discourse, authenticity is marked by such an array of values and experiences that the concept is almost impossible to define" (Whitmore 2020, 63).

35. Whitmore 2020, 58; see 56–58.

36. Whitmore 2020, 63.

37. Ozkirimli 2000, 110, 116-7, 130-133, 144.

38. On national cultural roots in religion and dynasty, see Anderson 1991, Chapter 2; on flags and anthems, see Smith 2010, 37. Anthony D. Smith, a renowned scholar of nationalism, wrote, "The ideologies of nationalism require an immersion in the culture of the nation [. . .] This accounts for the frequent cultural and literary renascences associated with nationalist movements, and the rich variety of the cultural activities which nationalism can excite" (Smith 2010, 7). Ethnomusicologist Bruno Nettl summarized the history of musical contributions to nationalism: along with folksong collecting in nationalist movements, "The creation of explicitly 'national' musics was a factor in the political nationalism in nineteenth-century Europe, but it was mainly art music that functioned as a kind of weapon in the international cultural wars. Over 100 years later, the expression of nationalism could be considered an important function of

music in the postcolonial era, but we are now talking mainly about music in the realm of popular culture" (Nettl 2005, 256).

39. Vertovec 2009, 2.

40. Ong 1999, 4; Seigel 2009, xiii.

41. Madrid 2011, 9.

42. D. Lopes 2008; Zheng 2010, 12.

43. Silverman 2012, 40–41. For ethnomusicologist Su Zheng, the continuous and intense interactions among subjects distanced internationally also makes transnationalism more appealing than diaspora (Zheng 2010, 12). On subtle distinctions between transnationalism and diaspora in music studies, see Shelemay 2006; Zheng 2010, 11–12; Slobin 2012; Solomon 2015; Lidskog 2016.

44. Krüger and Trandafoiu 2014, 17–18.

45. Vertovec 2009, 13–15; Appadurai 2013.

46. Ramnarine 2007; Bohlman 2011.

47. Pravaz discusses similar issues to those I do, concerning a demographically heterogeneous community of musicians who play Brazilian genres in Toronto, and she mentions their collective "transnational spaces" (Pravaz 2013, 282–283).

48. Ethnomusicologist Juan Diego Díaz, for example, has provided a robust study of Afro-diasporic "tropes" in Brazilian-jazz fusions in current-day Bahia, Brazil (Díaz 2021); see Chapter 4.

49. Gilroy 1993, 15.

50. For example studies, see Monson 1999, 2000; Stanyek 2004, 91; Feld 2012; Kubik 2017a, 2017b; Whitmore 2020.

51. See Afro Latin Jazz Alliance, "La Plaza | Letieres Leite & Orkestra Rumpilezz + Arturo O'Farrill + Steven Bernstein," posted to YouTube.com, https://www.youtube.com/watch?v=wrkzLdsnYlc, posted July 31, 2020, accessed August 14, 2023.

52. Jailton "Dendê" Macedo, interview with author, October 10, 2013; Amarildo Costa, interview with author, July 17, 2015; Edson "Café" Aparecido da Silva, interview with author, January 24, 2020; Fernando Saci, interview with author, May 21, 2021; Ana Fernandez, interview with author, May 28, 2021.

53. Musician-scholar George E. Lewis made a similar charge of "exnomination" against an "improvised music" scene in which white experimental musicians in New York City since the 1940s had not stated their indebtedness to African American improvisors, namely the jazz bebop musicians working before them (Lewis 2004a, 139–140). He extended this critique to include New York's "downtown" scene for using colorblindness, transcendence, and universality as justifications (Lewis 2004b, 164–166).

54. See anthropologist Pnina Werbner's elaboration of literary theorist Homi Bhabha's "vernacular cosmopolitanism," and my application of cosmopolitanism to explain Latin American art-music composers in the United States (Werbner 2008, 14; Gidal 2010, 46–48; see also Glick Schiller and Irving 2015; Robbins and Horta 2017).

55. To compare uses of cosmopolitanism in ethnomusicology, see Turino 2000; Gidal 2010; Feld 2012, 7, 90ff., 203, 229; Whitmore 2020; Stokes 2004, 62–65. I briefly surveyed varied applications of cosmopolitanism by musicologists (Gidal 2010). For examples in Brazil, musicologist Cristina Magaldi used cosmopolitanism to denote an international circulation of Eurocentric elite urban fashions that influenced Rio de Janeiro around 1900 and then, with influences from American cities, around 2000 (Magaldi 2008, 176–177, 181–182; 2009, 331). Ethnomusicologist Frederick Moehn drew on Thomas Turino's "cosmopolitan formation" when describing explicitly Brazilian creations that incorporated global trends: "Their music should be Brazilian *and* universal," he generalized the goals of a middle-class cohort of musicians in Rio de Janeiro (Moehn 2012, 5; see also 105, 115).

56. The quote about Mexican regional music is from Pacini Hernandez 2010, 152; the quote about "transnational life" is on page 12.

57. Pacini Hernandez 2010, 136. She explains the vernacular term "cosmopolatino" on page 106.

58. Connell 2002, 20; Piedade 2003, 56.

59. To reiterate, scholars have applied combinations of these and other concepts about globalization and music fusion to explain similar situations as this book describes. For one related example, ethnomusicologist/ethnochoreologist Sarah Town interpreted the dynamics of Cuban *timba* as a dynamic hybrid process and musical "intergenre," drawing on musicologist Danilo Orozco. She relates its developments by Cuban migrants in New York City to Afro-Atlantic "diasporic intimacy" (drawing on Paul Gilroy and Steven Feld), which she locates within cosmopolitanism,

and to the musicians' "bi- and multicultural identities" as they combine music associated with multiple countries (Town 2019, 108, 132).

60. Corona and Madrid 2008, 7. Also relevant to my focus on New York City, Corona and Madrid observe that urbanization "disrupts the meaning of the national"; and their volume presents the examples of Miami, Tijuana, and Rio de Janeiro as key sites to analyze postnational aspects of music.
61. Atkins 2003, xiii, xx, xxi.
62. Seigel 2009, xiii.
63. Ong 1999, 21; see also Smith 2010, 134.
64. On class and cosmopolitanism, see Gidal 2010, 47.
65. Ong 1999, 92, 101; Werbner 2008, 14.
66. Romero Lubambo, interview with author, January 23, 2018.
67. A complete discography is on his website: http://www.romerolubambo.com/music.html, accessed October 8, 2019.
68. Lubambo, interview.
69. Lubambo, interview.
70. Anat Cohen, interview with author, June 14, 2017.
71. Stanyek 2011, 122.
72. Vitor Gonçalves, interview with author, July 24, 2015.
73. Gonçalves, interview.
74. Clarice Assad, interview with author, August 6, 2015.
75. Itaiguara Brandão, email correspondence with author, November 28, 2018.
76. Nanny Assis, interview with author, January 15, 2020.
77. Patel 2008; Faudree 2012; Weidman 2014.
78. These developments overlap with the processual nature of developing both intercultural competencies and cosmopolitan identities (Spitzberg and Changnan 2009, 7; Glick Schiller and Irving 2015, 5).
79. Kisliuk 1997, 23.
80. Titon 1995, 289.
81. Titon 1995, 280, 290.
82. Deschênes 2018, 283.
83. Hagedorn 2001, 5–6.
84. Daniel 2005, 270.
85. Tenzer 2011, 383.
86. Miho Nobuzane, email correspondence with author, March 17, 2022.
87. The accompanying musicians changed at these regular weekly shows of Brazilian jazz, including Hélio Alves, Itaiguara Brandão, Maurício Zottarelli, Valtinho Anastácio, and others.
88. Miho Nobuzane, interview with author, August 11, 2015.
89. Nobuzane, interview.
90. On *afoxé* groups and their use of the *ijexá* rhythm and these instruments, see Henry 2008, 169–175.
91. Miho Nobuzane, personal communications (email), May 22 and 23, 2016.
92. The strongly Afro-diasporic aspects of jazz and the Brazilian music that Nobuzane plays (samba, bossa nova, *afoxé*) also reflect performance scholar T. Roberts's point that playing African American genres with African Americans in the United States helps Japanese immigrants assimilate to Afro-Americanized American culture (Roberts 2016, 61).
93. Richard Boukas's Brazil-focused projects include his duet with clarinetist Louis Arques, titled Diálogos Duo. They perform 100 original movements by Boukas in nine suites, which, in his words, "explore a vast scope of urban, folkloric and regional genres: samba, *choro*, the Northeast (*baião, maracatu, frevo, marcha, toada*), music of Minas Gerais, *gaúcho* traditions of the south, and so on" (email communication, March 10, 2022). See "Richard Boukas: Guitarist, Vocalist, Composer, Educator," website, https://www.boukas.com/, last accessed June 1, 2023. See also https://www.boukas.com/dialogos-duo.
94. Billy Newman, interview with author, January 26, 2018.
95. "Analytic Approaches to World Music Conference 2016," Richard Boukas website, accessed March 21, 2022, https://www.boukas.com/aawm2016.
96. Livingston-Isenhour and Garcia 2005, 6–7, 203.
97. Richard Boukas, interview with author, July 21, 2015.

3

"Bossa Nova York"

Popularity, Singers, and Anxieties

On a Friday night in January 2018, bassist Nilson Matta presented his "Brazilian Voyage" show at the jazz nightclub Dizzy's Club. His ensemble featured singer Fabiana Masili, Craig Handy on tenor saxophone and flute, Jay Ashby on trombone, Julian Shore on piano, and Fernando Saci on a hybrid drum set with Brazilian percussion (see Figure 3.1). Guitarist Romero Lubambo joined them for three songs, two overlapping with Masili. One was a beautiful rendition of "Dindi," music by Antônio Carlos Jobim and lyrics by Aloysio de Oliveira, composed around 1959. Masili and Lubambo began the ballad without meter; Handy responded on flute and Saci added quiet cymbal rolls. At the first chorus, to the lyrics "Ah, Dindi," Saci and Matta established steady time, a common approach when performing this song. Masili stretched and compressed the rhythms and timing of the melody, sometimes singing lyrics ahead of their usual placement and sometimes later, as she expressed the song's tender confession of ineffable love. "*Ah, Dindi / Se soubesses o bem que eu te quero / O mundo seria Dindi / Tudo, Dindi, / lindo, Dindi.*" In Ray Gilbert's idiomatic translation, "Oh, Dindi / If I only had words I would say / All the beautiful things that I see / When you're with me / Oh, my Dindi."

Jobim and de Oliveira wrote the song for singer Sylvia Telles, nicknamed "Dindi," who recorded it in 1959. In 1965, Jobim, Astrud Gilberto, and Elza Soares each released renditions. Jobim recorded it again as a duet with Frank Sinatra in 1967, then in 1980 with Claus Ogerman's orchestration, and yet again in 1981 for a voice-and-piano concert. Illustrating the song's longevity in the United States, famous American singers not of Brazilian descent have recorded English covers through the decades: Perry Como (1966), Paul Anka (1967), Willie Bobo (1971), Carmen McRae (1977), Billy Eckstine (1979), Sarah Vaughan (1979), Singers Unlimited (1979), Ella Fitzgerald (1981),

SamBop NYC. Marc Gidal, Oxford University Press. © Oxford University Press 2024.
DOI: 10.1093/oso/9780197619049.003.0004

Figure 3.1. Nilson Matta's Brazilian Voyage ensemble at Dizzy's Club, January, 2018. Left to right: Fabiana Masili (vocals), Craig Handy (sax), Matta (bass), and Fernando Saci (drums and percussion). Not pictured: Jay Ashby (trombone) and Julian Shore (piano). Photo by author.

Nancy Wilson (1984), Shirley Horn (1987), Natalie Cole in Portuguese (1996), Jane Monheit (2000), John Pizzarelli (2000), and Johnny Mathis (2005).[1]

After Matta's show, Lubambo and his wife, the singer Pamela Driggs, praised the Brazilian singer Leny Andrade's approach to "Dindi." Driggs told me that Andrade sang it so slowly, it was unimaginable how she could pull it off so well. Andrade and Lubambo had played duets at Dizzy's Club in 2011, and again in 2013, that included "Dindi" captured on video.[2] To preface the song for the crowd, Andrade universalized its message by language, gender, and sexual preference: "Dindi is the most important person we have in *our* lives," pointing to her heart. "We know who is Dindi for us. We know. Everybody knows. Sometimes you don't say anything. But you know. You know who is Dindi."

"Leny is special," Matta said. Andrade had previously sung with Matta's Brazilian Voyage at Dizzy's Club. "She did 'Dindi' with a lot of feelings and sophisticated thoughts."[3] Her version of "Dindi," along with that of Rosa Passos (recorded in 1991), inspired Matta and Masili to present the song in

2018. Matta said, "I like playing this very slow tempo. So, at Dizzy's I played it with a very slow tempo. That's why it's very difficult to play." In short, like so many other popular songs by Jobim, most everyone performs "Dindi," each musician presenting the classic in a personal, individualized way while inspired by the composer and other singers.

Bossa nova in general and the compositions of Jobim in particular are the most popular type of Brazilian-jazz fusion, and Brazilian music in general, that are performed and recorded in contemporary New York. This seems to have been the case since the early 1960s, whether it started after the international popularity of the earliest recordings in 1958 and the 1959 film *Black Orpheus*, or since the landmark 1962 concert of bossa nova at Carnegie Hall, or since the proliferation of recordings made inside and outside of Brazil during the early 1960s, notably the 1964 smash record *Getz/Gilberto* (Verve). Even today, Saci, the percussionist in Brazilian Voyage, foregrounded the emphasis on bossa nova and singing in New York as the city's distinctive approaches to Brazilian jazz compared to São Paulo and Rio de Janeiro, based on his experiences.[4] Whatever historical, sociological, or commercial forces contributed to the global explosion of bossa nova, a major reason is that Jobim's compositions are widely considered to be beautiful, whether or not listeners understand the Portuguese lyrics.[5] Jobim said of bossa nova, "It's serene and it has rhythm and it has love and romance and everything."[6] David Treece, in his detailed study of early bossa nova song lyrics, attributes the repertoire's lasting appeal aesthetically to "a profoundly utopian as well as critical response to the experience of modernity."[7] Producer François Zalacain, label owner of New York's Sunnyside Records, called bossa nova "universal music," hence its popularity.[8] Bossa nova as a "universal language" was also used to explain the collaboration of Brazilian and US musicians in New York on Sergio Mendes's 1964 album *Bossa Nova York*—which also titles this chapter—with Jobim, Phil Woods, Art Farmer, and Hubert Laws.[9] Dom Salvador, an influential Brazilian-American pianist in New York, speculated on bossa nova's popularity as familiar, simple, and accessible: "I think it became very famous because it's very easy for people to understand. It's not too complicated."[10] Familiarity to American audiences helped bossa nova to succeed, Salvador believes. "The thing is that bossa nova was successful because it has a lot to do with the American music. That's why they understood it better."

Jobim composed a wealth of songs between the late 1950s and early 1970s, alone and with lyricists, many of which became hits and are covered by singers and instrumentalists inside and outside of Brazil. "Chega de Saudade," "Desafinado," "Garota de Ipanema," "Águas de Março," "Água de Beber," "Insensatez," "Corcovado," "Triste," "Samba do Avião," "Wave," "Samba de Uma Nota Só," "Ela é Carioca," and "Dindi" are among the frequently performed and recorded of Jobim songs. Others that are also performed, rearranged, and recorded in the New York scene include "Por Causa de Você," "Caminhos Cruzados," "O Morro Não Tem Vez", "Se É por Falta de Adeus," "Inútil Paisagem," "Chovendo na Roseira," "Passarim," "Fotografia," "Sue Ann," and "Ligia." The many Jobim tribute projects include more from his oeuvre. Inside Brazil, by the 1970s, trends and tastes in popular song styles expanded and moved away from bossa nova, though bossa novas continued to be composed and heavily influenced Brazilian Popular Music, known as MPB.[11] Despite changing trends in Brazil, however, in New York, to where Jobim moved in 1987, his music has not budged from its place of prominence. Beneath the adoration, musicians in the Brazilian music scene in New York have mixed feelings about bossa nova's popularity. Nevertheless, they all love, respect, and perform Jobim's music, whether the hits or lesser-known gems.

The way that bossa nova songs are performed in contemporary New York City is not necessarily different than anywhere else, although local musicians have their individual styles and the influence of jazz accompaniment is often strong and explicit. The market for bossa nova may also not be considerably different than elsewhere outside of Brazil. However, to examine the music, example singers, performance settings, marketing, and opinions about bossa nova in New York offer multi-sided and contextualized perspectives on bossa nova in a market dominated by jazz. This chapter begins by describing varied approaches of performing "Dindi," as an example bossa nova song. A comparison of three singers then illustrates a range of styles and relationships to jazz with respect to musical interpretation, improvisation, and experimentation. The dominant stereotype of female Brazilians abroad as hyper-sexualized, mixed-race samba dancers is then contrasted with an alternative, though overlapping, image of bossa nova singers who express subdued, conversational intimacy and romance. Discussed last are anxieties, in other words, some musicians' mixed feelings about bossa nova's preeminence in New York among Brazilian-jazz fusions and other Brazilian genres.

Although bossa nova can generally be described as a Brazilian-jazz fusion, bossa nova has complicated and debated relationships with jazz as well as with other styles of Brazilian jazz. Most histories of Brazilian jazz include bossa nova as a key milestone, inspiring so-called instrumental bossa nova or samba jazz and attracting global attention, although Piedade presents bossa nova as an overlapping parallel stream to Brazilian jazz.[12] Bossa nova developed within a musical culture in 1950s Rio de Janeiro that included jazz, blues, and American popular song, and bossa nova showed stylistic and aesthetic similarities to cool jazz of the 1950s, if not direct influences.[13] On the other hand, Jobim seems to have been less directly influenced from jazz than his peers and fans were. He said himself that the similarities between his bossa novas and jazz were unintentional and coincidental, owing to similar African and European musical roots and hybridity; and commentators and music analysts often emphasize the European-classical basis of his compositions.[14] Supporting Jobim's points, music scholar Peter Freeman offers an appealing middle-ground interpretation, based on his extensive music analysis of Jobim's oeuvre: Jobim's music was original while eclectic in influences, analogous to the eclecticism of George Gershwin, to whom Jobim is often compared. Jobim drew on his piano training and appreciation of art-music composers Chopin, Debussy, Ravel, and Stravinsky, as well as Brazilian popular genres like samba, *choro*, *modinha*, and *baião*. He was also inspired by prior Brazilian composers, principally Heitor Villa-Lobos.[15] Extending Freeman's eclectic interpretation to bossa nova, while including jazz, pianist-singer Eliane Elias has explained that the originators of bossa nova were indeed influenced by jazz, while Jobim also drew on classical music: "Jobim—he's the father of Brazilian standards—he loved the American songwriters. I mean, I can talk about other writers he loved. He loved Ravel, he loved Chopin. But he loved Cole Porter [and] Gershwin. João Gilberto was also completely taken by jazz. João Donato, who is a writer pre-bossa nova, he loved Stan Kenton. He even had a picture of Stan Kenton on his night table, I mean right where he slept. He really loved his music."[16]

As bossa nova developed past its genesis and its international renditions, there were mutually inspiring and productive interactions and collaborations between Brazilian and American musicians: Dizzy Gillespie, Charlie Byrd, Herbie Mann, Stan Getz, and others.[17] Yet bossa nova has had a life of its own, or lives of its own, inside and outside Brazil.[18] This chapter points out that some bossa nova singers have contrasting affinities with jazz and its performance practices of improvisation, musical complexity, and displays of virtuosity. Some of the varied renditions of bossa nova feature jazz characteristics, while other versions seem intentionally distanced from jazz. Indeed, definitions of "samba jazz" as a stylistic label—explored in the next chapter—tend to embrace these very elements of jazz, as well as instrumental music over vocal music, in contrast to bossa nova.[19] Dom Salvador, for example, views bossa nova as less complicated than the samba jazz that he has championed, characterized by instrumental music, more improvisation, and faster tempos. "People understand [bossa nova] better. It's a very nice style of music, but it's not really the real jazz that I'm looking for or play, because what we play is more complex music."[20]

In other words, discursive contrasts between bossa nova and samba jazz overlap with distinctions made between bossa nova and jazz, situating bossa nova closer to Brazilian popular song and samba jazz closer to US American jazz. This categorization parallels the long-standing attitudes of jazz historians who view instrumental music as authentic jazz and vocal jazz as less authentic, despite being more popular among audiences and consumers; importantly, this bias against vocal jazz has contributed to sidelining and excluding female musicians from the jazz world.[21] Furthermore, the popularity of bossa nova as a form of Brazilian jazz may function to include and empower more female singers in the Brazilian jazz world. Ironically, however, bossa nova continues to be the main Brazilian genre embraced in jazz scenes worldwide, including in New York.[22] If bossa nova is not jazzy enough for samba-jazz proponents, the resentment appears lost on jazz fans. Bossa nova has thereby opened doors in the jazz scene for musicians to perform samba jazz and other Brazilian-jazz fusions, such as *baião* jazz, *choro* jazz, *frevo* jazz, jazz renditions of *MPB*, and music of and inspired by enigmatic artists like Hermeto Pascoal. Musicians featured in this chapter argue that the commercial viability of this stylistic diversity is only possible in the jazz market thanks to bossa nova's inroads and continued popularity. Because bossa nova made it into the jazz canon, it has led musicians and audiences to discover other Brazilian-jazz fusions. Nevertheless, some musicians who specialize in Brazilian jazz find bossa nova overly popular in New York's jazz scene, and suspect this popularity may be stalling opportunities for them to play other Brazilian-jazz fusions. This begs a debated dilemma: has bossa nova's success in jazz been too much of a good thing for Brazilian jazz? Or is Brazilian jazz viable in New York thanks to bossa nova?

Musical Interpretations of "Dindi"

When performing bossa nova in contemporary New York, musicians usually stay close to Jobim's compositions while offering their own musical interpretations, improvisations, and arrangements. The instrumentalists often play the original melodies and save their expressions of individuality for improvised solos. Luciana Souza, Greta Panettieri, Clarice Assad, and Bebel Gilberto are among the singers in this study who tend to add improvised solos to their arrangements, similar to scat-singing with lyrics or wordless syllables, a hallmark of improvised jazz singing. Betty Carter once explained: "I'm a jazz singer, there's no doubt about it. [. . .] I reach, and I take liberties. I do a lot of stuff—and it's mine. What you hear is me and my thinking at that moment and the musicians behind me. They're reaching and growing at the same time."[23] Singers typically express their artistic selves through musical "interpretation" of melodies and lyrics, a term commonly applied to their individual creativity during performance, and a term used in both the United States and Brazil (*interpretação* in Portuguese).[24] Interpretation commonly refers to the ways that singers, as well as instrumentalists, perform song melodies with variations, nuances with rhythms, pacing, and tempo; selective use of dynamics, vibrato, melisma, glissandos, and ornamentations; exploration of notes in relation to the chords and scales; gradations of timbre and intonation; structural reorganization; and phrasing, as jazz critic Will Friedwald writes, "how melodies are divided into breath-sized chunks."[25] Substituting and repeating words, and choosing lyrics among different versions, offer singers further artistic decisions.[26] Commentators speak of musical and lyrical interpretation synonymously with terms such as rendition, variation, styling, melodicism, embellishment, phrasing, rephrasing, and paraphrasing, sometimes in combination or contrast with improvisation. Adding to these features, singers of Brazilian songs in New York may also alternate Portuguese lyrics and English translations in order to connect with English-speaking audiences. Adnet explained to me that when she sings in Portuguese for a non-Portuguese-speaking audience, she may emphasize aspects of the lyrics without becoming excessive or literal in her gestures.[27]

Musical interpretation is easier to generalize than to isolate conceptually or decode meaningfully. Ethnomusicologist/jazz scholar Lara Pellegrinelli has pointed out that distinguishing between interpretation and improvisation can depend on a song's tempo, making ballads such as "Dindi" ripe for more noticeable variations than songs with medium-to-fast tempos. Moreover, she argued that the interpretation-improvisation dichotomy masks anxieties concerning song texts in the jazz community, which relate to gendered biases against singers that are common among instrumentalists and critics. A compounding issue is the myth that singers only sing about themselves through other people's lyrics. Instead, Pellegrinelli conceived a "dialogic" relationship between singers and lyrics: "Singers do not so much interpret the texts of songs as create spaces within them and between them, mediating between themselves and their texts, the trope of repetition and revision. This is what allows them to continue revisiting the same repertory, whether on the same evening or over the course of decades."[28] Following Pellegrinelli, interpretation can be understood as dialogic mediation, repetition, and revision. Yet the Brazilian singers discussed here are agents and subjects in the interpretation-improvisation divide in jazz discourse. Jarrold Levinson, a philosopher of aesthetics in art, identifies aspects entangled within the concept and analysis of "interpretation" in jazz singing. He distinguishes a singer's "performative interpretation" of the song's lyrical meaning and musical characteristics from a performance of the singer's personality. He makes further distinctions between what a singer intentionally "communicates" and unintentionally "conveys." These efforts may differ from listeners' varied interpretations of a singer's performance.[29] Singers of bossa nova songs have an additional communication challenge when they sing in Portuguese to non-Portuguese listeners. It seems that deciphering interpretation may prove beyond the technical lens of musical analysis if not impossibly complex and subjective.

As an initial foray, however, this section describes a few technical aspects of musical interpretations by comparing renditions of "Dindi" by several singers relevant to the current New York scene. None strays far from the melody, though they vary in phrasing through rhythm and timing, and some embellish liberally. Even versions of the sheet music show comparable rhythmic variations. As mentioned, rhythmic timing is just one musical element through which to compare interpretation; it focuses our window for a brief analysis but provides a limited view. On the other hand, Friedwald highlights rhythmic nuance as the key element that distinguishes jazz-styled interpretation; so these singers use rhythm to individualize their interpretations.[30] Other comparisons might also describe emphasized words, articulation, accenting, dynamics, timbre, and so on, paired with explanations from the singers and listeners. To move from musical sound into the realm of meaning, the comparison of three singers later this chapter considers how they generally strive to communicate mood, emotion, or meaning and how they relate to the interpretation-improvisation dichotomy in jazz discourse.

This comparison begins with sheet music. The Jobim Archive in Rio de Janeiro has four versions of the score online, with excerpts transcribed in Figure 3.2, using $\frac{4}{4}$ meter: labeled [1] in the figure is his son Paulo Jobim's arrangement, published in *Cancioneiro Jobim*, an official collection of the maestro's works; [2] two manuscripts in Jobim's hand from 1962 and 1964, which are nearly identical; and [3] a published score with a 1965–1966 copyright.[31] The main differences for the present concerns are the rhythms used for the quickly paced syllables, such as, "If I on-ly had words I would say all the beau-ti-ful things that I see." Just as the singers interpret the line at slightly different paces and rhythms, the scores notate the rhythms with different combinations of triplet-quarter notes, dotted-eighth notes, and eighth notes (in other words, sixteenth notes grouped in 3-3-2 patterns); and combinations of quarter notes and consecutive eighth notes (sixteenth notes in 4-2-2 patterns). Jobim's manuscripts [2] nearly always use 3-3-2 rhythmic patterns in dotted-eighth and eighth notes, whereas his son's arrangement [1] mostly uses triplet eighth notes, an approach the son also employs to arrange other songs.[32] This basic 3-3-2 rhythm and its variation as 2-3-3 (see Figure 3.3), as well as combinations of these rhythms, are common in bossa nova, samba, and samba's predecessor genres, as well as prominent in many Afro-Latin-Atlantic traditions.[33]

Figure 3.2 continues with my transcribed excerpts of five singers on recordings as they sang the first half of the first chorus, using $\frac{4}{4}$ meter for consistency: [4] Jobim himself (1965); [5] Astrud Gilberto (1965); [6] Leny Andrade (1994); [7] Luciana Souza (2012); and [8] Maúcha Adnet (2019).[34] Absent from the transcriptions are the accompaniments, whose playing may have influenced the singers' musical decisions. The rhythmic variety among the singers is much greater than those in the scores and, of course, no one sings the notes in the scores precisely or exclusively. Gilberto [5] sang rhythmically closest to the published scores, whether notated as quarter notes and tied eighth notes, or as triplet-quarter notes. Because Jobim [4] and Gilberto [5] sing the English lyrics whereas the others sing in Portuguese, the rhythms differ due to the words and their syllables. The versions in Portuguese tend to approximate combinations of sixteenth and eighth notes rather than triplets; though when Andrade [6] sang with pianist Fred Hersch, her subdivisions approach a triplet-feel. Jobim's [4] singing reflects his manuscripts by anticipating the first downbeat with a pick-up eighth note, which several other singers also do. Adnet [8] and Jobim [4] use similar phrasing, which is not surprising since she developed her approach while singing in his

Figure 3.2. Comparison of excerpts from "Dindi," music by Antônio Carlos Jobim, Portuguese lyrics by Aloysio de Oliveira, English lyrics by Ray Gilbert. The first half of the chorus as notated in three scores and as interpreted by five singers on recordings, numbered as follows: [1] Paulo Jobim's published arrangement; [2] Antônio Carlos Jobim's identical manuscripts from 1962 and 1964; [3] Jobim's published score, 1965–1966; [4] Jobim singing (1965);

Figure 3.2. Continued
[5] Astrud Gilberto singing (1965); [6] Leny Andrade singing (1994); [7] Luciana Souza singing (2012); and [8] Maúcha Adnet singing (2019). Transcriptions by author.

Sources: Scores are from "Musicas," Instituto Antonio Carlos Jobim, https://www.jobim.org/jobim/ handle/2010/10868, first accessed from previous version of the website on November 12, 2019.

Figure 3.2. Continued

Recordings: Antônio Carlos Jobim, *The Wonderful World of Antônio Carlos Jobim: The Brazilian Mood with Nelson Riddle* (Warner Bros., 1965); Astrud Gilberto, *The Astrud Gilberto Album* (Verve, 1965); Leny Andrade, featuring Fred Hersch, *Maiden Voyage* (Chesky Records, 1994); Luciana Souza, *Duos III* (Sunnyside, 2012); Duduka Da Fonseca and Hélio Alves, featuring Maúcha Adnet, *Samba Jazz & Tom Jobim* (Sunnyside, 2019).

ensemble. Adnet's [8] rendition falls closer to sixteenth- and eighth-note combinations, synching with her accompanists on guitar, piano, and drums who play rhythms using these subdivisions.

Rhythmic subtleties aside, Andrade's [6] phrasing stands out with a dramatic entrance from the interval of a tenth below, from D to F in the octave above. She does this at the start of each full phrase of the chorus, more dramatically as the song progresses. McRae, Vaughan, and Fitzgerald sang similarly wide intervallic leaps, though not as repetitively as Andrade; perhaps they inspired her.[35] I have not heard a singer imitate this aspect of Andrade's approach. However, just as Andrade's rendition is unique, when listening to these versions, general differences among the others should be recognizable. This reinforces the general point that singers take liberties with their interpretive presentations of the melodies as a means of artistic expression, whether or not they improvise solos.

Another contrast are the tempo differences among these renditions of "Dindi." Jobim [4] and Gilberto [5] sang at a pace of 90 and 85 beats per minute (bpm), respectively, whereas the recent performances inspired by Andrade [6] feature much slower tempos, mostly around 60 bpm. Souza [7] sang it the slowest, at 45 bpm, though Shirley Horn also sang it dramatically slow, at 50 bpm. As Driggs pointed out during our conversation at Dizzy's Club, Andrade not only sings "Dindi" slowly, but elongates the first syllable of the chorus, which delays the remaining lyrics and pushes her phrase to end two measures later than the others. Souza extended this approach, enhanced by her markedly slower tempo. She also prolonged and elided the lyrics "*quero o mundo*" and then contrasted this with a quickly descending lyric "*seria Dindi.*"

Although I do not know how or why all these singers developed individual interpretations, I can provide insights from Souza. She explained to me that she and Romero Lubambo often develop their interpretations of songs by initially playing them either really quickly or really slowly, and sometimes removing parts of the song to find a core, as they did here.

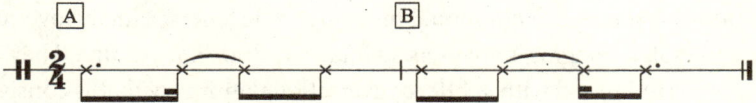

Figure 3.3. A common rhythm in samba, bossa nova, and myriad Brazilian and Afro-Atlantic music traditions, transcribed here [A] and with a common variation [B].

Our idea of either going too fast or too slow is to see if we can do a new reading of a piece. [. . .] When I teach, I always talk about that you can add things, but you can also remove things. So, both Romero and I did a lot of removing on "Dindi." [. . .] He's usually somebody who adds a lot, Romero. And so the challenge for us was to remove, if we take everything away, what are we left with here? So, he plays very little, he comps very little. It's almost single line for him really. It's very sparse and vacant almost. And so that was just to leave that kind of space and see what would happen. I think that it is a new reading. I think it offers a new reflection on this person, on this woman Dindi.[36]

This brief comparison provides a range in singers' interpretations of one song through a limited window of music description. Jobim's original recordings and Andrade's slower rendition seem to have influenced the other singers. Souza's explanation of her creative process with her accompanist suggests that singers have intentional strategies to develop individualized interpretative goals through the music.

Three Bossa Nova Singers and Their Accompanists

Maúcha Adnet, Luciana Souza, and Vinícius Cantuária, all of whom lived in New York during the 2000s, sing bossa nova and other repertoires. A comparison of their interpretive approaches reveals varied relationships with bossa nova and jazz, including the interpretation-improvisation dichotomy. Souza strongly identifies with jazz as well as Brazilian music, whereas Adnet identifies with bossa nova more than with jazz; yet the two singers utilize improvisation differently. Though Adnet does not improvise, she encourages the improvisations and jazz inflections of her accompanists. Cantuária, who views bossa nova and jazz as closely related genres, has collaborated with many non-Brazilian musicians to create an aesthetic intersection as well as to interpret Jobim's songs. The three singers' aesthetic goals overlap as they communicate a range of emotional meanings to listeners, usually love songs with a nostalgic longing known as *saudade* in Brazilian culture. They also create a relaxed mood with subtle, conversational intimacy that is consistent with the bossa nova aesthetic that Jobim, João Gilberto, and lyricists established. When they introduce their songs, they explain the meaning, general or specific, similar to Andrade's introduction to "Dindi" mentioned earlier. All three are lighter-skinned, whiter Brazilians, and probably perceived that way in Brazil and the United States. To compare more singers in the local scene would certainly paint a fuller picture about interpretive, improvisational, and performance styles. Nevertheless, these three successful vocalists situate bossa nova singing with respect to jazz and other Brazilian-jazz fusions.

Maúcha Adnet: Interpreter of Brazilian Song

When considering the categorical labels jazz and bossa nova, improvisation and interpretation, Adnet regards herself as a singer who interprets Brazilian songs while also critiquing pigeonholing discourses. Adnet has told interviewers that she is a Brazilian singer but not a jazz singer.[37] When we spoke in 2016 she elaborated that these labels do not suit her.

> I'm not quite like a jazz singer because I don't feel like I am a jazz singer exactly. And I'm not exactly a bossa nova singer and I'm not a samba singer. You know, I'm a singer from Brazil, obviously, with that as my strong side in terms of the music. But you know it's a little funny that everything has to be labeled.[38]

The way she views her musical self has also changed over her years living in New York.

> At first I felt that I wasn't an improviser and then that doesn't make me a jazz singer, but also because I don't sing jazz masterfully mainly. [...] I never thought of being a jazz singer anyway because I was a Brazilian singer in Brazil and I wasn't even singing by myself in Brazil.

Adnet was one of half a dozen singers in Jobim's ensemble Banda Nova for the last decade of his life, 1984 to 1994, and moved to New York when he did, in 1987. From Jobim's apartment overlooking Central Park, his "view with a room" as he called it, Adnet used to sing with him. There, Jobim's wife Ana filmed them singing a lovely duet of "Curare" by Bororó, in late 1987 or 1988, and used in the film *Casa do Tom*, Adnet recalled.[39] It was also not until she moved to New York that she began to perform solo, thereby gaining the flexibility to interpret as she pleases. Nevertheless, she treats melodies conservatively.

Now people say that I am a whatever, a Brazilian jazz singer. It's fine with me. I don't really care what the title is anymore. I just don't want people to get the wrong sense if I say, "Yeah, I'm a jazz singer" and then people imagine scatting, and I don't do that. [...] I like "interpretation" because I think I concentrate on the lyrics and I love the melodies and the harmonies. [...] The melody is something to be respected, not changed. I don't like that about some jazz singers who change the melodies so much that you can't even learn a song listening to them.

Her self-consciousness about jazz with respect to improvisation resonates with conflicting attitudes toward jazz singers who do not improvise or scat-sing, which Pellegrinelli discussed.[40] Yet, in this quote, Adnet also explains why she preserves Jobim's melodies closer than other singers, such as Andrade.

Singers communicate more through interpretation than through the phrasings transcribed in notation, Adnet points out. In order to present songs convincingly, she believes that life experiences will affect subtleties in performance. "I see those young, beautiful singers singing beautifully with beautiful voice and beautiful feelings—of course they will grow and they will be happy, they will suffer, and they will put that into songs and make us feel more and more emotional. Because you have to live life a little bit to be able to pass something in a song. [...] You have to be also a little sad to be able to put that in a song, to pass that." To express herself more naturally, Adnet selects material she can relate to with ease. "You pick songs that really are already telling you something and make you tell something. It gives you the opportunity to throw some emotional moments to the audience. And if somebody feels something, that's good. [. . .] It's really about making somebody feel something. I think that's the main thing for any musician when they play, singers or not singers." For these reasons she says, "The repertoire is always your partner as a singer. [...] It's the repertoire I chose for that moment and it could be a song that everybody else has recorded." Adnet seeks out new songs that speak to her, that she likes, that she can interpret her own way and communicate authentically to audiences. Returning to the distinctions that Levinson disentangled within the term "interpretation," Adnet is concerned with each processual step from selecting songs to moving listeners.

Adnet's first two recordings under her own name focused on Jobim's influence, starting with *Songs I Learned From Jobim* (Venus Records, 1997), containing other composers' material, and then *The Jobim Songbook*

(Kind of Blue Records, 2006). Her duet album with pianist Hélio Alves, *Milagre* (Zoho Music, 2013), covers several songs by Jobim, including his arrangements that she sang with him (see Figure 3.4). Adnet and Alves include other Brazilian composers and arrangements by the two of them as well as those by her brother Mário Adnet, Paulo Jobim, and others. I heard Adnet and Alves perform at Mezzrow's, a narrow basement club in the West Village that features piano jazz, run by the owners of Smalls Jazz Club. Adnet also played hand percussion, not only during Alves's solos but while she sang. Vibraphonist Chuck Redd joined them twice. On *Milagre* and during the show, they played Jobim's "Gabriela," a seven-and-a-half-minute medley from 1983 that she sang with his group—not your typical Jobim hit.

Adnet has been accompanied by Jobim himself on piano and pianists who improvise more than he did, like Alves, Dom Salvador, Bill Charlap, Hugo Fattoruso, and Alfredo Cardim. She contrasted Jobim and Alves as the composer/arranger versus the improviser. "They had very different backgrounds in so many ways. Jobim, everything he did on the piano, he had the mind of a composer and arranger. Everything he composed the arrangement would

Figure 3.4. Maúcha Adnet (vocals) and Hélio Alves (piano). Photo by Nick Suttle, reproduced courtesy of Suttle.

come together with the song. He would compose arrangements." She sang an example phrase that might seem improvised but was part of his arrangement, as a counterpoint or response. "You may take it out and change the intro because people try to make songs different, but I think it's such a beautiful part of the song, I would never take that out. [. . .] Hélio doesn't have the mind of an arranger when he's on the piano even though he is an incredible improvisor. So he does, for instance, 'Caminhos Cruzados,'" by Jobim. "He does the intro and he's improvising as he's doing his intro. Beautiful and he never does it the same." Not only does Alves change the song's introduction, but Adnet will start at different times, which affects his improvisations, she explained. "Everything is pretty structured but it's also pretty free because it's only the two of us. So wherever I go, he comes with me, and sometimes I come with him too. But usually he has to pay attention to me because I'm doing the melody." This freedom to be flexible within the song structure, while maintaining its integrity and inheritance from the composer, is part of what she loves about duets and singing in general. Adnet appreciates improvisation and jazz approaches to performing bossa novas, and she works with collaborators in a market that produces Brazilian-jazz fusions. Still, she feels most comfortable as a vocal interpreter of Brazilian song, including but not limited to bossa nova. Above all, her main goal is to "pass" emotion and meaning to audiences through song, despite language barriers, and while preserving original melodies and even counter-melodies.

Luciana Souza: Jazz Singer

While Maúcha Adnet considers herself a Brazilian singer, Luciana Souza strongly self-identifies as a jazz singer (see Figure 3.5). Souza combines repertoires and stylistic characteristics of jazz, bossa nova, and other American and Brazilian genres as well as setting poetry to original compositions. She was raised in São Paulo in a household filled with music and poetry, where LPs of jazz singers and big bands were played routinely, bolstered by her father's work at a radio station. She also benefited from informal, playful music lessons from Hermeto Pascoal, her godfather.[41] She moved to Boston to study jazz, first at Berklee for a bachelor's degree in Jazz Composition and later, after four years in São Paulo and Rio de Janeiro, at the New England Conservatory of Music for a master's degree in Jazz Studies.[42] Then she moved to New York City in 1998, where she delved into the jazz,

Figure 3.5. Luciana Souza. Photo by Kim Fox, reproduced courtesy of Souza.

avant-garde, and contemporary classical scenes rather than the Brazilian jazz scene in which Adnet, Lubambo, and Alves were fixtures. Befriending these musicians, she began to collaborate with Lubambo and percussionist Cyro Baptista. In 2006, she relocated to Los Angeles where, in addition to starting a family, she continued the career trajectory she had established in New York, recording under her own name primarily with Sunnyside Records. Some albums focus on either Brazilian or American songs, while others mix sources, united by her artistic voice. Around the year 2000, for instance, she created and released *The Poems of Elizabeth Bishop and Other Songs* (2000) with a jazz combo; *Brazilian Duos* (2001), with bossa novas for voice and guitar; and *Norte e Sul (North and South)* (2003), which intersperses originals with American and Brazilian songs, including Jobim's hits "Chega de Saudade" and "Corcovado."

Souza uses different guitarists for accompaniment, including her father Walter Santos, Toninho Horta, and Marco Pereira, but most frequently she performs and records with Lubambo. He recalled, "we developed this duo thing that was unbelievable."[43] Even after she moved to Los Angeles, they continued to play concerts. "She calls me and I say, 'Oh, yes, let's do it!'" She arranges her material, while Lubambo helps to shape them. "You put your own colors in the arrangement. You see the basic things and you put your own energy on the arrangement."[44] When speaking of Lubambo, Souza emphasizes jazz. "We happened to make Brazilian music, but it was deeply infused with jazz also."[45] She continued, while noting her bonds with other guitarists:

> I think we have parallel journeys, and I think he's a real soulmate of mine, you know, a brother really. [. . .] I think Romero is different because he is so informed by jazz, but also rock. And some of the other players are not. [. . .] I liked that he is messy and adventurous, while Marco [Pereira] is beautifully methodical and careful. So each one of them just represents a different aspect of playing guitar. They are all deep, deep musicians and deep souls. [. . .] I like the guitar player, but I also like the person who plays the guitar.[46]

Souza is perfectly comfortable drawing on her tastes and dual expertise in Brazilian and American songbooks and styles. Writers foreground her transnational identity and aesthetic more than she does, including my attention to it here. Zalacain, her record producer at Sunnyside, recalled one such story about *Brazilian Duos*, which was the first of six Grammy Award nominations she has received to date:

> You know the Brazilian musicians consider themselves jazz musicians and they're right. Even Luciana on *Brazilian Duos*, when we submitted the album for the Grammys we put it into the category of world music. I got a call from Neil Tesser, who is the curator of jazz and world music at the Academy. He said, "François, we're moving your selection to jazz," and I said, "Why?" "Because she is a jazz singer and the music is Brazilian." I said, "I am very glad that you said so." She got the nomination.[47]

Although both Bebel Gilberto and Luciana Souza sing many bossa nova songs on their albums, Gilberto's four Grammy nominations have been in global/world music categories rather than in jazz categories.[48] Meanwhile, Souza's six Grammy nominations have been in jazz categories.[49] Tesser and others at the Academy recognized differences between these singers or recorded performances that they associated with jazz, Brazilian music, or world music.

Souza's music and biography have inspired commentary in the US and Brazilian press about her transnational polymusicality as bridging categorical boundaries between the United States and Brazil, jazz and bossa nova.

Headlines from 2002 alone foreground this theme: "Coming to America, A new generation of immigrant musicians is rejuvenating jazz"; "A One-Woman Variety Show from Brazil"; "Luciana Souza Discusses Her Jazz Singing and Her Roots in Brazilian Music"; "She's Brazilian, Tempered by a Bit of Everything Else"; and "'I'm a Jazz Singer.'" As Souza made more albums that combined jazz and bossa nova (e.g., *Duos II* in 2005 and *Duos III* in 2012), as well as new musical settings of poetry (e.g., *Neruda* in 2004), and bossa nova–styled renditions of North American popular songs (e.g., *The New Bossa Nova* in 2007), journalists continued to spotlight her hybridity: "Jazz Singer's Style Blends in Some Brazilian" (2005); "*Luciana Souza atrai Grammy com jazz em português*" (2005) (Luciana Souza attracts Grammy with jazz in Portuguese); "Swept up by a beguiling, tragic voice, Luciana Souza reveals a synchronicity in the worlds of Chet Baker and her native Brazil" (2012); and "Crossing Borders with Allure" (2014). By the time I interviewed Souza in 2021, I simply asked her what she thought about the myriad descriptions of her with terms like "fusion, boundary crossing, the mixture between Brazil and jazz" and whether there are "pros or cons, or upsides or downsides" for her to be described that way? She affirmed:

> I think it's very accurate. I think it's impossible not to be a mixture or hybrid, I call it, of something [. . .] Brazilian born, of course, Brazilian raised, but then I spent most of my adult life in the US. And absorbing and consuming jazz, and being a part of it in some ways. It's impossible not to be boundary breaking or a hybrid. So, I don't take any offense with that. I think it's very accurate. I'm not a purist myself and I actually, that's why I'm a jazz musician. I consider myself a jazz musician beyond even being a singer. I love jazz because it has this open door, constant open door that just stays a jar for anyone who wants to push it open and breakthrough. And I think Brazilian music did that of course, with bossa nova, but it did that a little bit even with Carmen Miranda much before bossa nova.[50]

Souza has also pointed out the intertwined connections and musical/aesthetic similarities between the style of jazz she sings and bossa nova, not simply Brazilian music in general. In 2012, based in Los Angeles, she released *Duos III*, vocal-guitar duets, and *The Book of Chet*, a tribute to Chet Baker with a jazz trio. Both were nominated for Grammy Awards, for Best Latin Jazz Album and Best Jazz Vocal Album respectively. In an interview with Melissa Block on National Public Radio, Souza pointed out Baker's influence on early bossa nova, which in turn influenced her early develop-ment as a singer.[51] Lyrically she recognizes her preference across genres for songs about love and longing, related to the Portuguese concept of *saudade*. In a 2005 interview, after the release of *Duos II*, she said:

> I try not to hear music in terms of black or white, foreign or national, tra-ditional or modern. For me, the mission is to touch the heart, the soul, the senses. [. . .] True, there is a dialogue between two cultures, two ways of creating music, but Brazilian and American music have the same spirit.[52]

Regarding that "same spirit," interviewer Liane Hansen remarked about *The New Bossa Nova* (Verve, 2007), in which Souza sets North American pop-ular songs, "many of these songs seem like they have sadness at their core or something lost or longing to them." Souza concurred:

> I think you touched on it. I think a lot of the bossa nova lyrics have this sort of spirit what we called *saudade*, which is in sort an untranslatable word. It's a sense of melancholy, of longing of—and it's a sadness but it's a hopeful kind of sadness. Just the same sadness that one would have about love, you know. I've been destroyed by love and have built by love, but when you lose love and when you're hurting, you still have hope.[53]

Longing is among the moods that Souza often conveys through music, whether in bossa nova or jazz repertoire.

Vinícius Cantuária: Downtown-Scene Collaborator

Vinícius Cantuária, a male Brazilian singer who was based in New York, collaborated with many non-Brazilian musicians to explore overlapping aesthetics of João Gilberto's iconic style of bossa nova and the experimental jazz of New York's so-called downtown music scene. His professional ca-reer began with success in the 1980s as a rock band singer, drummer, and composer ("Lua e Estrela"), working with *tropicália* icon Caetano Veloso in Brazil. He then worked as a singer, guitarist, composer, and percussionist/drummer in New York from the mid-1990s to the mid-2010s, after which time he returned to Brazil. Apropos of this chapter's topic, it was Jobim who encouraged Cantuária to relocate from Brazil to New York. In Manhattan, he connected with the downtown music scene, collaborating with circles of musicians connected to Arto Lindsay thanks to Veloso, their colleague in common. These collaborations with Lindsay, Bill Frisell, Ryuichi Sakamoto, Brad Mehldau, Brian Eno, Laurie Anderson, Jenny Scheinman, Jesse Harris, Melody Gardot, and others—including some Brazilians—produced a series of intriguing, creative, and beautiful albums, which generally feature a subdued guitar-based aesthetic that resonates with bossa nova. His music has been appropriately described as "urbane jazz bossas with a cosmopolitan flair."[54] His website's biography foregrounds his work in the "sphere of bossa nova and jazz," at times emphasizing his transnational affinities and global universality, such as combining "New York/cosmopolitan musicians" and Brazilian musicians to create "a unique-universal-Brazilian atmosphere."[55] When I interviewed him in 2015, he explained his creative process when working alone in his Brooklyn apartment studio and also his collaborative creations with Frisell and Sakamoto on the albums *Lágrimas Mexicanas* (2011) and *Indio De Apartamento* (2012). The Indian in the apartment is based on Cantuária, a Brazilian of mixed indigenous and European descent who, as a child, moved to Rio de Janeiro from Manaus, an inland Brazilian city on the Amazon and Negro rivers. Lyrics on these albums were also inspired by his interactions and observations of Latinx people in New York, with whom he felt a degree of kinship and empathy.[56]

When we spoke, Cantuária compared bossa nova closely to jazz, such that instrumentation can be a singular difference:

Bossa nova and jazz, they have a very strong relationship. So, when I play bossa nova on acoustic guitar, Bill Frisell, and his guitar, jazz guitar or country guitar, they are so close. And the same for piano. When I played with Brad Mehldau, Brad says, "Vinícius, this is so beautiful." He can understand the music, because bossa nova and jazz are very close, closer than people can imagine.[57]

He reduced their differences to instrumentation: "What's the difference between bossa nova and jazz? For me, the difference between bossa nova and jazz is that in bossa nova you play acoustic guitar and in jazz you play piano."[58]

When we spoke, Cantuária was releasing a new album entirely featuring Jobim's songs, recorded in both Rio de Janeiro and Japan, with Japanese and Brazilian musicians: *Vinicius Canta Antonio Carlos Jobim* (Song X Jazz &

Sunnyside Communications, 2015).[59] His arrangements built on the classic sound of João Gilberto: quiet singing with strumming acoustic guitar. To this, Cantuária often added a second guitar, acoustic or electric, improvising solos or in response to the singing. Guitarists Frisell, Celso Fonseca, Chico Pinheiro, and Ricardo Silveira provided this accompaniment role. On some songs Cantuária sang duets with a female singer or added light samba percussion, piano, a sparse cello, or electronics. Jobim's hit songs only appear in the second half of the album, perhaps to mitigate the marketing conceit for this otherwise experimental musician. Although this Jobim tribute features a typical bossa nova sound—with embellishments—the singing and overall aesthetic is similar to Cantuária's hybrid projects.

Although Jobim was the most famous composer of bossa nova, the understated and intimate style of performing bossa nova was championed by singer-guitarist João Gilberto. As historian Bryan McCann summarized his sound: "Gilberto's new way of playing a deceptively simple, seductive rhythm on the guitar while softly crooning buoyant melodies—particularly those of Jobim."[60] Gilberto once said, in an oft-quoted interview from 1968 in the *New York Times*, "When I sing, I think of a clear, open space and I'm going to play sound in it. […] It is as if I'm writing on a blank piece of paper. It has to be very quiet for me to produce the sounds I'm thinking of. If there are other sounds around, the notes I want won't have the same vibrations." The interviewer, critic John S. Wilson, wrote that Gilberto "has gauged his art so skillfully that the listener is caught up in the mood and the effect becomes almost hypnotic."[61]

Among the singers of bossa nova in New York whom I have seen perform live, Cantuária has come closest to Gilberto's style, singing in a similarly hushed voice, accompanying himself sparsely on acoustic guitar with similar rhythms. Yet Cantuária also hires busier musicians in his live ensemble, such as Alves on piano and Jailton "Dendê" Macedo on percussion, whom Cantuária encourages to play with gusto at moments during shows (see Figure 3.6). He told an interviewer on NPR that his live shows feature more jazz influences, notably improvisation, than his recordings.[62]

Adnet, Souza, and Cantuária express a range of self-identifications with jazz, bossa nova, and their musical overlaps and compatibilities. They take different approaches to interpret bossa nova repertoire and collaborate with accompanying musicians. Their experiences also reveal ambivalence in the US music industry about placing bossa nova into categories of jazz and world music. Souza's and Cantuária's music focuses on intersections

Figure 3.6. Vinícius Cantuária at the Jazz Standard, March 17, 2016. Left to right: Hélio Alves (piano), Paul Socolow (bass), Cantuária (voice and guitar), Adriano Santos (drums), and Jailton "Dendê" Macedo (percussion). Photo by author.

of bossa nova and jazz through exploratory composition, improvisation, and a melancholic longing. Like the others, Adnet tries to communicate an honest emotional range to listeners, though intentionally maintains original melodies. Adnet and Cantuária leave the improvisation and jazz stylings to their collaborators. It is quite clear that bossa nova songs have been popular for singers, and the expert bossa nova singers based in New York have varied relationships with jazz. None of them perform in ways that suggest the Brazilian stereotype of a hypersexual Carnival samba dancer, discussed next; instead, they perform in ways that complement the subtle, quiet, intimacies of bossa nova's lyrics and music, a style epitomized by João Gilberto, Astrud Gilberto, and many other singers through the present.

Bossa Nova and Brazilian Femininity

This book's focus on Brazilian jazz, and bossa nova in particular, as performed in the United States offers an alternative, though overlapping, expression of the dominant sexualized and racialized image of female Brazilians abroad. Carnival samba has long supplied the dominant stereotype: sexualized bodies briskly dancing to samba music; primarily fit, young adult women in sequined bikini costumes with fanned feathers and high heels, shaking their hips with quick footwork. The dancer is assumed to be a brown-skinned woman who symbolizes Brazil's *mulata* racial category and national pride in racial mixtures of Portuguese, West African, and indigenous peoples. Dancing this role in Carnival parades are also whiter, blacker, and olive-hued brunettes who project Brazil's mixed-race categories: *parda*, *morena*, *mestiça*, and so forth (see Chapter 1). Anthropologist Natasha Pravaz wrote: "Whether during Carnival season or not, mulatas' bodies are on display for visual consumption and have become multifocal symbols eliciting associations that resonate both with colonial morality and with *mestiçagem*, the narrative of racial and cultural mixing as a cornerstone of nationhood."[63] As a stereotyped symbol of any nation in the Americas, a visibly mixed-race woman who dances energetically for public gaze also signifies a horrendous history of European colonialism, the trans-Atlantic slave trade, and sexual domination. Not unique to Brazil, legal scholar Dorothy Roberts summarized this history of white male control over Black women's reproductive rights in the United States that continued well after emancipation, which victim-blaming propaganda compounded through stereotypes of lascivious and promiscuous Black and brown women.[64]

Even within the Carnival parades of samba schools, however, this stereotyped feminine image is only one of the female roles, as ethnomusicologist Carla Sacon Brunet clarified in her study of Carnival in São Paulo (*carnaval* in Portuguese). *Passistas* are the solo dancers, usually female, in samba schools who perform the iconic role that embodies North American stereotypes of Brazilian women.[65] Possibly more important for the competition among schools, Brunet argued, is the flag bearer (*porta-bandeira*), who wears a long and wide dress while spinning and dancing in circles with a male partner. Although not explicitly racialized, she is taught to convey a refined sense of femininity that suggests whiteness. "The *porta-bandeira* reinforces ideals of modesty and grace stemming from Victorian [i.e., European] conventions, while the *passista* is often described as sexy, provocative, and exotic"; and the *porta-bandeira* cultivates her respectful femininity through dedicated practice, while the *passista* is presumed to possess inherent dancing talent—another racial stereotype—although also takes pride in her skills and dedication.[66] In samba schools are also groups of older women who perform the role of *baianas* (women from Bahia): they wear stylized versions of traditional turbans and billowing dresses over petticoats, and evoke Black women's attire in Candomblé ceremonies as well as street vendors, thereby performing Black Brazilian matriarchy.[67] In sum, as presentations of feminine archetypes of Brazilian social identities, the flag bearers perform whiteness, the *baianas* perform Blackness, and the *passistas* perform racial mixture, the most overtly sexual role of the three.[68]

Two internationally famous actresses have contributed to the North American imagination of the exotic, sexualized Brazilian women, epitomized by samba-school *passistas*: singer-actress Carmen Miranda, a white Portuguese-Brazilian who performed in Hollywood's mid-century films as a bubbly Afro-Brazilian caricature; and actress Sônia Braga, a medium-skin-toned *morena* who played sexualized roles in several hit films in the late 1970s and 1980s.[69] To a lesser extent, public perceptions of samba as sensual have also included male musicians and dancers: historian Marc Hertzman discusses two descriptions of male samba musicians in the 1920s, by Brazilian writers, as both sensual and either savage or mystical.[70]

This cluster of mixed-race female stereotypes has strongly influenced perceptions of Brazilian women in North American consumer markets, with implications for Brazilian immigrants.[71] Anthropologist Bernadete Beserra, who studied Brazilian women in Los Angeles during the 1990s, found the immigrants initially surprised by the ubiquity of degrading stereotypes about Brazil among Americans. A female Brazilian told Beserra, "The greatest advertisement of Brazil is the rear end," specifically that of a *mulata*.[72] Lacking power to challenge these stereotypes, some immigrant women selectively self-exoticize for personal gain.[73] Analyzing Brazilian female erotic dancers in New York City during the 2000s, anthropologist Suzana Maia explained that they perform stereotypes of Carnival samba dancers that they had learned in Brazil: "In constructing their migratory horizon, they have used to their advantage a gendered and racialized discourse of woman's body as national symbol. By appropriating nationalist discourses about the mixture of races as embodied in Brazilian women, their bodies have become an instrument of their move, a subject of commodification and desirability in the centers of power."[74] Ethnomusicologists have also explored how Brazilians and non-Brazilians in North American settings have navigated this dominant stereotype.[75]

However, this book is about Brazilian jazz, notably bossa nova and samba-jazz fusions, and not about Carnival samba with its dancing *passistas*, where this stereotype is most prominent. As Brunet underscored the variety of roles in samba schools that express Brazilian racialized and gendered identities, bossa nova presents yet another option. Musicologist K. E. Goldschmitt, drawing on Frederick Moehn, Michel Nicolau Netto, and John and Jean Comaroff, noted that the variety of Brazilian genres other than samba have

"varying relationships with national identity, branding, and race" and reinforce "Brazil's reputation for racial mixture" and "racial diversity."[76] Bossa
nova and the singers in this book present an alternative, though overlapping,
gendered and racialized image of Brazilians: a subdued, subtle expression
of sensuality, a quieter intimacy that some consider more modern, sophisticated, and associated with whiter demographics.[77]

Bossa nova developed in a middle-class youth scene of whiter musicians
and fans, both inside and outside of Brazil. Starting with Astrud Gilberto, the
internationally popular singers have often been lighter-skinned Brazilians of
European descent. As Chapter 1 explained, most singers in the New York
scene have been brunettes with southern European roots, though a few white
blondes and Black singers have also been successful in New York. New York–
based, white Brazilian singer Monika Oliveira critiqued the misunder-
standing bossa nova as sexy:

> Why do I think that in New York there's such a market for bossa? Because
> I think the New York audience, the public here is very sophisticated, very
> elegant and they like the music because it is that. Bossa is very elegant, it's
> calming, it's sensual. Not sexual, because you know I have some people say,
> "Oh it's so sexy!" No, it's not sexy. It's sensual. It's a carefree way of seeing
> life.[78]

Sophisticated, sensual, calm, elegant—these and similar terms recur in
descriptions of bossa nova's gendered cultural associations.

Among writers about bossa nova is a considerable diversity of opinions
around the contrasts and terms mentioned already, including the interlocking
concepts of exoticism, intimacy, sensuality, and sexuality as well as modernity and sophistication. Gilberto attributed her recording's popularity
in 1964 partially to its "romance," dreaminess, and "modernity" that provided reprieve for Americans following the tragic assassination of President
Kennedy, as Jim Farber reported in his obituary in the New York Times.
Summarizing other critics, Farber wrote, "Ms. Gilberto's whispery voice,
though limited in range and power, had a genuine ache and mystery to it, as
well as the ability to evoke images of summers imagined or lost."[79] Treece,
in his literary-cultural analysis of bossa nova, contrasted samba with bossa
nova and highlighted the intimate, conversational, and understated style of
bossa nova.[80] Love songs in general often correlate quiet intimacy and conversational settings, as writer Ted Gioia observed among forty-five songs in

his book-length survey of love songs.[81] When analyzing the two genres in the highly influential 1959 film *Orfeu Negro* (*Black Orpheus*), Treece described bossa nova as a modernization of samba.[82] Female Brazilian singers of bossa nova seem to have been interpreted through the lens of sensuality more than male singers. For example, in Ruy Castro's book-length narrative history of bossa nova, he only wrote "sensual" when describing female singers in the bossa nova milieu.[83] Similarly, in Chris McGowan and Ricardo Pessanha's survey of Brazilian music, they use "sensual" to characterize female singers Clara Nunes, Marina, and Danielle Mercury, but not to depict male singers.[84] The authors call bossa nova "intimate" and its style "conversational."[85] Goldschmitt presented two gendered notions of bossa nova reception in the United States and England, drawing on literary-cultural theorist Andreas Huyssen: jazz critics who valorized Afro-diasporic aesthetics in connection to progressive race politics, viewed bossa nova as over-commercial and adult-oriented, and therefore feminine and white.[86] Yet, samba and bossa nova also evoked the same hypersexualized Brazilian archetype to outsiders as did samba: "The association of bossa nova to empowered women who seduce, either on film or record, is reminiscent of both the racialized sexualization of Brazilian women (e.g., the *mulata*) as well as the broader trope of the dangerous Latina femme fatale."[87] Even though bossa nova expresses romance in more subtle performance practices than Carnival samba, ethnomusicologist Catherine Mercier found that Canadian audiences interpreted bossa nova as sensual because of singer's vocal timbres and the music.[88] This range of opinions suggests both distinctions and overlaps between gendered, sexualized, and racialized associations with bossa nova and samba in the US imagination. If a Venn diagram could represent these intersections, authors seem to view the middle realm in different proportions to the outer rings.

Having attended Brazilian jazz shows and interviewed musicians and presenters during the 2010s, I did not find that all Brazilian musicians present themselves or are always interpreted primarily through the lens of the sexualized and racialized *passista* stereotype from Carnival samba. My main impression is the opposite, that most singers of Brazilian jazz/bossa nova in New York do not perform as Carnival samba *passistas*, nor dance much at all while singing. Their performance styles, like bossa nova music, express intimacy but usually without sexual evocation. Likewise, the hypersubdued and quiet style of bossa nova that João Gilberto popularized seems to present an alternative masculinity to anything macho, aggressive, or physically sexual.

On the other hand, a few female singers seem intentionally to dance and perform sensually at times during their sets. Among the musicians in this book, Eliane Elias performs in ways that commingle such imagery, as Erin Putnam analyzed in her ethnomusicology master's thesis: in addition to playing piano with virtuosity, Elias is a white Brazilian with long blond hair; she performs barefoot (as featured in the film *Calle 54*), occasionally dances samba instead of playing piano, and sings a variety of bossa nova, sambas, and easy listening hits.[89] Elias might respond as she did in her quote in Chapter 2, that her dancing and the variety of genres and influences that she performs are all genuine expressions of her personality. Another example is the New York–based Dutch singer Fleurine. Her 2018 album *Brazilian Dream* (Pure Imagination Records/ Sunnyside Communications) and her live shows contain primarily covers and originals in a bossa nova style, including a bossa nova–styled rendition of Al Green's "Let's Stay Together." Although her music is stylistically consistent with bossa nova, her rhetoric differs. She called the love songs "sex bossas" during her onstage banter in a May 2018 show at Birdland that I attended; whether intended or not, this banter may have conveyed stereotypes of hypersexualized Brazilian women, although she is Dutch.

Regardless of the performers' intentions, Brazilian singers and instrumentalists may be perceived as foreign and exotic, perhaps situationally as sensual and erotic, sexualized and racialized, following Brazilian stereotypes abroad. Audience members unfamiliar with the music may initially project stereotypes on the musicians. But these first impressions may also transform over the course of a performance, while those already familiar with the genre may appreciate it in more complex, genuine ways.

Bossa Nova Anxieties

"We're going to keep it in Rio and play a different mood. We're going to play a bossa nova," saxophonist Lívio Almeida announced from the bandstand, leading his Brazilian-jazz dectet. There were cheers from the crowd in the intimate Zinc Bar's dimly lit room. "Yes, people like this here. And were going to play a tune by a very obscure, very not well-known Brazilian composer. We're going to play a guy named Antônio—"

As he paused an audience member yelled, "Jobim!"

"Oh, so a couple people know this guy, huh?" he responded, prompting laughs.

I later asked Almeida about his line. "Yeah, I've tried that joke a few times and it always works. It's just playing with the fact that everybody knows Jobim. Almost certainly, someone will know Jobim in the crowd. If I play a Luis Gonzaga tune, that might be a little harder. 'Do you guys know who Luis Gonzaga is?' Probably not so much. Milton Nascimento?"[90] American audiences usually don't know him by name either. But most of Almeida's audiences know at least the name Jobim and recognize his most famous melodies. This has translated into stable business for performers of Brazilian music, but with some slightly negative consequences, too.

There are mixed feelings among New York musicians who specialize in Brazilian jazz regarding the prominence of bossa nova. To be crystal clear from the outset about this sensitive topic, all the musicians I spoke with play Jobim's music, admire him, enjoy playing bossa nova, and think highly of the established musicians in New York who are known for championing the works by Jobim and his peers. Still, musicians with different tastes or broader repertoires also feel compelled to play bossa nova songs when they might prefer to play more varied material. The concern for some is not with the music or with musicians who play bossa nova, but with commercial pressures to play, record, and promote Brazilian music through the sole window of Jobim's bossa nova hits. About Brazilian music, the guitarist, singer, and educator Richard Boukas asserted: "The biggest misconception is that it's this narrow band of Jobim tunes, that's Brazilian music! Singer and rhythm section. . . . And when it comes to classical music, let's go there for a minute, the only composer that anyone can ever remember is [Heitor] Villa-Lobos."[91] He offered as an example the annual show at Dizzy's Club by Trio da Paz and Friends, noting that he admires and respects all the musicians involved and thinks they deserve the attention they have received. Boukas only takes issue with the show's marketing emphasis. He finds it unfortunate: "Among the great Brazilian musicians that are in New York, even they feel that in order to gig and present at the name venues like the Jazz Standard or Dizzy's Coca-Cola or the Blue Note—Jobim tribute. It's like, alright, enough! Brazilian music is bigger than Jobim."

I asked him: "Why are they doing this? Why? To bring in the crowd?"

"Yeah! They're playing it safe. The owners of the club who book it say, it has to be tunes that people recognize: 'Desafinado' or 'Girl from Ipanema,'" Boukas clarified, naming two Jobim hits that, indeed, I have heard at Dizzy's.

For another example, presenter Jane Stein told Adnet, "You *are* the girl from Ipanema," to justify advertising her 2011 concert at Ramapo College's

Berrie Center as "The Girl from Ipanema: Bossa Always Nova Featuring Maúcha Adnet & Samba Jazz." Stein knows that Adnet is not the same woman as the one whom Jobim's song describes, nor is she Astrud Gilberto, who popularized the hit. But Stein's goal was to familiarize Adnet to potential audiences and increase attendance.[92] Flutist and hobbyist promoter Junia Flavia d'Affonseca made the analogy to brand recognition when selling soft drinks: "It's like Coca-Cola or Tubaína," a Brazilian soda. "Coca-Cola you know, Tubaína you don't know. So, if you sell Coca-Cola you're going to make money but if you sell Tubaína, nobody's going to buy it."[93]

Brand recognition attracts audiences. However, by advertising a concert as a Jobim tribute or a bossa nova show, some musicians feel restricted artistically if they are interested in other styles or experimentation. One musician, whom I will quote anonymously, critiqued the situation this way: "It's hard to take that throne off bossa nova because, I wasn't here, but it seems like it was so huge that you know, it's easily marketable. [. . .] It's great that Americans are still mesmerized by bossa nova, but sometimes it gets a little bit like, more of the same." Keyboardist Vitor Gonçalves indicted a similar point in his critique of New York's Brazilian music scene as so heavily focused on bossa nova: "Maybe my criticism would be by being relatively small, [it] gets into a cycle and it doesn't breathe."[94] Monika Oliveira also struggled to expand the repertoire of her weekly Saturday night show at the Zinc Bar, which she maintained for most of the 2010s after singer Marianne Ebert returned to Brazil: "We pretty much got stuck on the bossa nova. [. . .] It's a style that came out in the '60s and we're in 2016," she laughed. "Brazil has so many other rhythms and these rhythms have to be explored, here! I mean we have to introduce people to these rhythms!"[95] She and other musicians intentionally try to introduce new genres in their shows. "It's time for us to listen to other things! Not to say to forget bossa, because bossa is a beautiful style. You know? Sophisticated, has hints of jazz and classical music, especially with Jobim." Oliveira's quote exemplifies musicians' simultaneous adoration for bossa nova and their desires to play other Brazilian styles in New York.

To rectify the situation, musicians have developed eclectic shows without branding them as bossa nova. An alternative approach is to create a musical tour of Brazil by including representations from different regions as well as stylistic variety. They make a point of narrating the tour from the stage along the lines of saying, "now we will visit the Northeast with a *forró* song." Oliveira intentionally programmed such a show as a response to feeling that her audience was becoming bored of hearing only bossa nova songs; they started talking, did not interact with the band, had no connection to the music, and left the show. Almeida narrates his dectet's show similarly to the audience, including his previously mentioned joke that they will stay in Rio de Janeiro to hear a bossa nova, one of several Brazilian genres that he has arranged for a jazz big band format. This brings us back to Nilson Matta's Brazilian Voyage show, a title that evokes a musical tour of Brazil. He created this name for an ensemble he formed in 1991 to accompany the opening party for an exhibition of Brazilian painters and sculptors at the Cooper Hewitt, Smithsonian Design Museum in Manhattan. "I try to play rhythms from Brazil of different styles from Brazilian music. So, from the Northeast, from the center, you know, ballads, bossa novas, something like that."[96]

In response to the critique that the local live music industry rewards bossa nova and hits by Jobim, the musicians who have had success with this situation—Adnet, Lubambo, Da Fonseca, Baptista, and others—defend it. They tend to argue four points: Jobim deserves all the respect he receives because he paved the way for all other Brazilian music to be recognized internationally. Jobim's hits are classics and should be played just as the canonic composers of the American popular songbook like George Gershwin are continually performed and reinterpreted. Jobim's music is wonderfully complex and varies well beyond his hits; they often highlight Jobim's stylistically expansive albums *Stone Flower*, *Matita Perê*, and *Urubu*. Lastly, they state that Jobim's popularity should not prevent anyone from playing other Brazilian music in addition. Of course this is precisely the complaint, that Jobim's ubiquity in New York does indeed stand in the way of other styles to be performed.

Adnet, Da Fonseca, and Lubambo pointed out that their annual show at Dizzy's Club, which is advertised as bossa nova, has changed over the years to include repertoire and influences from different Brazilian genres, with originals and covers, instrumental pieces and songs. "There's a lot of other things that we play also that is totally different," Lubambo said. "So, the people that are already there listening and they like it, 'Oh! This is different!' Yeah! It's different! There's other things, other sides of Brazilian music that we should show all the time."[97] Although advertised as bossa nova shows, their shows contain similar range of repertoire as the "Brazilian tour" shows. (This issue will return in Chapter 5 to introduce the live music industry in which they operate.)

Adnet offered all these arguments to defend the preeminence of bossa nova and Jobim's compositions in New York, including how they led the way to introduce audiences to other Brazilian repertoire and genres:

·I just feel that we have to be so thankful that the bossa nova has that power and that came to this country and all over the world with the force that came because that opens the door for everything else. I think that's something that people don't see because people were playing Brazilian music more and more *choro* and all the other stuff because of the door that bossa nova and samba opened. If that door didn't open, how would you get in? And I feel that way because we can play anything. We play *baião*, we play other styles, we don't only play bossa nova, samba, whatever, and even if we do, we play ballads.[98]

Adnet's argument seems convincing and conclusive. Aside from Afro-Hispanic-Caribbean-influenced Latin jazz, which, by contrast, was developed in New York, how many fusions of jazz with local music from other parts of the world have achieved bossa nova's level of success? Bossa nova seems more popular than Django Reinhart's jazz manouche, Indo-jazz, Ethio-jazz, South and West African jazz fusions, and Scandinavian and other European fusions—at least in the United States.[99] Perhaps jazz-influenced Tin Pan Alley songs and European cabaret music were more popular fusions during the 1910s through 1930s.[100] Rhythm and blues, if considered a jazz-pop fusion, may have eclipsed them all, especially when rebranded as rock and roll in the 1950s. Among international jazz fusions, bossa nova achieved undeniable success at being widely recognized, included in jazz songbooks, established as a standard performance practices of jazz musicians, and frequently presented in concerts and recordings in jazz markets. Despite the anxieties that this popularity creates for musicians, it is understandable that branding concerts and recordings with the term "bossa nova" or "Jobim" or "João Gilberto" or "Girl from Ipanema" attracts audiences and consumers whom musicians can then introduce to a range of other Brazilian-jazz fusions. The genre second in line is likely samba jazz, the topic of the next chapter.

Summary

This chapter discussed several topics concerning the popularity of bossa nova among Brazilian-jazz fusions in New York City and bossa nova's mixed relationships with jazz. Songs by Antônio Carlos Jobim are ubiquitous, while direct relationships between his eclectic music and jazz have been debated. A comparison of several renditions of the song "Dindi" by Jobim and Aloysio de Oliveira illustrated distinctive musical interpretations by five singers and nuances of three musical scores. Portraits of three prominent singers of bossa nova in New York—Maúcha Adnet, Luciana Souza, and Vinícius Cantuária—highlighted their connections to jazz practices of interpretation, improvisation, and experimentation. Turning to North American stereotypes of Brazil, bossa nova suggests alternative notions of Brazilian femininity and romantic intimacy when compared to the prevailing stereotype abroad of mixed-race, female dancers in Carnival parades and hypersexuality. Discussed last, local musicians have differing opinions about the prominent place of bossa nova in New York's jazz industry, which has caused anxieties for those who try to perform other types of Brazilian-jazz fusions.

Notes

1. Compiled using *Discogs.com, AllMusic.com*, and *Wikipedia*. Contributors to *Wikipedia* are accumulating vocal and instrumental covers of "Dindi": "Dindi," *Wikipedia*, https://en.wikipedia.org/wiki/Dindi, accessed November 12, 2019.
2. "Leny Andrade e Romero Lubambo—Dindi—Live," recorded and uploaded by Marcelo Maia, March 31, 2011, https://www.youtube.com/watch?v=YSbpp9Rjjak, accessed November 12, 2019.
3. Nilson Matta, interview with author, March 3, 2020.
4. Fernando Saci was a fan and college student of jazz in Brazil before moving to the United States in 2010 (to teach at Berklee College of Music) and to New York City in 2011 (interview with author, May 21, 2021).
5. Murphy 2006, 37; Treece 2013; McCann 2019.
6. McGowan 2012.
7. Treece 2013, 65. Drawing on work by Treece, Lorenzo Mammí, and others, Idelber Avelar and Christopher Dunn contextualized bossa nova in Brazil: "Emerging during the presidency of Juscelino Kubitschek [1956–1961], a democratic populist committed to state-driven development, bossa nova is associated with utopian national imaginary tied to the project of modernization. [. . .] Developed and performed primarily by white, affluent artists of Rio's south zone, bossa nova expressed a kind of domestic intimacy with lyrics that addressed themes of natural beauty, existential contemplation, and romantic love" (Avelar and Dunn 2011, 17).
8. François Zalacain, interview with author, Jan 19, 2018.
9. *Bossa Nova York* (Elenco 1964) by Sergio Mendes Trio, Antônio Carlos Jobim, Phil Woods, Art Farmer, Hubert Laws; liner notes available at https://www.discogs.com/Sergio-Mendes-Trio-Antonio-Carlos-Jobim-Phil-Woods-Art-Farmer-Hubert-Laws-Bossa-Nova-York/release/3916725, accessed August 16, 2023.
10. Dom Salvador, interview with author, January 4, 2018.
11. Reily 1996, 14; Piedade 2003, 47; Treece 2013, 123ff.; Borge 2018, 125–129; Goldschmitt 2020, 75.
12. Piedade 2003, 46–47; McCann 2007; Gomes 2010; Giller 2018.
13. Goldschmitt 2020, 32–37.
14. Béhague 1973, 212; Reily 1996, 6, 9; Piedade 2003, 44–46; McCann 2007; Avelar and Dunn 2011, 17; Treece 2013; Borge 2018, 89ff.; Freeman 2019, 10–11, 46–47.
15. Freeman 2019, 4, 5, 40, 46–47, 100, 129, 177, *passim*.
16. Claude Thibault and Myreille Bédard, "Eliane Elias Interview from the 30th FIJM—part 2—TVJazz.tv," July 3, 2009, Montreal, https://www.youtube.com/watch?v=wLs65APF66o&list=PL22EDC465AE01481A&index=2, accessed November 25, 2019.

17. Borge 2018, 114–116; Washburne 2020, 122–125.
18. Treece 2013, 63; McCann 2019; Goldschmitt 2020.
19. Saraiva 2007; Gomes 2010; McCann 2015; Giller 2018.
20. Salvador, interview.
21. Pellegrinelli 2005, 2008.
22. On bossa nova's enduring international popularity, see Goldschmitt 2020.
23. Michael Bourne, "Betty Carter. It's Not about Teaching, It's about Doing," *Down Beat*, December 1994, reprinted in *DownBeat—The Great Jazz Interviews, A 75th Anniversary Anthology*, ed. F. Alkyer, E. Enright, J. Koransky, A. Cohen, J. Cagle (New York: Hal Leonard, 2009), 268.
24. E.g., Perrone 1989.
25. Friedwald 1996, 130.
26. Friedwald 1996, xiv, 130; Siegel 2000; Willard 2000; Pellegrinelli 2005; Levinson 2013; Hargreaves 2014, 17–19.
27. Maúcha Adnet, personal conversation, Jazz at Kitano, New York, June 17, 2016.
28. Pellegrinelli 2005, 201, 269, 284–285.
29. Levinson 2013.
30. Friedwald 1996, xiv, 59.
31. "Musicas," Instituto Antonio Carlos Jobim, https://www.jobim.org/jobim/handle/2010/10868, accessed May 31, 2024; accessed on an earlier version of the website on November 12, 2019. These scores are all notated in common time except [3] is in cut time.
32. Freeman observed inconsistent rhythms in Jobim's published works, yet comments that Jobim was "assuming the allowance for individual stylistic interpretation is necessary to retain a sense of appropriate swing or '*balanço*'" (Freeman 2019, 126).
33. Brazilian musicologist Carlos Sandroni has explained the use of 3-3-2 rhythmic patterns in early samba and predecessor genres, and he has contextualized the "3-3-2 Paradigm" of related rhythms, notably the *tresillo, cinquillo*, and *habanera* rhythms, in other Afro-Latin-Atlantic traditions (Sandroni 2000; 2021, 9–13). On the 3-3-2 rhythm in samba and bossa nova, also see Béhague 1973, 210, 220, 222; and Freeman 2019, 111. About the 3-3-2 rhythm in early US jazz, see Washburne 2020, 44.
34. I do not have a recording of Fabiana Masili singing "Dindi," nor does she, she told me.
35. Fitzgerald's recording had influenced Andrade in the 1960s (McCann 2007, 36).
36. Luciana Souza, interview with author, May 18, 2021.
37. Eugene Uman, "Maúcha Adnet Interview," Vermont Jazz, No Boundaries Radio, WVEW FM (audio), November 10, [2016], https://soundcloud.com/ugeneermontazzenter/maucha-adnet-interview, accessed March 15, 2022.
38. Maúcha Adnet, interview with author, June 13, 2016.
39. Adnet, interview; "Curare (Bororó) com Tom Jobim e Maucha Adnet," uploaded to YouTube.com by curarenocorpo, October 3, 2013, https://www.youtube.com/watch?v=eS9d3ng95Gs, accessed June 25, 2021. For more on Jobim's "view with a room," see "A Casa do Tom en NY.mov" uploaded to YouTube.com by vermejor, October 4, 2010, https://www.youtube.com/watch?v=rNXp1ARPe2A, accessed June 25, 2021.
40. Pellegrinelli 2005.
41. Bill Beuttler, "She Breaks Down Musical Boundaries: Singer Receives Praise for Her Sound," *Boston Globe*, March 17, 2006: D15.
42. "About," Luciana Souza official website, https://www.lucianasouza.com/about, accessed November 24, 2021.
43. Romero Lubambo, interview with author, January 23, 2018.
44. Lubambo, interview.
45. Souza, interview.
46. Souza, interview.
47. Zalacain, interview.
48. "Bebel Gilberto," Grammy.com, https://www.grammy.com/grammys/artists/bebel-gilberto/2382, accessed June 24, 2021.
49. "Luciana Souza," Grammy.com, https://www.grammy.com/grammys/artists/luciana-souza/10113, accessed June 24, 2021.
50. Souza, interview.
51. "Luciana Souza: From Bossa Nova to Chet Baker," *All Things Considered*, National Public Radio, Washington, DC, August 31, 2012.
52. Eliseo Cardona, "Souza Displays Richness of Minimalism," *South Florida Sun-Sentinel*, Fort Lauderdale, FL, July 12, 2005: 1E.

53. "Luciana Souza: Revising Pop by Way of Bossa Nova," *Weekend Edition Sunday*, NPR Radio, October 21, 2007. Minor edits made by author for clarity.

54. Berendt and Huesmann 2009, 419.

55. Vinícius Cantuária website biography, http://vinicius.com/#bio, accessed August 5, 2015.

56. Vinícius Cantuária, interview with author, August 14, 2015.

57. Cantuária, interview.

58. Cantuária, interview.

59. "Vinícius Cantuária—Vinicius Canta Antonio Carlos Jobim," *Discogs.com*, https://www.discogs.com/release/11302299-Vinicius-Cantu%C3%A1ria-Vinicius-Canta-Antonio-Carlos-Jobim, accessed June 20, 2023.

60. McCann 2015, 172.

61. Many authors have referenced this quote, e.g., Ben Ratliff, "João Gilberto, 88, Architect of Bossa Nova Who Won Grammy Award, Dies," *New York Times*, July 8, 2019: D11.

62. David Dye, "Vinicius Cantuária on World Cafe," NPR Radio, recorded in 2004; July 19, 2013, https://www.npr.org/2013/07/19/203605115/vinicius-cantu-ria-on-world-cafe.

63. Pravaz analyzed the boundary-work that Brazilian *mulata* dancers navigate between symbolizing national identity and sexual immorality, based on fieldwork during the 1990s (Pravaz 2012, 114).

64. Roberts 2021. See also Wade 2009, Chapter 3; Omi and Winant 2015, 107–108. Valeria Ribeiro Corossacz studied the perspectives of present-day, upper-class white male Brazilians in Rio de Janeiro who had sexually harassed darker domestic servants, interpreting them through the lenses of race, class, gender, and whiteness (Corossacz 2017, Chapter 5).

65. Brunet 2012, 90.

66. Brunet 2012, 86; see also 93–94. In striving for respectability, Pravez found that *passistas* distinguish their dedication to a "highly skilled practice" from the work of nightclub dancers; and both these types of dancers distance themselves from prostitutes (Pravaz 2012, 114–115).

67. Brunet 2012, 100.

68. Brunet 2012, 106–107.

69. On Carmen Miranda's racialized and gendered performances, see Bishop-Sanchez 2016. See Beserra 2008 on Miranda's image in connection to Brazilian immigrant women in Los Angeles. On Sônia Braga's reflection of Brazilian nationalist notions of their own sexuality as well as North American images of Brazilian hypersexuality, see Legg 2015, 203, 209. On Braga's *morena* identity, see Legg 2015, 210–211.

70. Hertzman 2013, 110, 152.

71. The hyper-sexualized stereotypes are not much different from one of the stereotypes that Latina women (and men) navigate in the United States; they may embrace them or gravitate to alternative images (Wade 2009, 229–230). In Newark, New Jersey, hypersexuality is often associated with Brazilians and Dominicans, and women of color either try to disassociate themselves from hypersexual stereotypes or try to leverage them selectively (Ramos-Zayas 2012, 220, 222, 237).

72. Beserra 2008, 61.

73. Beserra 2008, 65.

74. Maia 2012, 8; see also 52.

75. Ethnomusicologist Catherine Mercier studied Brazilian music and dance in Toronto and Montreal, Canada, from the perspectives of non-Brazilian audiences and Brazilian performers; she found a general comfort with exotic sexualized stereotypes of Brazil because audiences' goal for pleasure supersedes their interest in genuine cross-cultural understandings and because performers' career goals benefit from self-stereotyping (Mercier 2013, ii–iii). Ethnomusicologist Cory LaFevers argued that Brazilian performers in Austin, Texas, occupy an exotic positionality based on sexualized and racialized stereotypes of Brazilians (LaFevers 2018, 122).

76. Goldschmitt 2020, 17.

77. To be sure, Carnival samba has also been popular in New York and these genres may be intertwined in audience's minds.

78. Monika Oliveira, interview with author, September 30, 2016.

79. Jim Farber, "Astrud Gilberto, 83, Dies; Shot to Fame with 'The Girl from Ipanema,'" *New York Times*, published June 6, 2023; updated June 7, 2023, https://www.nytimes.com/2023/06/06/arts/music/astrud-gilberto-dead.html, accessed June 19, 2023.

80. Treece 2013, 73.

81. I read forty-five instances of "intimate" in Ted Gioia's book *Love Songs* using the preview and search functions in Google Books (Gioia 2015).

82. Treece 2013, 171.
83. Castro 2000, 70, 169, 306.
84. McGowan and Pessanha 2009, 48, 133, 200.
85. McGowan and Pessanha 2009, 51, 55, 63, 77.
86. "I argue that since the machinations of the media industries (and industrial reproduction more broadly) can be coded as feminized and white [. . .], bossa nova's fad status facilitated the easy dismissal of Brazilian music. While bossa nova persisted long after its height of popularity, it lost some luster due to its links with commerce, whiteness, adults, and the feminine popular" (Goldschmitt 2020, 26–27, see also 48–51).
87. Goldschmitt 2020, 71.
88. Mercier 2013, 37. Mercier also connected the intimacy, pleasure, and sensuality of Brazilian music performance in Canada with Jocelyne Guilbault's concept of "public intimacy" (71).
89. Putnam 2012, 18–23.
90. Lívio Almeida, interview with author, January 13, 2016.
91. Richard Boukas, interview with author, July 21, 2015.
92. Jane Stein, interview with author, June 15, 2017.
93. Junia Flavia d'Affonseca, interview with author, June 8, 2016.
94. Gonçalves, interview.
95. Oliveira, interview.
96. Matta, interview.
97. Lubambo, interview.
98. Adnet, interview.
99. Nicholson 2002, 240ff.
100. Millard 2005, Chapter 5; Bohlman 2016.

4

Samba Jazz at Carnegie Hall

Genre Fusion in Instrumental Music

The year 2012 marked the fiftieth anniversary of the first bossa nova concert on the main stage at Carnegie Hall. Held on November 21, 1962, during bossa nova's global explosion, that show joined Brazilian innovators with US jazz musicians who were championing the new style on national and international stages. "It's my first time in New York and I'm very, very, very glad to be here," Antônio Carlos Jobim told the audience, in Ruy Castro's detailed account.[1] In 2015, also in November, a concert in Zankel Hall, Carnegie Hall's much smaller auditorium, celebrated a related fiftieth anniversary: *Rio 65 Trio* (Philips, 1965) was an influential album of samba jazz recorded in Rio de Janeiro by a trio of male musicians led by pianist Dom Salvador (see Figure 4.1), bassist Sérgio Barrozo, and drummer Edison Machado. Substituting for the deceased Machado was Duduka Da Fonseca, another expat from Rio de Janeiro and a fan of Machado and Salvador.[2] The album typified the small groups clustered in Rio de Janeiro and São Paulo, mostly trios of piano, bass, and drums, whose members combined samba and jazz during the 1960s. "Instrumental bossa nova" and "samba jazz" came to label their common practices, imperfect terms that overlap with bossa nova. Samba jazz is often described as instrumental and improvisatory renditions of bossa novas and other song repertoires that expanded during the 1960s, in Rio de Janeiro and São Paulo.[3] Several male innovators in this larger scene of bossa nova and samba jazz would move to the New York City area, not always permanently, to expand their careers: Dom Um Romão from 1965 until 1977, Airto Moreira from the late 1960s through mid-1970s, Eumir Deodato in 1968, Dom Salvador in 1973, Edison Machado from 1977 to 1990, Antônio Carlos Jobim in 1987,[4] Cesar Camargo Mariano in 1994, and temporarily João Gilberto and Sérgio Mendes.[5] The female pianist-singers Tania Maria and Eliane Elias also moved to New York during the 1980s.[6] Dom Salvador

SamBop NYC. Marc Gidal, Oxford University Press. © Oxford University Press 2024.
DOI: 10.1093/oso/9780197619049.003.0005

Figure 4.1. Dom Salvador at the River Cafe, February 2023. Photo by Maria Traversa, reproduced courtesy of Traversa.

had also helped to initiate a Brazilian funk movement in Rio, called "Black Rio," that took inspiration from Black pride movements.[7] Yet, in the United States, he pursued his interests in samba jazz and mainstream jazz, thereafter influencing many local musicians.

   This chapter explains musical aspects of samba jazz in technical terms as a fusion of samba and jazz. Dom Salvador, his composition "Gafieira," and the practices of drummers who have accompanied him provide the first windows into the musical characteristics of samba jazz as performed in New York City. To explain additional aspects are analyses of works by Elias and Cidinho Teixeira. The descriptions foreground stylistic characteristics and commonalities of progenitor genres as well as conventional ways they have come together in samba jazz. Highlighted are rhythms, uses of the drum set, harmonies (chords and chord progressions), bass lines, melodic phrasings, and group interaction. Also explained are combinations of overall grooves and the subtle swing feels from jazz and samba found in Brazilian-jazz fusions. This chapter primarily concerns musical characteristics, though Brazilian jazz will also be discussed as a fusion and genre. Readers should keep in mind the argument about contextualized significance made in the Introduction: the music can have different cultural meanings in the New York setting than it does in Brazil as well as for different listeners. Scholars have noted that Brazilian jazz in

Brazil implies a meaningful tension between Brazilian nationalism and American cultural and economic imperialism, whereas in New York, the demographically diverse musicians who play Brazilian jazz eagerly strive for intercultural collaboration and creation within a jazz-focused culture and market.

Anyone can reference another musical tradition superficially or mediocrely, but to combine and perform two traditions well usually requires high levels of competency in both genres and an understanding of their typical fusions. The examples and explanations here feature instrumentalists who have greatly influenced the New York scene. Tania Maria, Claudio Roditi, Paulo Braga, Romero Lubambo, Cesar Camargo Mariano, Portinho, Cyro Baptista, and others have also influenced local instrumentalists who play samba jazz. Their practices have informed musicians who developed skills playing Brazilian jazz by listening closely to them live or on record, sometimes playing with or for them, or studying their pedagogical materials. One person's fused creations can therefore contribute to shaping stylistic conventions as others adopt and adapt them further.

Samba Jazz

Dom Salvador has a clear view of the history of samba jazz, including his contributions along with those of his former collaborators. He told me, "I was one of the first guys there after bossa nova, to get the mixing of the American music and the Brazilian music, that became samba jazz. That's it. I was very interested to do that kind of style."[8] He clarified, "Of course, the samba jazz in Brazil came from Pixinguinha. From the 1920s they used to play, improvise, that kind of stuff." In Salvador's liner notes for his album *The Art of Samba Jazz* (2010), his brief history of samba jazz continues after Alfredo "Pixinguinha" da Rocha Viana Jr. (1897–1973):

> In the 1940's, this music already started embracing more modern harmonies and was increasingly sophisticated. Simultaneously, the Gafieiras (a kind of festival ballroom dancing style for the low and middle classes) were surging, especially in Rio de Janeiro, and the music was being orchestrated for bigger groups akin to the North American orchestras at the time. Around 1956–57, the group A Turma da Gafieiras was created and comprised excellent musicians.[9]

This group, with Machado on drums, is often regarded as initiating a new era of samba jazz, and indicates that the trailblazers of bossa nova were not the first to combine the two namesake genres in a contemporary way.[10] Salvador's liner notes continue the story and rationale for samba jazz as an alternative label to bossa nova along aesthetic lines:

> The Bossa Nova movement started in the 1960's. Heavily influenced by West Coast Jazz, it was based on beautiful melodies and harmonies, very smooth and romantic. During this period, many musicians wanted to move to create music parallel to Bossa Nova.

Salvador is not the only musician in New York who foregrounds the term "samba jazz" to describe his work.[11] Da Fonseca has called his music "samba jazz" for many years, as his album titles illustrate: *Samba Jazz Fantasia* (Malandro, 2002), *Samba Jazz in Black & White* (Zoho, 2006), *Samba Jazz— Jazz Samba* (Anzic, 2012), *New Samba Jazz Directions* (Zoho, 2013), *Samba Jazz & Tom Jobim* (Sunnyside, 2019) with Hélio Alves and Maúcha Adnet, and, for variety, *Jive Samba* (Zoho, 2015). Both Salvador and Da Fonseca differentiate their approach of combining Brazilian and jazz influences from bossa nova, although the boundary is blurred musically and rhetorically. Salvador, in his 2010 liner notes, calls samba jazz a "music parallel" to the bossa nova movement, notably among piano trios and larger groups, including those in which he and Machado participated. "I formed Rio 65 Trio, a new style of music," he told interviewer Essie Hayes. "At the time the Bossa Nova style of music was popular in Brazil. I put together Brazilian music with jazz—you know, bebop."[12] This connects with his explanation of "sambop," discussed in Chapter 2, as a fusion of samba and bebop.

Fusion and Genre

While it may seem commonsensical to consider bossa nova, samba jazz, and, in general, Brazilian jazz as fusions of different genres—mixtures of samba and jazz—they can also be understood as genres in their own right. They include musical and social conventions, and they connect stylistic practices and communities of people, all of which are hallmarks of contextualized conceptions of genre: genre-as-culture.[13] Musicologists Alejandro Madrid and Robin Moore offer an applicable definition: "We view genres as dynamic, socially defined categories in constant dialogue with broader social processes and transformed structurally and/or conceptually according to the needs of the moment."[14] Sociologist of music Jennifer Lena took a similarly socially grounded approach: "I define musical genres as systems of orientations, expectations, and conventions that bind together industry, performers, critics, and fans in making what they identify as a distinctive sort of music."[15] To mention here the perspectives of several ethnomusicologists, Acácio Tadeu de Camargo Piedade considered Brazilian jazz in Brazil to be a genre as well as part of the "supergenre" of Brazilian popular music, MPB. The central argument of Eduardo Lis's study about Brazilian jazz in North America is that it became a "new tradition" with its own idiomatic conventions: "Brazilian jazz today [i.e., 1990s] is more coherent and integrated as a music style than were its North American predecessors: 1960s bossa nova and 1970s 'Brazilian jazz-fusion.'"[16] This logic is consistent with other scholars who have described fusions as genres. Catherine Appert, for instance, regards Senegalese hip-hop its own genre by emphasizing the agency and self-consciousness of musicians.[17] Indeed, to approach Brazilian jazz as fusion and genre resonates with anthropologist Deborah Pacini Hernandez's argument that myriad genres of Latin popular music in the United States illustrate Latinx Americans' engagement and comfort with cultural hybridity, despite essentializing and bifurcating discourses in mainstream US culture.[18]

Kevin Fellezs has analyzed several aspects of musical fusion that are germane for analyzing Brazilian jazz. He considered the 1970s styles of jazz-rock fusion to be a genre, which he preferred to call "fusion" rather than "jazz-rock" or any hyphenation. Fellezs viewed this fusion as "in between genres," "transgeneric," and, drawing on literary critic Isobel Armstrong, "a broken middle" within dialecticism.[19] Fusion includes what Steven Pond called "fusing activities" or practices within a cultural and political context, which would include fashion and other subcultural characteristics that musicians and fans share.[20] Fusion in the 1970s implied crossing racial divides in US identity politics and even musically critiquing them through combinatory acts and expressing agency and empowerment. This was evident in musicians' self-expressions that strove to create something new while resisting essentializing limitations of involuntary social categories. By calling a musical fusion its own genre, one emphasizes not only a mixture of progenitor influences but also a developmental process of synthesis, an evolving set of conventions, and a shared identity. A cautionary point follows: analysts should not only point out musical aspects of contributing traditions, but show how they commingle as musicians formulate new music, perhaps congealing into new conventions. Furthermore, the musicians may naturalize these new combinations rather than remain preoccupied or aware of their roots or combinatory qualities. Theorists may isolate the constituent parts to highlight the contributions from jazz and samba, while musicians may see more overlaps and already fused conventions.[21]

In addition to these subjective perspectives, the genre labels themselves evoke meaning. In this respect, bossa nova and samba jazz are branded quite differently as fusions. To name a genre that implies combination, like "samba jazz," is to call attention to self-aware mixing practices in contrast to distinguishing a genre by name, such as "bossa nova" (new wave/trend). The fact that the label "samba jazz" explicitly conveys an international combination might contribute to its contestations in Brazilian debates about Americanization of national culture, and also to its acceptance in New York within jazz context, as explained in this book's Introduction. Responding to the "needs of the moment" (from Madrid and Moore's definition of genre), to advertise a show in the United States, the label "instrumental Brazilian music" is less likely than "samba jazz" to attract jazz fans to jazz clubs, which is the primary market for Brazilian jazz.

Ethnomusicologists have observed that musicians have applied their bimusicality, introduced in Chapter 2, to develop musical fusions of two traditions. Martha Ellen Davis described new musical fusions in Caribbean secular music as products of bimusicality among local musicians, a developmental process she witnessed over the span of twenty-five years.[22] Latin jazz musicians from Cuba and Puerto Rico developed skills in jazz that informed their efforts to fuse jazz with Afro-Hispanic-Caribbean music with which they already had expertise.[23] Musicians engaged in developing Indo-jazz, Zimbabwe jazz, and Scandinavian jazz fusions have been described similarly.[24] The creation of musical fusions combines competencies in multiple traditions, which leads to new competencies, as Benjamin Brinner noted, and depends on people's open-mindedness to such boundary-crossings.[25] On a grander scale, Bruno Nettl pointed out that society-large "multimusicalities" can foster new musical fusions, for example, West African popular-music genres known as highlife and *juju* and African American music in general, all of which mix African and European music.[26]

Related to bimusicality is Piedade's argument that Brazilian jazz results from a "friction of musicalities" among musicians with competencies in both Brazilian genres and jazz.[27] Piedade asserts, "we should not speak of complementarity, as many discourses naively do, since the nature of this friction is not constructive but deconstructive, full of tension and flexibility."[28] This "friction" metaphor evokes two traditions being rubbed against each other that produces fusion, Brazilian jazz. Similarly, anthropologist Anna Lowenhaupt Tsing coined the expression "productive frictions" to point to creative outcomes from cross-cultural interactions, a concept that ethnomusicologists have applied to the unexpected outcomes of collaborations.[29] Aleysia Whitmore, when explaining bands that combine West African and Cuban music, has shown that such frictions can manifest in pronounced or subtle ways; therefore, noticing or interpreting frictions depends on subjectivity and positionality.[30] As a metaphor for musical fusion, I find "friction" too limited. Instead, friction is one of many commingling interactions between the musical systems and stylistic conventions that occur when musicians create and perform Brazilian jazz. When combining two musical systems, however much they have already been intertwined, musicians sometimes play with their conventions by mixing and using complementary elements, while at other times their differences are starker and perhaps jarring. The musicians might create frictions, but just as well their music might feature overlays or combinations of elements, and selections of elements from both traditions that fit well together. There is often a syncretic quality where the same features could be interpreted from different perspectives as resembling different influences or indicating their fusion. The drumming practices in samba jazz, for instance, show a smoother blending of aspects from samba and jazz traditions. Examples here will illustrate a handful of scenarios, including frictions.

Jazz, samba, samba jazz, and Brazilian jazz in general can be contextualized in the circum-Atlantic both as cousin Afro-Atlantic or Afro-diasporic genres and as Afro-Euro-American fusions. The first frame emphasizes common African and Afro-diasporic qualities while the latter foregrounds African-European musical hybridity in American settings, although these frames are interrelated if not simply discursive. Regarding the Afro-Atlantic frame, ethnomusicologist Travis Jackson noted that music traditions of the Black Atlantic should be compared "less by specific retentions of African rhythms or melodies than by a shared conceptual approach to music-making among African diasporic populations."[31] Some commonalities in samba and jazz reinforce composer-scholar Olly Wilson's generalizations in the 1970s about African and Afro-diasporic music, such as propensities toward improvisation, percussive approaches, rhythmic syncopations, heterogeneous timbres, call and response, and cyclical forms.[32] As ethnomusicologist Ingrid Monson highlighted in Afro-Atlantic music, "riffs, repetitions, and grooves—as multilayered, stratified, interactive, frames of musical, social, and symbolic action" are also features in samba and jazz.[33] As this chapter will describe, differences between jazz and samba's syncopated rhythms are noticeable, even though both are African-derived with off-beat accenting, asymmetrical cyclical patterns, and shared circum-Atlantic rhythms. To play samba jazz, drummers have transferred the rhythms, accenting patterns, polyrhythmic structure, and timbres of samba percussion to the drum set in ways that overlap with approaches to conventional jazz drumming. Samba features a way of swinging notes, that is, playing beat subdivisions with consistent patterns of uneven durations, which differs from the consistent shuffle of uneven beat subdivisions in jazz swing. Specific pentatonic pitch sets and their uses is another topic that could be compared among these Afro-diasporic genres. As Afro-Euro-American fusions, striking similarities between mainstream jazz, bossa nova, and samba jazz include European-derived harmony, homophony, song forms, and timbres, often using practices developed by American jazz innovators, particularly African American musicians. Brazilian jazz features harmonic approaches of jazz (or similar to jazz) in chord progressions, chord extensions, chord substitutions, and types of cadences.[34] However, having just categorized these musical comparisons as African- and European-derived, advice from ethnomusicologists should also be heeded: avoid uncritically reinforcing these colonialist binaries while recognizing their social-political utility for Black empowerment; in other words, proceed cautiously when generalizing comparisons.[35] To summarize, Brazilian jazz as a fusion genre can be dissected as a combination of influences from other genres, while also appreciated as a consolidated dynamic genre with its own ever-changing conventions.

Dom Salvador

One of the main reasons that Salvador moved to the United States, like so many Brazilian-jazz musicians in that country, was due to his love of North American jazz, rather than an exclusive commitment to Brazilian music and Brazilian nationalism, or specifically to flee Brazil's military dictatorship that began in 1965.[36] "Always I had in mind in Brazil to come to the United States to really listen to my heroes," he told me.[37] Growing up in Rio Claro,

São Paulo state, and performing in São Paulo city, his influences during the 1950s were singer Carolina Cardoso de Menezes and pianist Dick Farney, both Brazilians, as well as Nat King Cole and George Shearing, pianists from the United States and England. He listened closely to American bebop and cool jazz, naming white male icons of the latter style: Chet Baker, Art Pepper, Dave Brubeck, Shorty Rogers, and Stan Kenton.[38] "I always liked American jazz, you know, the real thing."[39] He visited the United States in 1967 and 1968 before unintentionally staying for good in 1973. To learn the "American way to play jazz," he would visit nightclubs and listen to the professionals. His friend, the Black Afro-Brazilian drummer Dom Um Romão, already lived in New York and would take Salvador to hear music and meet people in the scene.

> When I came here, he knew everybody here. He introduced me to all the clubs he used to play: the Fez and especially the Village Vanguard. I used to go there every night to listen. I didn't pay. He introduced me to the guy [at the door]. I used to come every night to listen. Because my idea was to get that feeling, the way to play here. Of course, I learned a lot from that.

It took Salvador a long time to play with an authentic jazz "spirit." He recalled how depressed the music scene in New York was in the 1970s. "People weren't too much into Brazilian music," he said. Work was sporadic, but his group with Telmo "Portinho" Porto on drums did play for two years weekly on Friday and Saturdays at the Tin Palace, starting in 1974. "I played more Brazilian music, but mixed it up. I played jazz also." Da Fonseca, who moved to New York in 1975, said of that economically challenging decade, "Sometimes it was either beans or rice but not both."[40] A break from Salvador and Portinho's financial struggles in the new country came when the star singer Harry Belafonte hired them for his 1977 recording and tour.[41]

Soon after his tour with Belafonte, Salvador began a steady job as the house pianist in the upscale River Café restaurant, playing most nights of the week, which he has maintained since 1977.[42] Although Salvador did not need to find other gigs, he has played shows with his own ensembles in other venues and has accompanied other musicians; these have included jazz saxophonist Charlie Rouse, known for his work with Thelonious Monk in the 1960s. Salvador has a stable music career, though he bemoans the paucity of venues in the 2010s compared to previous decades. To release his 2010 recording, *The Art of Samba Jazz* (Salmarsi), his sextet of piano, alto and tenor saxophones, trombone, bass, and drums performed at Joe's Pub, the night-club attached to the Public Theater. In 2021, a biographical film about Dom Salvador, titled *Dom Salvador & The Abolition*, by Lilka Hara and Artur Ratton, was premiered before his concert at Summer Stage in Central Park, attended by friends, fans, and the public.

The choice to celebrate Dom Salvador at Carnegie Hall in 2015 owed to his 1965 album's seminal status as much as his long-term residency in the city and particularly the gumption of an enthusiastic fan. Augusto Ghiotto, a graduate student in physics at Columbia University at the time, with the help of the WKCR radio disc jockey Jassvan de Lima, an on-air champion of Brazilian music, had already brought Salvador to Columbia. Salvador recalled that Ghiotto became inspired to pitch the fiftieth anniversary con-cert to Carnegie Hall, whose administrators liked the idea. Salvador found the success of this amateur agent endearing and amusing, but was also anx-ious about the show. "I was scared because they gave me the date: one day after Thanksgiving. I said, 'Nobody is going to show up there.' That's what I thought. I was surprised because a lot of people came."[43] He reckons that 400 people attended the performance in Zankel Hall, which holds nearly 600. Rave reviews followed as well as a recording released by Universal Music in 2015.[44]

"Gafieira" by Dom Salvador

Dom Salvador's 2010 album and its release concert opened with "Gafieira," an original composition he has been playing for three decades, including at the Carnegie Hall concert. The tune and its recorded performances illus-trate general ways that musicians fuse samba and jazz characteristics; rather than superimpose or alternate between the styles, in many cases they syn-thesize aspects of both into something new. In this case, inspired by both bebop and the *gafieira* style of samba played by urban dance bands since the 1940s, Salvador's up-tempo tune allows performers to showcases their virtu-osity and their bimusicality. He composed "Gafieira" in 1982, first recording it with his quartet on *Rio Claro Suite* in 1984, and later he recorded it with his sextet in 2010 and the trio at his 2015 Carnegie Hall concert. Covers ap-pear on albums by pianist Hélio Alves (*Música*, 2010) and Da Fonseca (*Plays Dom Salvador*, 2018). After a complicated introduction with start-and-stop melodic ideas, chromaticism, and syncopated band hits, the main melody begins, evoking an older dance band. It is rhythmically characteristic of samba in its sixteenth-note based accenting and anticipated beats set in $\frac{2}{4}$ meter. The bulk of the piece has three melodic phrases that I am labeling A, B, and C with capital letters to read easily. Each is repeated twice to produce an Intro-AABBCC structure, which is also used for improvisation. Figure 4.2 shows my transcription of the initial melody of the A phrase, which different instruments play depending on the recording. Although tunes in the *gafieira* style are usually played at a medium tempo appropriate for dance, Salvador plays "Gafieira" at a fast tempo, between 126 to 128 beats per minute (bpm); in hot pursuit, Da Fonseca's cover with David Feldman on piano is around 128 bpm and Alves's is a hair brisker. Salvador explained, "I play fast because I do jazz, I incorporate jazz."[45] Likewise, he explained his chromatic har-monic movements as different from *gafieira*: "That's my way, my way to do it."[46] The tune would be at home in a bebop-style contest, where musicians aim to show off their fluency, agility, and speed, which is precisely what the soloists do on the recordings. Critic Thomas Conrad, writing in *Jazz Times*, likened the piece to acrobatics of "a daunting melodic and rhythmic obstacle course" added to a "traditional Rio ballroom dance."[47] Continuing his gym-nastics metaphor, Conrad praised Feldman's rendition: "He sprints, flies high, and sticks the landing." All the more so could be said of Alves's playing. Reviewing Da Fonseca's version for *Down Beat* magazine, J. D. Considine wrote, "it's the polyrhythmic group interplay on 'Gafieira' that make the strongest case for Da Fonseca's adoration of Salvador, and the listener's ad-miration for Da Fonseca."[48] The two covers retain Salvador's melodies and structures, rather than reinterpret them wildly, as if to show respect for the master and so that the younger musicians can prove their virtuosity with this inherited challenge. The circle of adoration reconnects to Salvador's grati-tude toward Da Fonseca for covering his music on album:

Figure 4.2. "Gafieira," excerpt from A phrase of melody, played on various instruments, between 126 to 128 beats per minute. Transcription by author.

I moved to New York City in 1973, and Duduka arrived in 1975. In 1980 I decided to form a new group in New York City, with Duduka on drums, Dennis Irwin on bass and Ion Muniz on sax and flute. At the first rehearsal, I was blown away by Duduka—he knew all the breaks and hits in my compositions and arrangements, and he'd never played in my band before. [. . .] To know that someone holds my music in such high regard and has produced such a deeply felt recording makes my heart sing.[49]

I will focus on ways that drummers have combined aspects of samba and jazz to develop conventions for samba-jazz drumming with flexibility for individual approaches. Thereafter, "Magali" by Cidinho Teixeira will further illustrate how musicians have combined samba and jazz. But first is an introduction to my use of pedagogical materials as sources for analysis.

Instructional Music Books

In addition to my interviews with musicians, analyses of musical examples, and studying secondary sources, a particularly informative resource has been the instructional method books written by and for musicians, which include recorded audio examples. Because several musicians in my study have written or contributed to these materials, they also provide insights into the musicians' music, conceptualizations, and pedagogical approaches. In short, they are the musicians' own musical introductions to Brazilian jazz in New York. Da Fonseca with Bob Weiner wrote *Brazilian Rhythms of Drumset*.[50] Guitarist Billy Newman wrote the guitar method book *Brazil: Your Passport to a New World of Music*.[51] Pianist Cidinho Teixeira with editors Janet Lemansky and Pedro Bermudez wrote *Brazilian Rhythms on the Keyboard*.[52] Scott Kettner wrote *Maracatu for Drumset and Percussion* with Aaron Shafer-Haiss and Michele Nascimento, and *The Essential Pandeiro Method*.[53] Bassist Itaiguara Brandão, percussionist Edson "Café" Aparecido da Silva, and drummer Paulo Braga contributed to *Inside the Brazilian Rhythm Section* by Nelson Faria and Cliff Korman; Korman is a New York pianist who moved to Brazil.[54] The books also share insights that the authors learned from their teachers, mentors, and musical heroes, many of whom are mentioned in musical explanations and examples. Although there are similar instructional books about Brazilian music, these particular sources clarify basic aspects of the authors' styles and outlooks.[55] Books like these also have the ability to influence the local scene, for at least one musician told me she worked through Teixeira's book while learning to play Brazilian jazz. Certainly, these materials are also limited in their ability to represent and explain music made by ensembles in professional settings where musicians interact, combine musical ideas differently, and change what they play.

These instructional books reinforce a few basic points about Brazilian music when compared to North American music—whether concerning samba, bossa nova, *baião*, *maracatu*, jazz, blues, or rock—points that have recurred consistently in my interviews and informal conversations with musicians. Professional musicians of Brazilian jazz in the United States and Canada also conveyed these comparisons to Lis in the 1990s.[56] First, in Brazilian music, the subdivisions of beats are usually conceived and notated as sixteenth notes, whereas eighth notes are more commonly used in the United States. The meter is written, conceived, and felt in $\frac{2}{4}$, meaning two quarter notes per measure, like a march, counted "one, two, one, two."[57] Whereas, $\frac{4}{4}$ meter, four quarter notes per measure, is the most common time in the United States, counted "one, two, three, four, one, two, three, four." These two points are related because popular compositions, such as sambas and bossa novas, are often written as sixteenth notes in $\frac{2}{4}$ meter in Brazil and eighth notes in $\frac{4}{4}$ meter in the United States, or sometimes in "cut time" meter (see Figures 4.3 and 4.4). Mathematically the meters are interchangeable enough to dismiss their differences; but each meter implies different ways of counting, subdividing beats, and feeling the music, a distinction that musicians often observe when comparing the two nations' music traditions and the chasm they must bridge when playing Brazilian-jazz fusions. Dom Salvador, for instance, spoke to me of $\frac{2}{4}$ and $\frac{4}{4}$ when differentiating approaches used in Brazil and the United States respectively, including rhythms,

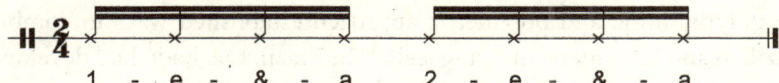

Figure 4.3. Sixteenth notes in $\frac{2}{4}$ meter with corresponding syllables.

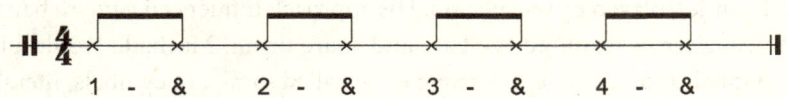

Figure 4.4. Eighth notes in $\frac{4}{4}$ meter with corresponding syllables.

accenting, and even swing feels. When counting and feeling Brazilian music in this way, a musician might subdivide a single beat as "1-e-and-a" for the constant flow of sixteenth notes, whether played or not, though drummer Maurício Zottarelli finds this way of counting sixteenth notes more typical in the United States than in Brazil.[58]

A second general point that the books explain is how musicians transfer rhythms from individual percussion instruments of traditional genres to the drum set, piano, guitar, and bass. As Kettner learned from his mentor, jazz drummer Billy Hart, the drum set is a "multi-percussion instrument."[59] He therefore prefers the term "trap drum set" (from a "contraption" of percussion instruments) to "drum set," tracing this development in the United States to early jazz of New Orleans. Therefore, Kettner's first book and Da Fonseca and Weiner's book for drum set progress from introducing the traditional percussion instruments, their roles, typical patterns, and idiomatic nuances, to explaining how to approximate them—and creatively play with them—on the drum set. Even instructional books for piano, guitar, and bass explain how rhythms derive from the same percussion parts discussed in the books for drums. It makes most sense, therefore, to feature the percussion and drum parts in this chapter's introduction to samba jazz.

Samba Jazz Drumming

Da Fonseca developed his drumming style inspired by Edison Machado as well as his knowledge of samba and influences from American jazz drummers Elvin Jones, Paul Motian, Jack DeJohnette, and others. Among the American jazz drummers in the 1960s who influenced Da Fonseca, Portinho, Airto Moreira, Paulo Braga, and other Brazilian drummers, Jones held a prominent position, perhaps partially, as Lis argued, because his flexible polyrhythmic and polymetric approach established ways to combine Brazilian and US American swing feels.[60] In Brazil, Machado had developed his personal style based on that of Luciano Perrone, from the prior generation.[61] Perrone had transferred samba rhythms typically played on multiple drums and percussion instruments in the samba schools of Rio de Janeiro to the drum set, played by one person. His approach influenced *gafieira* bands. Whereas Perrone featured the bass and snare drum, Machado would play the cymbals more, a style that came to be called samba of cymbals, literally plates, "*samba no pratos.*" Salvador and Da Fonseca said that Machado made this adjustment when recording the celebrated album *A Turma da Gafieira* (1957) because his snare drum's head broke.[62] Machado's style inspired other drummers to follow suit. The music critic Ben Ratliff described Machado's style as driven by the cymbals: "Machado's drumming was a duality: giddy and grounded. It came from the top down, fed first through the ride cymbal and always threatening to run ahead of the beat. At the same time it kept an independent, relaxed samba thump with his bass-drum foot."[63] This changes the timbre and lessens the patterns in the texture, and also leaves more room for drummers to interact with soloists and accompaniment patterns of other band mates. Da Fonseca, like Machado and other drummers, tends to combine such hits with samba patterns on the snare for emphasis or variation. Given how much translation to the drum set occurred in Brazil, some musicians call this style of drum set playing simply "samba" and not "samba jazz."[64]

Da Fonseca's samba-jazz grooves resemble the sound and approach of modern jazz drummers by combining aspects of samba and swing-based jazz, so-called straight-ahead jazz. Like other authors of instructional books, Da Fonseca explained how he translates Brazilian grooves from percussion to the drum set.[65] Notable in samba jazz are translations of conventions for the *surdo* and *tamborim* drums in samba, and not only to the drum set. Figure 4.5 shows this basic drum pattern, modeled on an exercise from the book, "Ride cymbal pattern #2—Tamborim pattern on ride cymbal."[66] The bass drum (notated below the bottom line of the stave) establishes the on-beats and pickup sixteenth notes, accenting the second downbeat. This is a signature feature of samba that mimics the largest *surdo* bass drums in Carnival samba schools, considered the heartbeat of the samba groove. The pickups "are in effect 'ghost notes' and are often felt rather than heard," Da Fonseca and Weiner explained.[67] This fundamental pattern played by the *surdo* drums also translates into bass lines in samba jazz, whether played by bassists, pianists, or guitarists (see Figure 4.6). Their basic pattern plays the

Figure 4.5. "Ride cymbal pattern #2" (from *Brazilian Rhythms for Drumset*) by Duduka Da Fonseca and Bob Weiner, transcribed by John Riley. Copyright 1991 Manhattan Music. All rights assigned to and controlled by Alfred Music. Used by permission of Alfred Music.

Figure 4.6. Basic samba rhythm for *surdo* drums shown on *surdos*, bass drum of drum set, and bass.

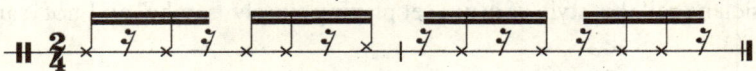

Figure 4.7. Basic samba rhythm for *tamborim* drum.

root and fifth of each chord on the two downbeats of each measure, accenting the second more than the first, and often anticipating these with sixteenth-note ghost notes of the previous pitch.[68]

Da Fonseca often transfers rhythms typical of the small *tamborim* frame-drum from samba ensembles to the ride cymbals (notated above the top line of the stave in Figure 4.5) and sometimes to the snare drum (in a middle space on the stave). As musicologist Carlos Sandroni has argued, the complex rhythms usually associated with the *tamborim*, probably African-derived, became a prominent feature of samba since the 1930s; hence, the so-called *tamborim* rhythm became structurally central in samba (see Figure 4.7).[69] For example, in the A phrase of "Gafieira," the pattern of sixteenth notes in groups of 2-2-1-2-2-3-4 resembles a *tamborim* pattern of sixteenth notes in groups of 2-2-1-2-2-2-1-2 (see Figure 4.2). Teixeira also prioritizes the *surdo* and *tamborim* when explaining how to transfer samba to the piano in his instructional book. He wrote twice, "The *tamborim* is the soul of Samba. The *surdo* is its heartbeat," and his book begins with pages of piano music that combine *tamborim* and *surdo* rhythms.[70]

The closed hi-hat (the lowest line on the stave), played with the foot, marks eighth-note off-beats (see Figure 4.5). These resemble the so-called backbeat common among African American genres, which are played on beats two and four in $\frac{4}{4}$ meter; however, at times Da Fonseca marks on-beats with the hi-hat.

Da Fonseca plays myriad variations to keep the music interesting and interactive, to complement the melodic lines and structural features, and to express his own ideas musically. He might redistribute samba rhythms between the snare and cymbals; play a pattern on the toms, sometimes to mimic the middle-range bass drums and toms in samba schools; alternate between sticks, brushes, and mallets; play accenting hits with the hi-hat instead of keeping constant time; and so on. Da Fonseca and Weiner notated variations that spread basic patterns over the drum set, and wrote twice that the rhythms and ordering one uses in performance should derive from the melody of the particular composition being played, which can be heard in his ensemble recordings. "As with other styles of Brazilian music, the starting point of the pattern often depends on the phrasing of the melody."[71] Faria and Korman, in their instructional book, made a similar point about drummer Paulo Braga's accompaniment in their samba example: "Paulo's skill and flexibility allow him to change the orchestration of his parts while maintaining the important elements of the rhythmic figures."[72] By "orchestration" they mean using different parts of the drum set. "Paradiddle combinations" and "broken paradiddles" are how Da Fonseca and Weiner described some variations such as a pattern distributed between the snare drum and hi-hat, or on tom toms, or on ride cymbal and toms.[73] This caveat is transferable to pianists who distribute rhythms between their hands.[74]

The result is that although drummers include identifiable elements from Brazilian genres, in this case samba, their overall sound shares basic elements of jazz drumming beyond simply the fact that they are playing a drum set. As is done in jazz, the ride cymbals maintain the beat subdivisions even though the rhythms derive from samba. The bass drum and hi-hat establish downbeats, upbeats, and metric time. Tom drums are used for fills and alternative patterns and timbres. The snare drum, bass drum, and crash cymbals are used to mark structural moments and respond interactively with the other musicians. Da Fonseca's drumming, like other drummers of samba jazz, resembles the sound and approach of modern jazz drummers even though he rarely plays the rhythms of mainstream jazz when playing samba jazz. More subtly, the swing feel—the cadence, sway, gate, lilt—of his drumming is that of Brazilian music, not of straight-ahead jazz.

Drumming on "Gafieira"

To compare the drumming in a few of the many renditions of Salvador's "Gafieira," Da Fonseca played on three recorded versions—in 1984, 2015, and 2018—while Zottarelli played on Salvador's 2010 recording and drummer Antonio Sánchez played on Alves's 2010 version. On Salvador's 1984 version, at the beginning of the melody's A phrase, Da Fonseca played a samba groove with snare-drum accents on the third sixteenth note of each measure, which usually coincides with the melody. On the closed hi-hat (and later on the ride cymbal) he played a *tamborim*-derived samba rhythm that follows the melody's rhythm, adding crash cymbals for the longer final notes. Meanwhile, he maintained the *surdo* part on the bass drum. Figure 4.8 transcribes the first two measures of the A phrase melody with Da Fonseca's drum part and the part played on a *cuíca* friction drum. He pointed out to me their use of the common *partido alto* rhythm in samba (see Figure 4.9).[75] On that recording, a *cuica* sounded the *partido alto* rhythm during the melody's A phrase (see Figure 4.8), from which Da Fonseca derived his ride cymbal pattern during the piano solo. Accompanying Salvador at his 2015 Carnegie Hall concert, Da Fonseca played the *tamborim* pattern that fits the A phrase, without the *partido alto* pattern.

To summarize a comparative example, without transcriptions, Zottarelli's style and rhythms differ from those of Machado and Da Fonseca, while influenced by Machado. He translates different samba instruments and rhythms to the drum set, though still in flexible ways. Zottarelli tends to use the *tamborim* pattern as part of the drummer's dialogue on the snare with the other musicians, while on the cymbals he more often plays consistent

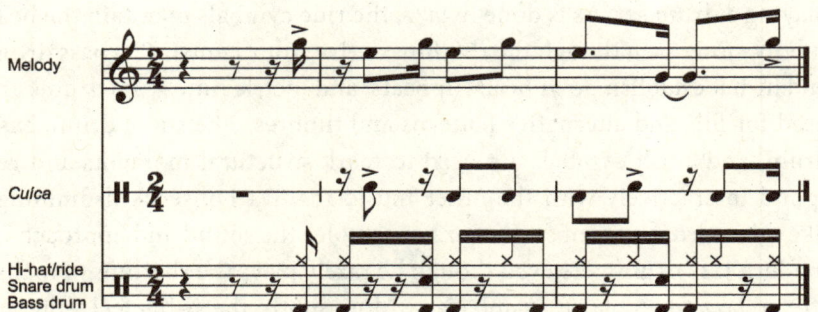

Figure 4.8. First two measures of "Gafieira" melody with Da Fonseca's drum part on 1984 recording. Transcription by author.

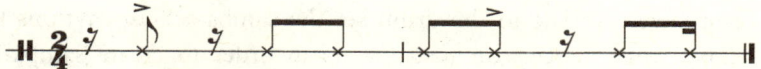

Figure 4.9. Common *partido alto* rhythm.

sixteenth notes that he associates with the shaker part in samba schools.[76] Like other drummers, he maintains the *surdo* pattern on his bass drum and closes the hi-hat with his foot on upbeat eighth notes, the backbeats. During the A phrase of Salvador's "Gafieira," Zottarelli plays the rhythm of the high-pitched *repique* tom drum from samba schools on his un-snared snare drum using a stick and a bare hand. He chose this approach to re-semble early *gafieira* drummers, notably Machado's early style and the group Quarteto Excelsior, a recording of which Salvador gave Zottarelli to study.[77] Listening closely to the album *A Turma da Gafieira*, Zottarelli noticed that Machado drew on *repique* rhythms more than the *tamborim* rhythm.[78] For the B phrase, Zottarelli shifts to the ride cymbal, often moving to its bell or closed hi-hat, playing a *tamborim* pattern. To accompany the solos, he fre-quently changes his patterns, not only at the ends of phrases and other struc-tural moments. Both drummers constantly interact with the soloists, while Zottarelli varies the timbres and rhythms more often. Musicians in the scene often compliment his complexity as well as dynamic range—Richard Boukas called him "the fireworks guy"—often contrasting his style to subtle, re-strained approaches of drummers other than Da Fonseca.[79] Lastly, Sánchez, a successful jazz drummer in New York from Mexico who plays on Alves's recording of "Gafieira," has a lighter touch than Da Fonseca and Zottarelli, using grooves similar to Da Fonseca's for samba jazz.[80] He usually uses a ride cymbal to maintain either a syncopated rhythm or constant sixteenths, and the snare drum for hits and broken paradiddles in combination with the ride cymbal and other parts of the drum set.

Without describing any more details, it is clear that there is significant overlap between the drummers' approaches to an upbeat samba-jazz piece that reinforces Da Fonseca and Weiner's instruction. The variety of samba-jazz styles of other drummers in the New York scene can be described in similar terms, while attending to the idiosyncrasies and decisions of each drummer. Salvador said that all the drummers he plays with are unique and incomparable to each other in terms of quality. Bassists Itaiguara Brandão and Eduardo Belo told me they can each identify the local drummers im-mediately upon hearing them.[81] The important conclusion here is that the drummers translate to the drum set the samba-school rhythms typical of particular percussion instruments in order to create samba-jazz grooves. This translation seems to include conventions of straight-ahead jazz drumming so as to create a fusion of characteristics from both genres. And drummers have made these translations in remarkably similar ways while expressing their individual voices and decisions, such as which samba instruments, rhythms, and timbres to emphasize using different parts of the drum set. Other musicians recognize the drummers' stylistic differences, which informs when and how they choose to work with the drummers. The basics of these styles are explained in some instructional books, while their recorded performances in ensembles showcase the complexities, nuances, and interactive aspects of the drummers' music. The next section concerns the different swing feels typical of jazz and samba, which can be heard both in the drums and other instrumentalists, and how musicians commingle grooves and swing feels while creating Brazilian jazz fusions.

Commingling Grooves and Swing Feels

Music scores of jazz and samba in Western notation mask a critical point: musicians with expertise in these styles do not play notes of the same notated values with equal durations, but instead they play them unevenly with swing feels. Even when instrumentalists play notes in a so-called straight manner—that is, with even durations—they inevitably play with some unevenness because, above all, humans are not machines and, more to the point, many music traditions have conventional gates and sways, which musicians and analysts call "swing." Jazz scholars have called this aspect swing eighth notes, swing quavers, swing rhythm, swing time, the swing ride-cymbal pattern, and shuffle.[82] The have also elaborated diverse aspects, definitions, and interpretations of swing.[83] Jazz swing features a conventional lengthening and shortening of paired eighth notes in a long-short pattern and sometimes a short-long pattern. By contrast, the swing feel played in samba and other Brazilian genres typically features a pattern of long-short-medium-long durations of beat subdivisions, usually conceived as sixteenth notes. This latter type of swing feel is called *balanço*, *cadencia*, or *suingue* in Brazil; the last of these Portuguese words approximates the English "swing." For convenience, I refer to these two general types of swing feels as *jazz swing* and *samba swing*. Other genres in the United States and Brazil share these swing feels, like the blues and *maracatu*, respectively, and different sub-styles or regional styles of samba can use ever-so-slightly different swing feels. I am also distinguishing swing from other aspects of grooves, such as the conventional rhythms, strong beats, repeating cycles, instrument roles, and instrumental interactions that vary by musical style. In short, the way I am using these terms is that music notation generally prescribes the rhythms of grooves, whereas swing feels pertain to micro-level timings of how the rhythms are performed. The particular swing feels of jazz and samba differ, as do their syncopated rhythms and notation conventions, yet they are related through their West African influences, practice of performing with an asymmetrical sway against a steady beat, and resulting ambiguity in between quadruple and triple meters.[84]

To expand and historicize these and related points mentioned earlier, consider the recollections of Eumir Deodato, a celebrated Brazilian-American keyboardist, arranger, conductor, and producer, about his initial experiences working with US musicians on Brazilian music in the late 1960s and 1970s in New York City. During that era, Deodato arranged music for US recordings of Antônio Carlos Jobim, Astrud Gilberto, Luiz Bonfá, Maria Toledo, Milton Nascimento, and João Donato, as well as Jobim and Frank Sinatra's second duet album (*Sinatra & Company*, Reprise, 1971).[85] He encountered the contrasting conceptualizations and notation conventions between Brazilian music and US jazz when he directed big bands and strings to accompany Brazilian musicians. Moreover, the American musicians, unless instructed otherwise, habitually added a jazz swing feel instead of playing notes evenly, let alone with a samba swing. He noticed that within a couple years, when he arranged for Sinatra and Jobim's collaboration, studio musicians were playing Brazilian music without jazz swing, such that he had to instruct them to add it to jazz tunes when he desired.

The Brazilian music was always in $\frac{2}{4}$. Never in $\frac{4}{4}$. It was one of the major obstacles for bossa nova, for Brazilian music to take over, to take place in the United States. The second bad thing is that American music, as we know it, the so-called shuffle or swing, these are $\frac{12}{8}$ beats, not $\frac{4}{4}$. In other words, instead of four quarter notes, you talk about twelve eighth notes. Then you go, [sings triplets, clapping on ones, and sings a swing melody matching the first and third triplets]. That does not exist in Brazil, never did. In Brazil it would be, [sings similar melody on straight eighth notes, clapping on one and two]. Very different. The feel is different. Now one thing that wasn't a problem was doing [. . .] $\frac{4}{4}$ because $\frac{4}{4}$ is like $\frac{2}{4}$. Instead of using sixteenth notes as subdivisions you use eighth notes. So, you have 1 2 3 4, [singing as eighth notes] ta da ta da ta da ta da. And in Portuguese, in Brazil, you would have in $\frac{2}{4}$ [sings as sixteenth notes], da ki ta ki. And that's the feel of Brazilian music. [Sings a pattern in sixteenths], not [sings the same thing in eighths]. Very different. It's inherently eight sub-notes to each bar, or four per quarter note, which is sixteenth notes. By [the] Sinatra [album], everything was already squared out. Before that it was a problem. The very first record I did here was in 1968 and it was with Maria Toledo, who was Luiz Bonfá's wife, a very good singer, Brazilian singer [*Sings the Best of Luiz Bonfa*, United Artists Records, 1967]. And I used traditional big band plus strings. And in the station [recording studio], they wrote using eighth notes but they read it [sings with jazz swing]. It always intrigued me. Unless I told them specifically. [. . .] After a couple of years, bossa nova was recorded a lot in the United States, still is. By now they understand it, to the point that you have to write "swing," near where you write that the quarter note equals 120 [bpm]. Otherwise they read [straight eighths]. Before that it was swing unless noted "not swing." [. . .] It's one of those funny things.[86]

As Deodato mentioned, a rough way that musicians often gloss the difference between jazz swing and samba swing is that jazz swing derives from triplet subdivisions of beats whereas samba is based in quadruplet subdivisions of each beat. However, both these swing feels reside between triplet and duple/quadruplet subdivisions of beats, which is a key aspect of swing for music scholars.[87] In jazz swing, consecutive eighth notes on paper are played as if they are close to the first and third eighth-note triplets in a set of three: the lengthened note can last nearly twice as long as the duration of the shortened note. In Brazilian music, by contrast, the prolongation of sixteenth notes leans toward triplet subdivisions of beats in the first and fourth sixteenth notes in four-note groupings, and the shortening usually happens to the second sixteenth note.

Pertinent here are the explanations of swing feels by percussionist-pedagogues who have conveyed that rather than compare the swing feels as either triplet or duple/quadruple subdivisions of beats, it is more accurate to say that musicians play between these poles in myriad ways and to different extents depending on the musician, ensemble, piece of music, rhythms and accenting patterns, tempo, musical goals, personal whims, and other factors. Da Fonseca and Weiner mentioned swing and recommended playing durations between duple and triplet subdivisions. "One of the keys to understanding Brazilian music is feeling the pull towards a 'triplet pulse' against the $\frac{2}{4}$ feel of samba."[88] Kettner mentioned Brazilian swing in his books and on an instructional website, and we discussed swing at length in person.[89] In his *maracatu* book he compared a swing feel of any musical culture to an accent, dialect, or lilt. "Maracatu has a very strong lilt, and to make things even more interesting each group plays with varying degrees of this lilt."[90] In his second book about the *pandeiro* drum, he described his "SwingOmeter" concept to play swing feels from the United States and Brazil with "varying degrees," for which he has a software application to help students practice.[91] He also directed readers to percussionist-pedagogue Michael Spiro's instructional book, in which Spiro theorized that swing exists between $\frac{4}{4}$ and $\frac{6}{8}$ meters, not in four and not in six, but in between both, which Spiro calls "Fix Time."[92] Kettner uses a method to teach students to play with a Brazilian swing that he learned in Brazil, with syllables to accent and elongate the first and fourth sixteenth notes, comparable to Deodato's description.

Musicians commingle rhythmic structures and swing feels in various ways as they create and perform Brazilian jazz pieces. Most commonly, they alternate between conventional grooves and their swing feels, which adds interest, excitement, and opportunities for different rhythmic interactions. This alternation also positions samba jazz in the company of countless Latin-jazz tunes that switch between an Afro-Hispanic-Caribbean groove and a jazz swing groove, such as the influential "Manteca," co-composed by Chano Pozo and Dizzy Gillespie in 1947.[93] Other times musicians play momentarily or hint at a jazz swing feel during an otherwise samba groove, such as when improvising a solo. Overlapping swing feels can occur when ensemble members play with different swing feels simultaneously. Blatant or jarring overlaps are likely unintentional, however, since these mainly occur when musicians steeped in jazz improvise using jazz swing while a rhythm section maintains samba-based rhythms with samba swing. Perhaps to avoid such contrasts, musicians sometimes adjust their swing feels by lessening the durational micro-timings while maintaining the rhythmic patterns; such adjustments can bridge two styles more smoothly. Musicians I interviewed variously said that commingling swing feels should be embraced, accepted as inevitable, avoided, or regarded as unimportant. Some musicians view their mixtures as part of an aesthetic goal or the high value they place on intercultural collaboration. Meanwhile, other musicians try to avoid overlapping the two swing feels, at least on recordings, judging them as displeasing or inauthentic.

Examples by Eliane Elias

Because pianist-singer Eliane Elias has expertise playing both Brazilian music and jazz, she combines the two fluently in Brazilian jazz (see Chapter 2). Her complex arrangement of "Desafinado" by Jobim alternates sections in bossa nova, samba, and jazz grooves, in addition to a section in an R&B-styled even-note feel during which the bassist takes a solo. She has been developing this arrangement since the late 1980s, expanding it into a twelve-to-eighteen-minute closing number for performances. I compared ten of her recorded renditions, between 1989 and 2018—a commercial release is on *Eliane Elias Plays Live* (Blue Note Records, 2010). The progression of stylistic grooves in her arrangement have come to include these sections:

1. unaccompanied improvised piano solo without meter
2. presentation of the song's melody in a bossa nova groove
3. improvised piano solo in a faster-tempo samba groove
4. slower tempo section with improvised bass solo at first in an R&B groove and then in a samba groove
5. restatement of the song's melody in a jazz groove instead of a bossa nova groove
6. unaccompanied improvised drum solo
7. closing vamp in a samba groove

The restatement of the song melody includes a twist: it starts in jazz swing but switches to samba at the point in the melody that corresponds to the song's lyrics (though not sung), "That this is 'bossa nova'" ("*Que isto é 'bossa nova'*"). Much more could be said about this arrangement including its harmonic changes, her improvisations, and subtle changes over the years.

Elias also moves between swing feels during performance. In her recording of Antônio Carlos Jobim and Aloysio de Oliveira's song "Dindi," with bassist Eddie Gomez and drummer Jack DeJohnette (*Eliane Elias Plays Jobim*, Blue Note Records, 1990), she and her ensemble hint at and later shift to jazz swing. She plays most of the piece as a ballad with nearly even eighth notes, as does her rhythm section in their accompaniment. She shifts to a jazz swing feel during her solo as DeJohnette follows with a swing feel in the cymbals (timecode 3:05–3:32). At the end of the arrangement, the outro vamp switches to a jazz swing with her improvised bluesy riffs on top (from timecode 4:08). Gomez plays triplet-note embellishments in his walking bass line that strongly imply jazz swing, which DeJohnette and Elias echo in response. Nearly two minutes later the improvised vamp fades out.

An example of Elias hinting at jazz swing during a bossa nova groove can be heard in her composition "Little Paradise" (*Dance of Time*, Concord, 2017). She adds jazz and blues-style phrases here and there throughout the recording but includes jazz swing during her piano solo (3:10–4:00). These and many other examples of Elias moving between samba swing and jazz swing feels speak to her fluency with styles from both musical traditions and combining their characteristics to create artistically interesting and expressive work.

Jazz Harmony in "Magali" by Cidinho Teixeira

Samba and jazz characteristics have been combined not only in rhythms and drumming but also in melodies and harmonies, as illustrated in a complex composition by an impactful local musician. Milcíades "Cidinho" Teixeira (1942–2020) was an anchor in New York's Brazilian-jazz scene, a musician's musician whose biography has not received the attention of Salvador, Deodato, Elias, Mariano, and other prominent musicians in this book. Not an extensively recorded musician, Teixeira directly influenced the next generation primarily through his weekly Brazilian jazz shows at the Zinc Bar (see Figure 4.10). For the purposes of this chapter, his music exemplifies the marriage of samba rhythms and jazz harmony in samba jazz.

Growing up in Rio Grande, a small port city in the southernmost Brazilian state of Rio Grande do Sul, Teixeira began playing music on the accordion at age eleven and playing accordion and piano professionally by age fifteen. His father neither believed in his musical calling nor respected his musical activities until he heard from professional musicians that his son was the best pianist in Porto Alegre, the state capital.[94] Teixeira had learned to play by ear and taught himself to read music in adulthood. His father was an amateur singer and exposed him to American jazz on records of pianists George Shearing and Nat King Cole. Hermeto Pascoal and Luiz Eça, key pianists in

Figure 4.10. Cidinho Teixeira at the Zinc Bar. Photo by Poby, reproduced courtesy of Poby.

the early scene of samba jazz/instrumental bossa nova, later became major influences and inspirations. North American jazz pianists Barry Harris, Bill Evans, Oscar Peterson, and McCoy Tyner also caught his attention. After he lived temporarily in Buenos Aires, where he learned Cuban music, and São Paulo, Teixeira's first major relocation was to Rio de Janeiro in 1965. There he played regularly at Chico's Bar, where, in the 1970s, Bill Evans heard and watched Teixeira play. Teixeira, Evans, and the singer Leny Andrade are in a photo that later hung in his New Jersey home. Nearby on the wall is a photo of Teixeira and Gilberto Gil, for whom he played on his funky albums *Refavela* (Philips, 1977) and *Refestança* (Som Livre, 1977). With Gil, Teixeira toured Africa and performed live as recently as 2009. Johnny Alf, Jackson do Pandeiro, Tim Maia, Gal Costa, Simone, Djavan, and Eliana Pittman are other celebrity musicians he accompanied, as well as leading his own band, Som Tropical.

Teixeira moved to the United States, along with his sister, the singer Vera Maria Teixeira, around 1985, after a sojourn in Italy and a stint on an American cruise ship around the Bahamas. The Teixeiras played with other Brazilians as well as regularly with the US-born Americans Paul Meyers and

Greg Jones. Similar to Dom Salvador, Teixeira also had weekly engagements playing piano in restaurants for years at a time, as he recalled in 2019, although forgetful of dates: "I played ten years at Via Brasil. [. . .] I played five more years at [Churrascaria] Plataforma. I played three more years at Tribeca, and then I went back to Via Brasil and played seven more years there. I have been playing Brazilian music for a living in the USA for 34 years."[95] His most locally influential engagement was Brazilian jazz on Sunday nights at the Zinc Bar from the late 1990s until 2013.[96]

Teixeira explained in his instructional method book, *Brazilian Rhythms on the Keyboard*, fundamental approaches to playing piano in Brazilian genres. The book contains many original compositions that show how he incorporated Brazilian rhythmic vocabulary and instrument roles with complex jazz harmony and changing meters. With respect to harmonic vocabulary and improvisation skills, Teixeira believed that these are the aspects of his playing that improved the most during his years in the New York area, through study as well as observation. "I studied two years with Charlie Banacos," he told me.[97] Banacos was an influential theorist and pedagogue of jazz harmony and improvisation, who authored textbooks starting in the early 1970s. "The study improved my technique, improved my view of improvisation. To this day I still look at the books I have by him."

The first samba song Teixeira provided in his book, "Magali," is also a harmonically complex arrangement of his oldest composition. It shows influences from jazz harmony and a rhythmic approach from samba that he explained, a testament of this highly influential musician in New York's Brazilian jazz scene. The melody was inspired by a childhood crush:

> "Magali" was the name of the first song I wrote. It was about a very beautiful girl I met, a blonde named Magali. I had never written anything before. But the love was so great that I sat on the piano and when I noticed, I was playing it. And this song is not an easy one, it even started with compound steps, and the melody is beautiful as well because it was made with so much love. The song is very beautiful. And I loved this girl so much. She was the love of my life. And to this day I play this song.[98]

He used to play "Magali" during his years at the Zinc Bar, while hosting weekly nights of samba jazz. His accompanists recalled the trial by fire of learning it on stage without rehearsal.[99] A seven-minute version appears on the recording *Brazilian Night—Live at Zinc Bar by Cidinho and Friends*

(2004). He played a solo version as the opening number on a live show (radio-broadcasted and webcasted) featuring Gilberto Gil in São Paulo in 2009. It is rhythmically complicated due to the changing pace of melodic phrases, bass lines, and metric feels; it has a section in $\frac{3}{8}$ meter in the midst of $\frac{2}{4}$ meter. Harmonically it has several modulations and robust chord qualities. Since he said that his harmonic vocabulary expanded in the United States, as a first composition, it was either very advanced for his age or, more likely, he developed the harmony over the years, resulting in the published version in his 2011 book.[100] This published version is remarkably similar to his contemporary recorded performances.

I will describe parts of "Magali" starting with the form, melody, and complex jazz harmony, and then his rhythmic approach, which he teaches in the instructional book. Along the way, I include a loose interpretation of it as an instrumental love song. If this is too technical to read, skip ahead to the last paragraph of this section. "Magali" can be divided into two sections that I will call A and B. The A section has three four-measure phrases and repeats before the eighteen-measure B section. The first phrase moves slowest of the three and sets a dramatic mood, as if a proclamation of his passion for Magali. This leads to the second phrase, set in $\frac{3}{8}$ meter, like a fast waltz, which may be expressing her beauty or his dreams to dance with her. The phrase repeats a riff of rapidly ascending sixteenth notes in A minor, which repeats sequentially over ii-V chords in descending major keys. Possibly further describing Magali or responding to his dance fantasy, the third phrase returns to $\frac{2}{4}$ meter with another repeated sixteenth-note riff that ends on the sixth scale degree, as did the previous phrase. The melody of the third phrase smoothly leads back to the first phrase for the A section's repetition, and after that into the B section. The contrasting B section begins with an elongated melody, interrupted with a series of swift-moving ideas. Under this melody are ii-V-I progressions in A minor that also function in F major, the temporary landing point before resolving to A minor.

In Teixeira's webcasted performance with Gil looking on, he plays an improvised solo for one chorus between renditions of the melody. Using samba-based patterns, in the right hand he plays chord tones and some chromatic passing notes in sixteenth- and eighth-note figures. Meanwhile, in his left hand he plays bass notes and chords on downbeats and often the anticipations of beat two. The fact that he stays so close to the chord changes of the version in his instructional book, including specific chord extensions, confirms the book's accuracy. Yet, he varies the changes during his solo a few times. Typical of jazz conventions, chord-scale theory in particular, Teixeira uses the Lydian mode to improvise over the major chords in the A section. In the B section, he makes minor changes that are also common for jazz variations.[101]

Moving from harmonies to rhythms, the bass lines of "Magali" include a few patterns that Teixeira had introduced in prior pages of the book and are typical of samba jazz and related genres. The bass lines in the first and third phrase of the A section, and in the B section, apply two rhythmic patterns that he emphasizes in the samba and bossa nova sections of his book, in addition to the *surdo* pattern. Because the *surdo* rhythm is crucial to samba, he advises using these alternate patterns only if a bass player is present to play the *surdo* pattern, which would free the pianist to play other rhythms. In practice, he plays these rhythms on solo piano, such as during the webcasted performance of "Magali." The first is the samba pattern associated with the *tamborim* drum, already explained with respect to Da Fonseca's drumming. The second is a short, syncopated figure common in Brazilian music: a beat divided into a sixteenth note, an eighth note, and a sixteenth note (see Figure 4.11-A). Teixeira calls it "the golden groove," applicable to both samba and bossa nova because it sounds good at any tempo and is appropriate for either right or left hands, he explains.[102] Teixeira and his coauthors write in large print, "Looking for a hot Samba? Use the golden groove!" and "Looking for a cool Bossa Nova? Use the golden groove!"[103] Mário de Andrade, a pioneering and influential Brazilian ethnomusicologist, discussed this "typical syncopation" preceding two eighth notes (see Figure 4.11-C); using this combined rhythm, he compared European and American approaches to syncopation and noted the figure's prevalence in Afro-Euro-American dance genres around the turn of the twentieth century: Brazilian *maxixe*, *catira/cateretê*, and samba as well as North American ragtime and foxtrot.[104] Add to these genres Brazilian *lundus*, *modinhas*, and early sambas,

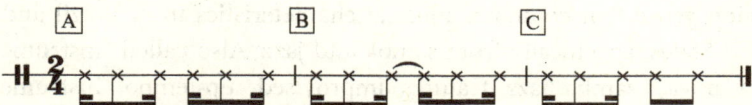

Figure 4.11. [A] Common syncopated rhythm that Cidinho Teixeira called the "golden groove." [B] Repetition of the rhythm combined with tied middle notes. [C] A common syncopation according to Mário de Andrade. Transcription by author.

as musicologists Gerard Béhague and Carlos Sandroni have discussed, while other musicologists have noted this characteristic syncopated pattern in samba jazz.[105] Teixeira often ties a repetition the golden groove to create a measure-long combined pattern of 1-2-2-2-1 sixteenth notes (see Figure 4.11-B). Another way to hear and conceive Teixeira's combined pattern is the middle portion of the *tamborim* pattern, but starting on beat two. It first appears in his book played in the left hand with the *tamborim* pattern in the right, an intriguing combination that reveals how he alternated offbeat sixteenth notes with moments of simultaneity.[106] On the pages leading up to "Magali," Teixeira prepared the student by explaining how to play samba in odd meters and how to apply both the *tamborim* and golden groove patterns to the bass lines in "Magali."[107] In these notated versions, he distributed the golden groove between both hands, similar to Da Fonseca's "broken paradiddles." With these instructions in mind, Teixeira's golden groove is visible in the bass clef of "Magali": the opening phrase of the A section is clearly the syncopated figure distributed to both hands. The golden groove in the bass line can be heard in the webcasted version in the first phrase of the A section and during his solo in the third phrase of the A section and in parts of the B section.

Teixeira's composition, explanation in his instructional book, and solo piano performance of "Magali" show simultaneous combinations of key samba rhythms and complex jazz harmony, applied to the piano, from the perspective of a highly influential figure in New York's Brazilian jazz scene. Many musicians from different musical backgrounds listened carefully to his art, and some even played with him, as they developed their appreciation and skills performing and creating Brazilian-jazz fusions.

Summary

This chapter was intentionally technical to explain ways that samba jazz is a fusion genre that combines musical characteristics from Brazil and the United States, specifically from samba and jazz. Also called "instrumental bossa nova," samba jazz features improvised, up-tempo, instrumental music that is related to bossa nova. The analyses of example works by influential local musicians—Dom Salvador's "Gafieira," Cidinho Teixeira's "Magali," and Eliane Elias's compositions and arrangement of Jobim and de Oliveira's "Desafinado"—have introduced basic, complex, and subtle characteristics of samba jazz. To explain the genre as a musical fusion, the analyses added layers at each stage: starting with samba's percussion rhythms and their orchestration on the drum set in ways that parallel conventional jazz drumming, to the different ways that musicians commingle grooves and swing feels from different traditions. This samba-jazz drumming style developed in Brazil, even before the famous Edison Machado, while New York–based drummers Duduka Da Fonseca and Maurício Zottarelli illustrated later developments and nuanced approaches. "Magali" showed samba rhythms played on piano and complex harmonies that are typical of jazz. Improvisation and group interaction are other important areas, explored in other studies, that can show combinations of jazz with Brazilian styles.[108] To support the explanations, the chapter utilized instructional method books written by several local musicians as well as academic studies and original analysis. In addition to the notion that musical fusion can be considered a genre, the music in this chapter should also be interpreted with a point made in this book's Introduction: the cultural significance of Brazilian jazz likely differs between New York City and São Paulo. To generalize, Brazilian musicians in New York try to assimilate musically and culturally in order to build careers in the jazz industry, whereas scholars of jazz and Brazilian jazz in Brazil have emphasized the music's entanglements with Brazilian nationalist responses to tense US-Brazil relations and Brazilian anxieties about US cultural imperialism. This book has focused on bossa nova and samba jazz because of their prominence in New York City. Yet there are other Brazilian genres that musicians in Brazil and the United States have combined with jazz—commonly, *choro*, *baião*, *maracatu*, and *MPB*, as well as *afoxé*, *maxixe*, *marcha*, *frevo*, *xote*, *toada*, and Brazilian *tango*. In fact, *maracatu* is the focus of Scott Kettner's first instructional book, while *afoxé* and *choro* were part of the compositions by Miho Nobuzane and Richard Boukas, respectively, described in Chapter 2. Readers can consult the instructional books to learn from the perspectives of New York–based musicians about these genres' particularities and their combinations with jazz and other US American genres.

Notes

1. Castro 2000, 251.
2. Ratliff 2015.
3. Castro 2000; McCann 2007; M. S. Gomes 2010; Mateus 2014; McCann 2015. Samba jazz was also called "instrumental bossa nova" and "hard bossa nova" (Connell 2002, 77–78).
4. Jobim had lived in Los Angeles from 1964 to 1966 and from 1972 to 1974 (McGowan 2012).
5. McGowan 2012. Ethnomusicologist Andrew Connell summarized the motivations of Brazilian musicians to emigrate: "For many of these musicians, the opportunities for work in the U.S. and

Europe often proved to be greater than in Brazil, inspiring Antonio Carlos Jobim's oft-quoted remark that the quickest road to success for Brazilians was the road to the airport" (Connell 2002, 94).

6. For a longer list of influential Brazilian musicians who immigrated to the United States, see Quintero et al. 2014, "2. Brazilian American Music."
7. Dunn 2016, 156–157.
8. Dom Salvador, first interview with author, January 4, 2018.
9. Dom Salvador, *Art of Samba Jazz*, liner notes, 2010.
10. Barsalini 2009.
11. Roberts 1999, 240.
12. Hayes 2006.
13. Holt 2007; Lena 2012.
14. Madrid and Moore, 2013, 8.
15. Lena 2012, 6.
16. Piedade 2003, 42, 53; Lis 1996, 3.
17. Appert 2016, 280.
18. Pacini Hernandez 2010, ix–x, 2–3.
19. Fellezs 2011, 4–8, 12.
20. Pond 2005, ix; Fellezs 2011, 16.
21. Appert 2016, 282.
22. Davis 1994, 146.
23. Fernández 2003; Washburne 2020; Lapidus 2021, Chapter 5.
24. Pinckney 2003; Williams 2003; Holt 2016.
25. Brinner 1995, 84.
26. Nettl 2005, 58.
27. Piedade 2003, 2005. Piedade developed this theory earlier than these publications and it has influenced musicologists who analyze Brazilian-jazz fusions, e.g., M. S. Gomes 2010.
28. Piedade 2003, 55.
29. Tsing 2005, 3; Reily and Brucher 2018, 9.
30. Whitmore 2020, 5.
31. Jackson 2002, 92.
32. Wilson 1974, 1998. Ethnomusicologist Jason Stanyek extended Wilson's "heterogeneous sound ideal" to other aspects of musical interaction in Pan-African music and musician collaborations (Stanyek 2004, 114–115).
33. Monson 1999, 32. This chapter does not connect common musical features to the Afro-diasporic cultural contexts as her article does.
34. Reily 1996.
35. Drawing on ethnomusicologist Kofi Agawu's deconstruction of the historical overemphasis on "African rhythm" as a biased "ideology of difference" that privileges European above African peoples, ethnomusicologist Juan Diego Díaz critiqued "tropes of Africanness" about Afro-Brazilian music, including Brazilian-jazz fusions in Bahia, Brazil. These tropes include rhythmicity, percussiveness, embodiment, spirituality, spontaneity, and collectivism. Not entirely repressive, he argued, these tropes have been used musically and discursively to differentiate African culture both negatively, in persistent European colonial hegemony, and also positively for Black empowerment. For example, he wrote about rhythmicity, which I described to compare Afro-diasporic traditions: "To summarize, African rhythmicity is an essentialism that reinforces an ideology of difference, one that may perpetuate unbalanced power relations and exoticize Africans and members of the diaspora, but also support black empowerment" (Díaz 2021, 34; see also Chapter 2 in his book).
36. Roberts 1999, 240.
37. Salvador, first interview.
38. Dom Salvador, second interview with author, April 1, 2020.
39. Salvador, first interview.
40. Eduardo "Duduka" Da Fonseca, interview with author, July 22, 2016. Historian Bryan McCann also found that musicians of Brazilian jazz contended with economic depression in 1970s New York City (McCann forthcoming).
41. Drummer-percussionist Telmo "Portinho" Porto, from Rio Grande do Sul, Brazil, also played with Salvador at the Tin Palace and in Belafonte's group as well as with ensembles led by Dom

Um Romão, Gato Barbieri, and Charlie Rouse in the 1970s. In the 1980s, he accompanied Belafonte on two more tours, as well as Tania Maria, Astrud Gilberto, Paquito D'Rivera, Herbie Mann, and many others. Porto, interview with author, August 4, 2022.

42. Hayes 2006; Thayler 2011; Kassell 2018; McCann forthcoming.
43. Salvador, first interview.
44. Ratliff 2015.
45. Salvador, second interview.
46. Salvador, second interview.
47. Thomas Conrad, "Duduka da Fonseca Trio: Plays Dom Salvador (Sunnyside)," *Jazz Times*, October 18, 2018.
48. J. D. Considine, "Duduka Da Fonseca Trio Plays Dom Salvador (Sunnyside)," *Downbeat*, June 2018.
49. Liner notes quoted by Marc Myers, "Duduka Plays Dom Salvador," *JazzWax* (blog), May 23, 2018, https://www.jazzwax.com/2018/05/duduka-plays-dom-salvador.html, accessed October 29, 2019.
50. Da Fonseca and Weiner 1991. Da Fonseca also played drums on Jamey Aebersold's play-along book-recording, *Antonio Carlos Jobim* (Aebersold 2000).
51. Newman 2002.
52. Teixeira 2011.
53. Kettner, Shafer-Haiss, and Nascimento 2013; Kettner 2022.
54. Faria and Korman 2001.
55. Faria 2005; Figueiredo and Oliveira 2009.
56. E.g., Lis 1996, 15–16, 42–48.
57. Sandroni 2021, 15.
58. Maurício Zottarelli, interview with author, December 11, 2019.
59. Kettner, Shafer-Haiss, and Nascimento 2013, 54.
60. Lis 1996, 114–117. Da Fonseca, interview; Porto, interview.
61. Barsalini 2009; Gomes Maia Tomé Pimentel 2019.
62. Dom Salvador, second interview. Da Fonseca, interview.
63. Ratliff 2015.
64. E.g., Telmo "Portinho" Porto inferred this point during our interview.
65. Da Fonseca and Weiner 1991.
66. Da Fonseca and Weiner 1991, 30.
67. Da Fonseca and Weiner 1991, 12.
68. Daniel Ribeiro Campos explained in his master's thesis the conventional and idiosyncratic nuances of Brazilian bassists who contributed to the development of samba jazz in 1960s Brazil, including Sérgio Barrozo from Dom Salvador's trio (Campos 2014).
69. Labeling this development in 1930s samba as the "Estácio Paradigm"—after the innovative samba school—Carlos Sandroni explained the history of the so-called *tamborim* pattern and its variations, the musicological literature about the rhythm, and samba recordings in which the rhythm is played on other instruments and exists in vocal melodies (Sandroni 2021, 13–18, 182–196). For examples of the *tamborim* rhythm in Brazilian samba-jazz melodies, see M. S. Gomes 2010 and R. T. Gomes 2012.
70. Teixeira 2011, 12, 35.
71. Da Fonseca and Weiner 1991, 42.
72. Faria and Korman 2001, 29.
73. Da Fonseca and Weiner 1991, 53.
74. Faria and Korman 2001, 28.
75. Eduardo "Duduka" Da Fonseca, telephone conversation, April 12, 2021.
76. Zottarelli, interview.
77. Dom Salvador, second interview.
78. Zottarelli, interview.
79. Richard Boukas, interview with author, July 21, 2015.
80. Audio available on Spotify: https://open.spotify.com/track/5wWYzz6BFPFVp3saboReVZ?si=cvSDKITqSeWdXsGNmM68pA.
81. Itaiguara Brandão, email correspondence with author, November 29, 2019; Eduardo Belo, interview with author, April 11, 2020.

82. Gridley 1988, 364; Monson 1996, 52–57; 2002, 114; Friberg and Sundström 2002; Butterfield 2011.
83. Among many examples are these: Schuller 1989, 223–225; Floyd 1991, 273; Berliner 1994, 244–245; Washburne 1998, 161, 163; Jackson 2002, 85; Butterfield 2010.
84. Kubik 1999, 77, 93; 2010, 50; 2017; Pressing 2002; Polak and London 2014; Gerstin 2017, 12, 15, 16.
85. Eumir Deodato's credits are on AllMusic.com, https://www.allmusic.com/artist/deodato-mn0000212614/credits, accessed June 3, 2021.
86. Eumir Deodato, interview with author, August 11, 2011.
87. Studies that have influenced my understanding of the topic are these: Gerischer 2006; Lindsay and Nordquist 2007; Naveda et al. 2011; Butterfield 2011; Díaz 2014, 153; Gerstin 2017, 12.
88. Da Fonseca and Weiner 1991, 12.
89. Scott Kettner, interview with author, September 18, 2019.
90. Kettner, Shafer-Haiss, and Nascimento 2013, 11.
91. Kettner 2022, 14.
92. Spiro 2006.
93. Washburne 2020, 99–100, 119; Goldschmitt 2020, 33–34.
94. Cidinho Teixeira, interview with author, September 27, 2019.
95. Teixeira, interview. Translation by author and Nadja Batdorf.
96. The last listing in *Hot House Jazz* magazine is February 2013. Archives of http://www.hothousejazz.com, accessed November 17, 2019. In the 1990s, Portinho played drums with Teixeira at the Zinc Bar, with Sérgio Brandão on bass, and at Plataforma; but Portinho was the bandleader at Plataforma, where he played on Friday and Saturday nights for twenty years until the pandemic halted live music there. Porto, interview.
97. Teixeira, interview.
98. Teixeira, interview. Translation by author and Nadja Batdorf.
99. Zottarelli, interview.
100. Teixeira 2011, 54–55.
101. To support my point using technical terms, Teixeira maintains the initial A minor chord without the subdominant in the melody. Instead, his quick figures over the A minor lead to a climatic ii-V preparation for F major, which he establishes as a major-sixth chord instead of the augmented chord written in the instructional book. The last noticeable reharmonization during his improvisation moves from A minor to A dominant via G minor instead of A major (sus 4), which he plays along with descending bass notes.
102. Teixeira 2011, 33, 37, 40.
103. Teixeira 2011, 37, 38.
104. Andrade 1999, 475–477.
105. Béhague 1973, 210. Sandroni 2021, 28–30, 40, 171ff. For more on the use of these samba rhythms in bossa nova, see Reily 1996, 4–5; Freeman 2019, 109–114. Marcelo Silva Gomes explained that widely differing tempos of fast-paced Carnival samba, slow bossa nova, and medium samba jazz can affect the relative durations of notes within this syncopation, sometimes rendering it as a triplet (M. S. Gomes 2010, 52–54). On the use of this syncopated figure and other samba rhythms in pianist Cesar Camargo Mariano's samba-jazz work, see R. T. Gomes 2012, 27–28; Mateus 2014, 11–12, 37–38, 57–58.
106. Teixeira 2011, 33.
107. Teixeira 2011, 51, 53.
108. On improvisation in samba jazz, see Piedade and Bastos 2007; M. S. Gomes 2010, 60ff.

5

From CDs to Covid-19

Professional Agency in Volatile Industries

Each August since 2005, the ensemble Trio da Paz (Peace Trio) has played a weeklong engagement at Dizzy's Club Coca-Cola, the nightclub-style performance venue of Jazz at Lincoln Center, titled "Trio da Paz & Friends Play the Music of Jobim, Getz, and Other Brazilian Classics." Their residency expanded to two weeks and in 2010s the club dropped Coca-Cola from its name. Guitarist Romero Lubambo, bassist Nilson Matta, and drummer Duduka Da Fonseca, three white male Euro-Brazilians, established themselves as a mainstay in the New York Brazilian jazz scene since forming their trio in 1985, the year that Lubambo and Matta moved from Brazil to New York. Da Fonseca, who had immigrated in 1975, invited them to jam in his basement.[1] Matta suggested the trio's name, based on a soccer tournament.[2] In 2016, they released *30*, their thirty-year anniversary album, on the New York record label Zoho Music, which received a Grammy Award nomination for Best Latin Jazz Album. The longevity of their collaboration alone is noteworthy, making them iconic of Brazilian jazz in New York. Their music is even more impressive, beautiful and inspiring to witness. These three outstanding musicians know each other's playing and their repertoire so well that their musical interactions, responsiveness, flexibility, and tastefulness flow naturally. By the 2010s, they no longer rehearsed before shows. Each member has incorporated elements of samba, bossa nova, *baião*, other Brazilian genres, jazz, Western classical, and other interests in their own personal ways. For this chapter, their annual show serves as a springboard to discuss the commercial markets for live and recorded Brazilian jazz in New York during the 2000s and 2010s. This section will describe this trio of successful musicians, their income-generating routines, and the marketing strategy for their annual residency at Dizzy's. It will also foreground a highly visible venue that presents their work to attract a paying audience, as well

SamBop NYC. Marc Gidal, Oxford University Press. © Oxford University Press 2024.
DOI: 10.1093/oso/9780197619049.003.0006

as provide comparisons to other venues and a sketch of local audiences for Brazilian jazz.

This chapter explains the agency, strategies, and decisions of musicians, record producers, and live-event presenters as they navigate capitalist markets for live and recorded Brazilian jazz in New York. People work in music industries because of their passion for the music, to support financially their lives centered on music. Yet because they operate in a capitalist system, they must exercise business savvy to survive, let alone to accomplish their ambitions. They are not pawns in the system, though, despite the industry's tremendous force and volatility. Even in conservative working situations, such as performing well-known bossa novas and Brazilian classics at Dizzy's Club, the musicians have creative latitude and exercise agency to decide how to arrange, interpret, and improvise music; they intentionally include styles unfamiliar to typical audiences and in general perform artistically expressive, exciting, and entertaining shows that emotionally satisfy themselves and audiences. Current perspectives of scholars about music and business tend to view workers as creative agents who interact with powerful and shifting capitalist systems, markets, products, and practices.

Music professionals—meaning musicians and industry personnel—work in music industries that have changed dramatically every decade or so, generally in ways that hurt their livelihoods. Still, many of them persevere, responding to paradigm shifts and prioritizing their art, while some have switched professions or relocated for pragmatic reasons. The 2000s saw declining revenue in both recorded music and live music for Brazilian jazz in New York. Musicians therefore relied increasingly on earnings from live performances. Although streaming music increased revenue to the music industry and star musicians in the 2010s, it has not helped the niche musicians in this book financially. Despite diminished returns, musicians in this study continue to record albums, for personal and promotional reasons. Then the pandemic in 2020 crushed what remained for most of them, their live income and savings, forcing some to take drastic actions, pursue technologically aided ventures, risk their health to earn money, or wait out the storm with government aid and hope. The perspectives of musicians and businesspeople help explain changes in the live and recorded music markets, how musicians have survived financially, and how presenters and producers dedicated to Brazilian jazz must balance personal tastes with business acumen to stay in business. As the other chapters in this book have explained, these music professionals exercise creative agency as they navigate and sometimes shape culture—in this case, business culture—in order to achieve their personal and professional goals.

Trio da Paz & Friends at Dizzy's Club

The annual residency at Dizzy's was billed as "Trio da Paz & Friends" because the trio has a circle of musicians who have been playing with them for over two decades. A night I attended during the trio's tenth annual residency, their collaborators included singer Maúcha Adnet, trumpeter Claudio Roditi, and saxophonist Harry Allen, all established figures in the New York Brazilian jazz scene and regular guests with the trio (see Figure 5.1). Others in this circle are pianist Hélio Alves, percussionist Cyro Baptista, clarinetist/saxophonist Anat Cohen, trombonist Jay Ashby, and vibraphonists Chuck Redd and Joe Locke. They are regular featured guests at the trio's shows and, vice versa, the trio members are guests in each of the other members' shows. This reciprocity expands the paid engagements for all the musicians since each one can headline a show locally without compromising the others' contracts. Not only does the larger circle of friends diversify shows musically,

Figure 5.1. Trio da Paz and Friends at Dizzy's Club Coca-Cola, Jazz at Lincoln Center, August 2016. Left to right: Romero Lubambo (guitar), Maúcha Adnet (vocals), Nilson Matta (bass), Harry Allen (saxophone), Claudio Roditi (trumpet), and Duduka Da Fonseca (drums). Photo by Maria Traversa, reproduced courtesy of Traversa.

but it expands the appeal of recordings by advertising "special guests." Rick Warm, who ran the independent record label Malandro Records at the turn of the millennium and specialized in New York Brazilian jazz musicians, noted this as a productive marketing strategy to increase sales.[3] Some special guests are not part of their inner circle, though they are part of their professional networks, including better-known musicians like Cesar Camargo Mariano, Herbie Mann, Joe Lovano, Dianne Reeves, Randy Brecker, and Joanne Brackeen.

Trio da Paz members have also achieved a level of success with multiple types of work that have afforded them stable careers compared to most musicians in the local Brazilian jazz scene. On the one hand, they play well-paying shows in the New York area because they each have name recognition, as does their trio. Because venues use radius clauses in contracts that dissuade a headliner from booking multiple shows too close in time or proximity—commonly ninety days and fifty miles from a venue—each trio member also arranges shows under his own name.[4] One night you might see Da Fonseca's ensemble with Matta on bass, and within ninety days you might see Matta's Brazilian Voyage ensemble in another venue with Lubambo as a guest. Despite this strategy, they cannot schedule enough well-paying local gigs to earn enough money to afford their middle-class lifestyles. So they must perform outside the New York region and internationally to earn money from more shows, which often pay higher wages, too. As bassist Nicki Parrott summarized the situation, "I get paid to get on an airplane," pointing out that if she travels to a show she gets paid more.[5] Drummer Maurício Zottarelli said that one usually has more engagements in a shorter time span while touring than when at home because booking agents try to maximize revenues in order to offset expenses during a tour.[6] In Trio da Paz, Lubambo seems to travel far more than the others, in fact, far more than many musicians I met. He mainly tours regularly with jazz singer Dianne Reeves; and between tours and segments, he flies to other live and recording engagements. He once left a cruise ship gig to fly back to New York for Reeves's annual Valentine's Day concert at Jazz at Lincoln Center.[7] Alves performs and records with Da Fonseca and Matta without Lubambo, under the name the Brazilian Trio; together since 1993, their first album was nominated for a Grammy. For Matta's Brazilian Voyage show, he rotates a still broader range of musicians, which also expands his professional network.

Playing music in live performances is the primary way these musicians, like most others in New York's Brazilian music and jazz scenes, earn livings in the 2000s through 2010s, between the steep decline of the recorded music industry since 1999 and the Covid-19 pandemic in 2020; more about these events later. Supplementing their performance income, they sell their CDs after shows while greeting audience members, which serve as souvenirs for audiences. All three members of the trio also teach in various settings, including Matta's multi-day workshop, "Samba Meets Jazz."[8] Lubambo, it seems more than the others, is hired to record on other musicians' projects, as will be discussed.

As noted above, "Trio da Paz & Friends Play the Music of Jobim, Getz, and Other Brazilian Classics" was the full publicized title of the show. The venue advertises the most famous composer of the best-known genre of Brazilian jazz to attract a wide audience of jazz fans, Latin- and Brazilian-music fans, tourists, and anyone else who might consider attending. The headline communicates to anyone unfamiliar with the band that they will play Brazilian music, songs by Antônio Carlos Jobim, recognizable songs, and music popularized in the United States by jazz musicians like Stan Getz in the early 1960s—in short, bossa nova plus more. Including Getz's name connects the show directly to jazz and thus the venue's mission as well as the spirit of international collaboration. Getz was an American jazz saxophonist who helped promote bossa nova worldwide through his break-out collaboration with guitarist João Gilberto and his then-wife, singer Astrud Gilberto, playing bossa nova compositions by Jobim. Their 1964 album *Getz/Gilberto* (Verve) won the Grammy Award for Album of the Year, a rare accomplishment for music other than pop.[9] JALC might have simply advertised the show as "Bossa Nova!" but their headline expands the point to include "Brazilian classics," accurately stating that the trio also covers mainstream songs in other styles. Indeed, the trio fuses many Brazilian styles with jazz in covers and originals. One night I attended, August 18, 2015, their set included Jobim's "Ela é Carioca" and "Wave" as well as originals by Lubambo and Matta and well-known songs by other Brazilian composers: Moacir Santos's "Nanã" and Johnny Alf's "Céu e Mar." Getz recorded none of these songs, as it turns out. Lubambo emphasized their variety:

We don't play only one type of Brazilian music. You went there. You saw it. We play some very traditional Tom Jobim bossa nova, we also play *baião*, we play instrumental music without a singer, we play with Maúcha. So we try to put one hour and fifteen minutes of a lot of different ideas of Brazilian music. And they seem to like it a lot. They seem to love that. And every year we have more people coming. I mean, really, it's a lot of people that come. We do twenty-four shows in two weeks.[10]

Lubambo's point resonates with opinions included in Chapter 3 about bossa nova: performers and presenters of Brazilian-music shows in New York often use the genre's familiarity with non-Brazilians to attract audiences, but the musicians also perform other genres. Jassvan de Lima, the radio host of a forty-five-year-old Brazilian-music show in New York called "Som do Brasil" (Sound of Brazil) on WKCR, Columbia University's station, described his approach similarly: since he reckons that only a quarter of his audience is Brazilian and because the station focuses on jazz, he begins his shows with bossa nova or samba jazz recordings from the 1960s before playing recent recordings, other genres, and live guests. This way, "I can turn them on to *so many things*," he said.[11]

Before closing the set with Jobim's "Wave," Adnet told the audience confidently, "You all will know this," without specifying the song. Whether they knew the song by name or recognized the melody, the audience enjoyed it, bobbing their heads and smiling more than to the other songs. Audiences often appreciate familiar bossa novas, particularly those associated with the performer, such as when Bebel Gilberto sings hits from her smash album *Tanto Tempo* (2001), as I witnessed. Cyro Baptista recalled that when he played regularly with Astrud Gilberto, audience members would "*cry*," he emphasized, when she sang "Garota de Ipanema" (The Girl from Ipanema), which she helped to popularize on that *Getz/Gilberto* album.[12] Even more experimental singers like Luciana Souza and Clarice Assad will close shows with Jobim's hits, sometimes singing in English. As musicians and presenters have explained to me, they attract audiences by advertising that which is most familiar, and they might begin and end shows with well-known songs; but once an audience is there, then musicians introduce a wider range of music than they had expected. They might include original music, songs by lesser-known composers, unfamiliar Brazilian genres like samba, *baião*, *choro*, or *frevo*, or even genres not associated with Brazil but that are popular in Brazil.

The specific audience and their experience of the annual show of Trio da Paz and Friends corresponds to the venue, though they share commonalities with other Brazilian jazz shows. Jazz at Lincoln Center has become a hub for mainstream jazz in the national spotlight, and possibly a metonym for jazz approaching the notoriety of the Blue Note nightclub.[13]

Its website address is even jazz.org. Unlike the Blue Note, located on the ground floor of a narrow Greenwich Village building, JALC resides five stories up a skyscraper north of midtown, in One Columbus Circle, formerly the Time Warner Center and currently the Deutsche Bank Center, opened in 2004, a year before the trio's engagement began. The Mandarin Oriental hotel, Whole Foods, and an upscale shopping mall are other commercial tenants. Two of JALC's three performance spaces have floor-to-ceiling window backdrops overlooking southern Central Park and Columbus Circle's cityscape, framed by the Trump International Hotel & Tower and the Museum of Arts and Design. Dizzy's Club, the smallest space, is a beautiful, immaculate space with curved walls resembling the Guggenheim Museum on the Upper East Side. There are clear views of the stage from every seat, excellent sound, a contemporary dinner menu, and professional service. The club is run so efficiently that I often feel there is no room for encores beyond the allotted time frame, which counts down on a digital clock facing the band. Given the venue's elite brand and high rent, the cost for admission plus the minimum food and drink orders and gratuity reaches the upper end of cost for jazz clubs in Manhattan, in company with the Blue Note.[14] In expensive clubs like Dizzy's, some patrons order modestly—fries and a beer, or cheesecake and red wine—while many patrons order entrées and share a wine bottle. Brazilian jazz shows I saw there in the 2010s set me back $80 while one could easily spend over $100 if dining. Still, tickets are less expensive than most Broadway musicals and concerts by the New York Philharmonic. At Dizzy's, the audience is nearly full, with a mix of regulars, locals, casual attendees, and tourists, a mostly whiter, middle-aged-and-older clientele.

This demographic mix compares similarly to Brazilian music shows I have seen at the slightly less expensive nightclubs Birdland and the Jazz Standard. At Brazilian shows at inexpensive clubs downtown, which also pay musicians less, such as Zinc Bar, Cornelia Street Café, DROM, NuBlu, and Le Poisson Rouge, the age ranges of audiences are younger, twenty-to-forty-somethings. Those clubs typically serve beer in bottles, not necessarily food, and have older furniture and minimal table service. However, audience members I have spoken with remain a mix of fans, friends, regulars, casual attendees, and tourists—simply on different budgets. I have met regular attendees at both Dizzy's and Cornelia St. Café, in western Greenwich Village, who live nearby and attended shows without knowing who or what was playing, but they trusted the club's curation. The music was excellent at both shows, with a $60 difference to attend. The Cornelia Street Café and Zinc Bar lack backstage green rooms for musicians, such that musicians and audiences, who often includes other musicians, can and do mingle off stage. At the Jazz Standard this mingling happened at the bar between sets, where other musicians can sometimes sit without paying to enter, helping them to network, discreetly hustle gigs, and learn from the music—"the hang," as this is known among jazz musicians.[15] While the inexpensive venues help less-affluent audience members and musicians attend shows, and support a music scene's artistic development, the well-paying venues like Dizzy's Club help its musicians earn a living and promote Brazilian jazz to a larger and broader audience through the jazz market.

Music Markets in Paradigm-Shifting Industries

The musicians and music-industry professionals who produce Brazilian-jazz fusions in New York exhibit individual and collective agency in markets for live and recorded music whose parameters fluctuate with paradigm shifts in the music industry. To start with the big picture, scholars in the fields of popular music studies, musicology, and business have been converging to reinterpret earlier conceptualizations of music, culture, societal institutions, and capitalist industries as a holistic system. Timothy D. Taylor, a leading voice in political-economic musicology, argued that neoliberal capitalism should be conceived as a cultural system, not only as an economic system: as both a "social form [that] profoundly shapes people's relationships to each other, and their relationships to cultural forms such as music" and as cultural with respect to its capitalist values and practices.[16] This intellectual history largely began with Theodor W. Adorno and Max Horkheimer's "culture industry" theory.[17] Writing in the 1930s and 1940s in response to fascism, Adorno and Horkheimer depicted the culture industry through a Marxist lens, akin to manufacturing, in which corporate workers produce and disseminate commodities for mass consumption that support unconscious conformity. The industry perpetuates status-quo values by reproducing mainstream products in standardized forms with negligible deviation and development.[18] Although a largely mechanistic and manipulative scenario, Adorno and Horkheimer valued individual agency to create art that strived to be "autonomous" from the mass cultural production of capitalist hegemony.[19] Adorno later summarized:

The total effect of the culture industry is one of anti-enlightenment, in which, as Horkheimer and I have noted, enlightenment, that is the progres- sive technical domination of nature, becomes mass deception and is turned into a means for fettering consciousness. It impedes the development of au- tonomous, independent individuals who judge and decide consciously for themselves. These, however, would be the precondition for a democratic society which needs adults who have come of age in order to sustain itself and develop.[20]

Later scholars have critiqued as well as developed aspects of Adorno and Horkheimer's political-economic arguments. Popular-music scholars in the 1990s and recent musicologists and ethnomusicologists have studied how music, musicians, industry professionals, and consumers/audiences partic- ipate in global capitalism by actively navigating, interpreting, or influencing the system that shapes their behaviors, rather than solely as the passive laborers and consumers that Adorno and Horkheimer's theories imply. For instance, Keith Negus argued against mechanistic views of the music corporations' influence on society, foregrounding the decisions of industry professionals and also proposing a dialectic in which "an industry produces culture and culture produces an industry," a two-way street where "cultural formations" shape music industries as much as the industries shape culture.[21]

Because this book is mainly an ethnographic and musical study of musicians, with some attention to record producers and concert presenters, my focus is on cultural production rather than the finances, distribution, con- sumption, reception, or interpretation within music markets. This chapter therefore compares to studies that highlight agency asserted by musicians and record industry professionals.[22] In this literature, music professionals are considered "cultural agents" and "market actors" who creatively navi- gate industries.[23] Corporations and their workers "shape industrial processes in Brazil," as K. E. Goldschmitt described.[24] Taylor describes social ac- tors pursuing their own ways through a conventionalized system: "culture patterns provide pathways, choices, for subjects. Capitalism as a cultural system offers its own patterns, its own programs, and entrepreneurialism, consumption, and much more."[25]

While the musicians and industry professionals in my study certainly exercise free will in their business decisions, they operate within business paradigms that have been changing every decade or so. This is nothing new, since volatility, uncertainty, and disorder were key features of the music industry throughout the twentieth century.[26] While some market actors have actively disrupted and shaped the entire music system, the music professionals in this book respond to the existing systems as they change and when they stabilize. They have plenty of room to express agency, develop their musical products, and make career choices, as scholars have shown in other areas of the music industry in order to correct Adorno and Horkheimer's notions that musicians and consumers are pawns in the capitalist system. Jason Toynbee argued that musicians as laborers have significant creative freedom compared to other industry models: "the logic of the music industry's own structure as a capitalist cultural industry has, paradoxically, pushed it into conceding a degree of creative control to musicians."[27]

The market definitely influences what genres musicians play when they want to try to earn a living. Because bossa nova is the most popular Brazilian-jazz fusion, the market rewards musicians, concerts, and venues that feature bossa nova much more than those who play lesser-known genres and experimental music. Musicians' artistic innovations rarely change the system dramatically; however, their minor creative contributions can affect what other musicians do, creating gradual change. And sometimes musicians influence what might become popular among audiences, in the rare cases of the bossa nova inventors or, say, Bebel Gilberto and her collaborators' fusion of bossa nova with electronica.

In sum, scholars of music and business have been highlighting the interactive, even dialogic, relationships between individual workers and capitalist institutions, assigning more agency to the workers without diminishing the powerful systemic forces. The next sections apply this dual-sided lens to examine how individual actors—musicians and music-industry professionals—have navigated volatile music industries for live and recorded music during the first two decades of the new millennium and into the Covid-19 pandemic.

Live Music Industry, Musicians, and Presenters

Several macro-level paradigm shifts in the new millennium impacted musicians' career opportunities and business strategies in the market for Brazilian jazz in New York. During the boom years of the 1990s, economic prosperity in the United States supported regular well-paying work for musicians in nightclubs, restaurants, festivals, and corporate events, recalled

the musicians I interviewed nostalgically. It was also the height of revenue for
the recorded music industry, mostly by selling compact discs (CDs), which
benefited musicians who recorded, those who collected royalties, and the
record companies that promoted Brazilian jazz. Meanwhile, despite Brazil's
return to democratic rule in 1985 from two decades of military dictatorship,
the 1980s are considered Brazil's economically "lost decade," a push factor
that increased emigration into the 1990s.[28] Brazil's economic prosperity and
confidence in the 2000s, as well as its socio-political and economic crises in
the 2010s, shaped the internal production, exportation, and international
trendiness of music from Brazil, as Goldschmitt has explained.[29] The dramatic changes in the 2000s affected Brazilian music in New York and elsewhere. Compared to the 1990s, the economic viability for music since 2001
diminished significantly, and musicians responded to struggles with new
career strategies and artistic expressions. Three major forces caused the
downturn, according to my interviewees and research: first, the aftermath
of the attacks of September 11, 2001, reduced concert attendance and restricted travel for musicians to visit and move to the United States as well
as the ability of many US-based Brazilian musicians to tour internationally.
Second, the economic recession of 2008 further reduced corporate spending
on live Brazilian music for events and payments to musicians from local
venues; although corporate sponsorship has increasingly sponsored art
music in the United States, which helps to explain the Coca-Cola Company's
sponsorship of Dizzy's Club.[30] Third, the increased availability of free music
and high-quality videos of live music on the internet reduced the public's
spending for recordings—music by local musicians and recording artists in
general—and may have negatively impacted attendance in live shows in the
small venues that present Brazilian music. All this was before the pandemic,
starting in 2020, halted live music performance and put one of the last remaining aspects of most musicians' careers on hold.

Despite these declines in the 2000s, Brazilian musicians continued to migrate to New York in the 2000s and 2010s, seeking artistic opportunities and
in response to ups and downs of Brazil's economy and perceived limitations
for them in its own music markets. Also mitigating these limiting forces, the
international success of Bebel Gilberto's album *Tanto Tempo* in 2000 and related albums that fused bossa nova with electronic ambient and dance music
boosted global interest in bossa nova.[31] This success trickled down to increase demand for Brazilian jazz and Brazilian music in general. Trio da Paz's
annual show at Dizzy's Club started thereafter, in 2005. Brazilian musicians

who established themselves in New York in the 1970s through the 1990s benefit economically by playing conservative music selections—bossa nova or samba jazz—and found supplemental work in related fields, like pop-music performance, jingle-writing and commercial music, and music education. Meanwhile, other musicians, often arrivals since 2001, have experimented with alternative sounds and business strategies to develop their professional careers in order to remain artistically satisfied and financially afloat. These changes in the New York music market over the decades partially explain my observation that musicians' opinions of the viability for Brazilian music can depend on when they arrived in the city.

Part of the reason that musicians tour, mentioned already, is that engagements in the local New York area do not pay most of them well. Annette A. Aguilar, who also teaches music in a public New York school, emphasized this point that musicians have to perform frequently and therefore cannot be too picky.[32] Some clubs pay well; for instance, Mark Morganelli of Jazz Forum Arts claims to pay musicians more than ever before and former agent Michael Solomon told me that musicians are still paid well by City Winery, where top acts like Eliane Elias and Bebel Gilberto perform.[33] But many musicians recalled that clubs that present Brazilian jazz are paying less than they did in the 1990s. The business model of a "door show" is particularly damaging, where musicians keep all or a percentage of ticket sales, and the venue keeps profits from food and alcohol sales. This model benefits musicians only if they have a following large enough to fill a club; yet many of the local Brazilian jazz musicians, especially the younger ones and newer arrivals, do not have fanbases. Low attendance also hurts the clubs because it decreases the food and alcohol revenue on which the venues depend. Much of the burden to bring an audience falls on the musicians even though the club may take out an advertisement, whether sporadically or for their entire monthly calendar, and market online via their email lists and social media. A staff member at Cornelia St. Café told Jorge Continentino to bring more people next time he played, disappointed with low numbers. This dynamic also encourages people to program music more likely to attract a following—bossa nova, in the case of New York—instead of the experimental music that Continentino's ensemble played that night.

Critical to the viability of a live music market are presenters, those who organize and promote shows, often working for the venues as talent buyers, but sometimes independently. They handle the business of operating live music venues profitably, either themselves or in coordination with other venue staff, and publicizing shows to prospective audiences. Ethnomusicologist Thomas Greenland devoted two chapters of his book about New York's jazz scene to business issues of presenters, venue owners and managers, and other professionals. This "web of interactive, interdependent, 'workers,'" drawing on sociologist Howard Becker's "art world" theory, tries to profit from live jazz in New York.[34] Based on many interviews with jazz presenters, Greenland's rich descriptions of the general situation and myriad nuances are highly applicable to the market for live Brazilian jazz, because it mainly exists within the jazz market. Though Greenland did not mention Brazilian jazz, he implies that it has value for venue managers in their "strategically eclectic" curation, such as "catering to separate sub-scenes on separate nights" in order to tap niche sounds, musicians, and audiences. In a revealing point from Greenland's research, the industry professionals he interviewed began as jazz fans and barely earn much profit.[35] The turnover in venues itself indicates the volatility of the live jazz market. Out of the 830 venues he counted by 2007, before the 2008 recession, within a decade "at least one hundred and thirty venues [15.7%] either closed or discontinued jazz programming, while more than a hundred clubs and locations [12%] either opened or initiated jazz programming."[36] Regarding interpersonal dynamics in this professional network, Greenland described many tensions between presenters and musicians as well as with audiences; but what emerges from their struggles are their co-dependencies and the compromises they make. Their actions keep afloat a fragile market that sustains many workers financially and meaningfully through a shared passion and commitment to live jazz. "Despite such conflicts of interest, examples of mutually beneficial working relationships between presenters and performers abound," he concluded.[37] Frank Christopher, who ran the jazz club Smoke, described what Greenland called "a network of partnerships" between performers, presenters and patrons who "work together synergistically."[38] Because of similarly interactive practices, popular music scholars have shifted from calling such positions as rigid "gatekeepers" to flexible "intermediaries."[39] The bigger picture of New York's jazz scene that Greenland and also ethnomusicologist Travis Jackson have painted depicts musicians, staff, and audiences working collaboratively within a capitalist system to achieve non-financial benefits from engaging with their favorite music. Still, they have to do this work strategically in order to make ends meet.

In the Brazilian music market, although presenters most often program and advertise samba or bossa nova because the styles attract larger

Figure 5.2. Mark Morganelli, trumpeter and executive director of Jazz Forum Arts, performing at his CD Release party for *Brasil!* on February 24, 2019. Left to right: Abelita Mateus (piano), Vic Juris (guitar), Morganelli (flugelhorn), Eddie Monteiro (accordion and vocals), and Graciliano Zambonin (drums). Photo by Bob Plotkin, reproduced courtesy of Plotkin.

audiences, some presenters choose what to curate based on their personal tastes as much as market demands. Regarding Brazilian jazz, consider the perspectives of trumpeter-presenter Mark Morganelli and guitarist-curator Billy Newman, who have dramatically different levels of investment as presenters. Morganelli has developed a career producing live music as well as recording albums and playing jazz and Brazilian jazz on trumpet and flugelhorn. He began by presenting jazz in Manhattan's loft spaces in the 1970s, where he founded his Jazz Forum loft.[40] He kept the brand name as he relocated his venue, most recently opening a music and dinner club in Tarrytown, in affluent Westchester County, north of Manhattan (see Figure 5.2). The club is less than thirty miles from the Village Vanguard, yet he still books jazz musicians who regularly play at the top Manhattan clubs, on Friday and Saturday nights, in addition to many musicians of Brazilian jazz on Sundays. Under the same brand name, he runs a corporate-sponsored outdoor music series during the summer, which is free to attend. For years he had booked shows at Birdland and has produced one-off concerts in larger venues like the Rose Theater, Jazz at Lincoln Center's largest auditorium. "I'm a huge fan of bossa nova," he said.[41] Despite a lifelong involvement with jazz, "my favorite composer is Antônio Jobim out of everybody I've played, like the Gershwins, Harold Arlen, Jerome Kern, Miles Davis." Why? "The melodies, the harmonies, the rhythms, his sensibility." Morganelli estimates that three quarters of his Brazilian presentations have been bossa nova, samba, or a combination of the two, mainly because they are styles that he likes the best. He has recorded an album with local Brazilian and non-Brazilian musicians, *Brasil!* (2019). When planning it, he said, "It will be mostly bossa novas, some sambas and maybe a *toada*." He has also been a champion of samba, hosting a weekly samba night in the 1980s and continuing to program Carnival-themed samba nights to this day. On the other hand, he said: "I don't particularly like *choros*. For me, they're too notey [*sic*]. . . . I'm overwhelmed and I don't want to hear more than one in a set." This is consistent with his overall approach when evaluating the risk of presenting concerts, which is to rely on his personal tastes and instincts. Because he has been successful as a presenter, he has every reason to trust his own taste, which for Brazilian music is mainly bossa nova. His aesthetic insights are also typical of baby boomers, who became interested in Brazilian music during the 1960s, when bossa nova was novel and popular. His tastes match those of his target audience, whose age and income levels can afford his mid-cost-range venue and one-off shows. In this case, presenter preferences have maintained a high number of bossa nova shows in the region relative to other Brazilian genres or sub-styles of Brazilian jazz, notwithstanding samba.

Billy Newman also relies on his personal tastes when he curated shows for the Brazilian Music series at Cornelia St. Café in the West Village during the 2010s, before the venue closed (see, e.g., Figure 5.3). He did this for the sake of promoting Brazilian music, not as a career move. Unlike Morganelli, Newman has only occasionally curated shows and decidedly does not prefer bossa nova. He gravitates to *choro*, erudite acoustic guitar music, instrumental Brazilian music, and experimental projects. Introducing a show at Cornelia in January 2016, Newman said something to this effect: "We are not trying to do what people expect Brazilian music to be. It's not bossa nova." He sought to expand audience's awareness of Brazilian music's breadth and make room for musicians to play different music, including their own music.[42] To be sure, musicians occasionally played bossa nova tunes. Two composer-performers rearranged "Garota de Ipanema" in "a totally twenty-first-century style and

Figure 5.3. Richard E. Miller Trio at Cornelia Street Café, 2017. Left to right: Itaiguara Brandão (bass), Miller (guitar), and Sergio Krakowski (pandeiro). Photo by author.

totally different," he explained. Rubens Salles performed "a really inverted version of 'Ipanema' in seven [$\frac{7}{8}$ meter] with different chord changes"; and during the same night Arthur Kampela performed a "deconstructed bossa" also different from the original. Programmatically, Newman's approach fit the Cornelia St. Café, where I saw some of the most experimental projects related to Brazil. Luciana Souza recalled that it was an avant-garde venue she frequented, before 2006. Newman's approach falls short financially, however, because the audiences are minimal, the cover is only ten dollars, and audiences do not spend much money at the bar; so the musicians barely made any money from their cut of the door revenue and the club could hardly survive. The club closed at the end of 2018, after forty-one years of business, due to a rent increase and despite public outcry.[43] Notwithstanding Newman's ideological stance, he has learned to be flexible curating music. He loves *choro* and guitarists, for example, such as Rio-based guitarist Rogério Souza, who is a close friend and collaborator. But he acknowledges, "most people don't even like *choro*."[44] He also sought to diversify musician demographics by programming a wider range of styles. Interestingly, these two presenters' programming also overlap at times: Morganelli has presented Rogério Souza at the Jazz Forum, and Newman himself has performed there at least twice.

Clearly, these two presenters are primarily in the business of live music because of their passion for the music, which also drives their programming decisions. Still, they must use business savvy for their commercial projects to survive. The example situations from the performance venue within the Cornelia St. Café restaurant partially shows that experimental music is riskier than mainstream genres, though a rent increase is what drove the longstanding venue out of business. Newman had to be flexible with his curation to be more inclusive and attract a larger audience. Morganelli is a success story, having decades of experience to inform how he balances the business and artistic sides of his performance venue and concert series. He has found ways to run his various event series and nightclub as a nonprofit organization with corporate and government sponsorships as well as ticket revenue, while paying staff and musicians what he regards as decent rates. I have never heard from musicians anything negative about his business dealings and would be surprised if he is portrayed as unfair. He transitioned his outdoor series and venue to nonprofit status to help them stay solvent, a strategy shared by many jazz venues.[45]

The Record Industry and Musicians' Needs

As with the live music industry, the recording side of musicians' businesses changed dramatically between 1990 and 2020; yet local musicians of Brazilian jazz and the owners of independent labels that support their projects have strategically navigated the topsy-turvy market to support their broader goals, both artistic and commercial. Although revenue from record sales contributed significant earnings for recording artists in the twentieth century, the rapidly declining record industry during the 2000s diminished revenue for musicians and labels.[46] This reached the lowest level in 2014.[47] The declines started with the spread of MP3 and related file formats online via file-sharing services, famously Napster and Bit Torrent; the situation was compounded by increasingly available high-band internet connectivity, faster home computers, and rampant piracy, meaning that people did not pay copyright holders for music.[48] Apple's iTunes Store, begun in 2003, provided a legal system for digital downloading that compensated copyright holders; yet it only slightly reduced piracy levels as ratios of legal-to-illegal downloads adjusted from 1:40 to 1:37.[49] Sales of digital downloads via the iTunes Store did not generally replenish revenue for artists, other than for the most popular musicians.[50] Eumir Deodato told me that his decreased earnings from recordings was one reason he resumed playing live music and touring in the 2000s.[51]

That was the 2000s. By 2015, revenue in the recorded music industry had begun to rebound thanks to legal streaming services as well as revenue from licensing music to advertising and other media, synchronization, publishing, vinyl records, and (although decreasing) digital downloads. Replacing downloads as the primary distribution system for digital music, the increased use of streaming music in the United States since 2011 began to increase revenue for the record industry, but not significantly for niche-music artists.[52] In the early 2010s, nearly 80 percent of streaming revenue went to 1 percent of recording artists, despite "long tail" predictions that music online would support vastly more niche musicians than previously.[53] Streaming music also combated piracy by offering consumers seamless legal alternatives, simultaneously incentivizing its use and discouraging piracy.[54] This has been good news for streaming services and record companies, but revenues have been paltry for musicians compared to physical music sales and even to legal downloads. Musicians still may earn around 14 percent of revenue from recording royalties, as they did from sales of CDs and downloads on the iTunes Store, but the minuscule amounts earned from each stream mean that they depend on scaling numbers of streams and a longer timeline of earnings.[55] Since 2000, the rise of digital distribution methods shifted the record industry back to a focus on singles over albums, and increased dependencies on playlists and other promotional placements. Goldschmitt found that Brazilian musicians in Anglophone markets stand to benefit significantly if their music is included in playlists on streaming services, which can depend on curator selections, algorithms, machine learning, inclusion in world-music compilation albums, and non-transparent deals between record labels and streaming services: "algorithms and social media now direct the attention of publics, amplifying existing power structures with the occasional, unexpected musical breakthrough."[56]

Among the musicians in this book, it appears that the highest-streaming tracks on Spotify are those either included in an official Spotify playlist or the first tracks on albums. For example, as of July 2021, Eliane Elias's highest streaming tracks on Spotify, "Little Paradise" (21.3 million streams) and

"Time Alone" (11.8 million), are those included in Spotify's curated playlists "Jazzy Romance" and "An Elegant Affair." Most other tracks from her albums *Dance of Time* (Concord, 2017) and *Dreamer* (Bluebird, 2004), which contain these two tracks respectively, have received between 200,000 and 500,000 streams, between 1 and 2 percent the volume of "Little Paradise." Elias also appears on forty-four compilation albums in Spotify and fifty publicly available playlists, ten of which are Spotify-curated playlists. A counterargument is that this situation compares to the relative attention that hit songs that have always received, overshadowing other songs on the albums whose sales the hits drive. Yet a key difference for musicians and record labels is that these streams of singles boost curated playlists more than an artist's albums, let alone album revenue. Moreover, Elias's success is not generalizable to all the recording artists in New York's Brazilian jazz scene, not only because they do not have as large an online audience but also because playlist curators do not include their work as much or prominently as they do the work of star artists. Hence, the CDs that Trio da Paz sells at their shows in the 2010s likely constitutes a higher percentage of their overall recorded music sales than was the case during the 1990s.

So why bother recording music anymore? These changes made label professionals and musicians re-evaluate and revise their reasons to record as well as their business practices. Despite the dramatic decline of revenue from recordings since 2000 and its gradual recovery from digital distribution services since then, musicians in this study still choose to record albums for several reasons. First, artistically they want to document their latest creations, ideas, skills, and collaborations, like a memoir of their musical developments. After all, without recorded documentation, music is otherwise an ephemeral experience and most of their creations are performed rather than written in notation. This resonates with the value among New York musicians to produce their own artistic works, not solely to accompany other projects or to have steady work performing or recording music for others. Second, they produce albums to promote themselves in order to build their reputation and to receive live performance engagements. There has long been a reciprocal relationship between recorded and live performance. New albums serve as calling cards, publicity vehicles for critical attention, possibly awards, and to expand a fan base. Festivals in Europe want artists to have new albums, Anat Cohen noted, which she routinely releases before an international tour.[57] Third, during my research period, the musicians were selling their CDs at shows, usually themselves; like merchandise, they are valuable for audiences as mementos of the event, for future listening, and morally to support an artist to whom they now have a personal connection. Smaller, lighter packaging has helped musicians bring them to shows, especially when traveling and touring, Deanna Witkowski explained.[58] The audiences have to have a CD player at home or in their car, which is decreasingly common, especially among younger consumers and anyone using the latest technologies. These reasons suggest that baby boomers and Generation X have internalized and thus have been perpetuating a late-twentieth-century value in recorded albums, rather than singles, as a musician's noblest products, signs of professional productivity and prestige, and as a format for distribution, listening, and collection.

In the new millennium, musicians are no longer dependent on record labels, although many still work with them, notably a handful of independent labels in New York City that feature Brazilian jazz. Various types of record labels and relationships with artists have supported the New York Brazilian jazz scene since the late 1980s, though their business agreements changed in the 2000s. Occasionally, major labels and their subsidiaries become involved in such releases of star musicians: Concord Jazz's Concord Picante imprint released *Brasil from the Inside* by Trio da Paz (1992); Eliane Elias has recorded for Blue Note, Bluebird, Columbia, ECM, and Concord Jazz; Verve released Luciana Souza's *The New Bossa Nova* (2007); and Bebel Gilberto records for the major labels Verve Records and Sony Music Group's Masterworks label. More often, independent labels in New York that primarily focus on jazz either produce or help distribute local recordings of Brazilian jazz; they sometimes distribute in the United States recordings from Brazil and elsewhere. Pianist, composer, and producer David Chesky created Chesky Records, which features innovative techniques to produce high-definition recordings and has produced a number of Brazilian albums since the 1990s by Lubambo from Trio da Paz as well as singers Ana Caram, Leny Andrade, and Badi Assad.[59] Rick Warm founded Malandro Records and produced a couple dozen Brazilian jazz recordings between 1998 and 2002, including albums by Zé Luis Oliveira, Richard Boukas, Da Fonseca, Matta, and Trio da Paz itself. François Zalacain founded Sunnyside Records in 1982 as primarily a jazz label, and continues to produce a number of Souza's and Lubambo's albums as well as Vitor Gonçalves's first album in the United States. Zoho Music, founded by Joachim "Jochen" Becker in 2003, has released an extensive series of Latin jazz and also Brazilian jazz albums by Trio da Paz, its members' solo projects, harmonicist Hendrik Meurkens, and others. John Zorn's Tzadik Records, Jana Herzen's Motéma Records, and Robert Corroon, Mike Marshall, and David Zarinsky Jr.'s Adventure Music are other local labels that have released albums of New York–based Brazilian music. Outside New York are the labels Maxx Records, several Japanese labels, Brazil's Biscoito Fino, and others that have contributed to documenting Brazilian jazz by New York–based musicians. During the 1990s, these labels used to pay initial expenses to produce albums, including the cost of flying musicians from Brazil to New York for recording sessions; yet by the 2010s, Zalacain explained, it became standard practice to license complete recordings from the musicians for distribution, shifting the burden and expense of production to the artist. "Basically, today the modus operandi, the way that we can work with many musicians, is to license the albums from them. That means they do the album, they pay for the recording either from their money or crowd funding or whatever it is, and we license. [. . .] They own the masters."[60] The flip side of this change, Maúcha Adnet observed, is that when musicians pay for the record production, the record label staff has less creative input and, depending on the contract, less control over the album's future than they did during the 1990s and previously.[61] On the other hand, musicians who cannot afford to front their production costs may relinquish control when contracting with record labels, as Adnet and Nanny Assis each did with their first solo albums.[62]

Self-producing and self-distributing records are methods that musicians increasingly undertake, especially since they know the income from records will be minimal. Many opt for the do-it-yourself route to maintain control over the process as well as revenue, to avoid unfavorable contracts with record companies, Scott Feiner told me, or simply because labels did not become interested in supporting the recording project, another musician admitted.[63] Through learning and experiencing these activities, they gain the skills and resources to release albums by friends and like-minded musicians. Anat Cohen and Oded Lev-Ari's company Anzic Records falls into this category, on which Da Fonseca has released two albums in addition to Cohen's own recordings. Chesky Records functions similarly by releasing Chesky's own recordings. Still, despite the increasingly available tools to self-produce and self-distribute recordings, there are musicians who prefer to have a record company handle the business arrangements, mainly distribution and publicity, even though it cuts into the musician's revenues from record sales.

Musicians and Venues during the COVID-19 Pandemic

Starting in late 2019, the Covid-19 pandemic began to ravage through countries unevenly and with varied responses; and by 2021, countries began slow recoveries at unsteady rates. The numbers of infected cases in the United States declined after vaccinations began to be administered in January 2021, though subsequent waves hit the United States and around the world.[64] When the pandemic fully arrived in the United States, in March 2020, parts of the country began issuing stay-at-home orders except for essential workers in order to reduce infections and overcrowded hospitals. With those government regulations for the sake of public health and safety, the live music industry came to a standstill. Performances were canceled, concert venues closed (some permanently), restaurants and bars with live music closed for indoor customers, recording studios and rehearsal spaces closed, and consequentially professional musicians lost nearly all live-performance work.[65] Musicians who perform live Brazilian music and jazz mostly work freelance, from show to show, gig to gig, without job security. Musicians, the original "gig workers," no longer had work in the "gig economy," an economy based on temporary positions.[66] Because people were socially distancing, musicians also stopped creating and rehearsing music together in person, instead collaborating remotely with the aid of impressive though inadequate communication and recording technologies.[67] Sociologists Jo Haynes and Ian Woodward summarized the pandemic era and its volatility as "what happens to music and culture when public spaces of creativity, collaboration, production, social interaction and community are disrupted and pathologized. In the current moment, we are likely to think about the COVID-19 pandemic, but exogenous or external shocks are in fact recurrent features of social and economic change."[68] Thus, within the timeframe covered in this book, the pandemic was the latest but unlikely to be the last upheaval that the music industry would face.

To subsist financially, the musicians I studied had to replace their income and lower their expenses in ways similar to other professional musicians, by some combination of teaching online, recording remotely, livestreaming/webcasting performances for small fees, composing for commission, organizing events, and doing non-musical work.[69] They variously relied on personal savings, public welfare, and small grants from nonprofit organizations; and to reduce their expenses, some moved to less expensive residences and regions, including outside the United States. The musicians I talked to utilized these approaches to different extents and levels of enthusiasm. Many musicians initially experienced heightened anxieties and depression due to the crises; the Brazilians were also worried about their families in Brazil.[70] I have not met Brazilian musicians in the United States who suffered from Covid-19 itself. The musicians I know who were most deeply impacted were those whose immigration status in the United States was at risk; they could not utilize public assistance as much as US citizens could, and some Brazilians had to return to Brazil due to limited finances or visas. Those in the most precarious positions resorted to work that compromised their health or morals in order to earn money. On the other hand, although it was a horrible year for everyone, musicians in the United States were likely to suffer less than those in other countries; and improvements because of vaccinations indicate that musicians should gradually recover their livelihoods. These findings are not unique to Brazilian music, Brazilian-jazz, or Brazilians working abroad; instead, these trends relate to professional musicians and international workers in general.[71]

Among the musicians I interviewed, those with US citizenship were able to endure financially with the help of federal relief funds and state unemployment aid in combination with other financial support and minimal income. The musicians worst affected by the pandemic economically were those with immigration statuses coincidentally in flux during the pandemic.[72] They tended not to receive government welfare, neither money nor food subsidies. Brazilians could not rely on family support from Brazil because their families earn much less with the currency exchange. Due to tightening and lengthening of visa applications and renewals under the administration of President Donald Trump (2017–2021), Brazilian citizens experienced prolonged processes, which for some became too long for them to remain legally in the United States. Because the US embassy in Brazil was only processing visa applications for emergencies, those who had to return to Brazil temporarily were not expecting to return to the United States. I explained bassist Amanda Ruzza's situation in the Introduction. Brazilian pianist Felipe Viegas had a one-year extension after a student visa had ended. But his application process for a new type of work visa was taking too long, and he had to return to Brasília, where he was resigned to remain.[73] Bassist Eduardo Belo had a particularly tumultuous year navigating life in the United States during the pandemic. A young adult from Brasília, he was working with an O-1 visa for foreign workers with extraordinary skills, and had been saving money to pay the legal fees for a green card (approximately $7,000) and also to record an album ($4,000). But the lack of work led him to spend those savings for living expenses. Serendipitously, Belo had to renew his work visa and encountered more scrutiny than previously, requests for evidence, and a lengthier wait time (thirteen weeks) than previous renewals. He did not want to apply for state unemployment benefits, although he was eligible, in case taking public assistance would make him seem like a "burden of the state" and hurt his future green card application. He did accept the federal stimulus check because it was intended for taxpayers. Belo was also out of an apartment because the pandemic drove him and his roommates away from expensive New York City. Unable to commit to a single residency while he waited for the O-1 visa renewal caused him to move ten times during the year before finding stable housing. Meanwhile his girlfriend ended their relationship.[74]

Musicians replaced some of their lost revenue through alternative business activities, mostly in music, although to various extents. Those who had diverse revenue streams beforehand expanded easily into non-performance activities such as online teaching, recording remotely, and, for a few, composing for commissions. Clarice Assad, for example, performs and composes; therefore, she said, "I had agreed to write many works for the 2021–2022 season and I was able to live comfortably with it. [. . .] Renting works for 2020 virtual performances was also a way to generate income, as well as selling scores from my website."[75] A notable difference among musicians was between those who began new ventures, often that utilized technology, and those who chose to wait out the pandemic by surviving with social welfare (public or private), personal savings, and family support. Musicians had to weigh financial pressures with their professional goals and skill sets to decide how to proceed. Some of them told me that musicians who play gigs in restaurants and other low-paying engagements could receive more funds from government welfare than they had earned previously on their own. This resonates with complaints of conservative politicians about overly generous public assistance. For example, during the pandemic, pianist Vitor Gonçalves started to learn computer programming, thinking he should switch professions. He was earning minimal income from online teaching, livestream performances, and remote recording sessions. However, the level of financial support he and his wife, a singer, began to receive from the federal and state governments, and food and rent subsidies provided most of the support they needed to wait out the pandemic and remain in the music industry, which is their life passion.[76]

Musicians expressed different levels of comfort and enthusiasm for embracing new technologies widely used during the pandemic. Two musicians, who chose to remain anonymous, worked hard at first to situate themselves teaching on web-based video conferencing software; but otherwise they found that they were a bit depressed and not musically productive, and instead waited for live music to return. By contrast, several musicians not only pivoted to teaching and performing online but reinvented aspects of their careers and lifestyles with technology and otherwise.[77] Guitarist Richard Miller, who had moved from New York to San Diego before the pandemic, created a weekly livestream concert series. This series brought him visibility that led to new work creating livestream events for non-music companies.[78] His collaborator, singer Vanessa Falabella, joined him in San Diego, renting out her apartment in Manhattan during the pandemic. She taught group classes online to non-Brazilians on how to sing Brazilian music properly. Once in southern California, she found new work as a voice-over artist for Portuguese overdubs of Mexican telenovelas. The two became inspired to compose music together and did so prolifically, which they performed in livestream concerts and began recording projects.[79] These are the most extreme cases of music-career transformations with technology during the pandemic compared to similar stories I heard, including the many who made the ubiquitous remotely recorded video collages.[80]

By May 2021, although most of the world continued to suffer without sufficient vaccines, including Brazil and Canada, nearly half the US population was partially vaccinated and nearly 40 percent were fully vaccinated. State and city governments responded by lifting restrictions on indoor venue capacities. Venues began to program shows following local guidelines and audiences began to attend, signs that the live music industry was gradually resuming. For example, once vaccinated, Mark Morganelli, Eddie Monteiro, Nanny Assis, and his son Daniel Assis flew from New York and Florida to New Orleans to play Brazilian jazz with local musicians for the opening of an indoor venue called Jazz at the Blue Dog on April 30, 2021.[81] Following Covid protocols, the room had a Plexiglas barrier between the stage and audience, and capacity was not yet 100 percent; yet none of the band members wore masks because they were vaccinated. The next week, Nanny Assis traveled to New York to record in a studio with other musicians for the first time since before the pandemic.[82]

Illustrating the fluctuating situation for venues during the pandemic, Morganelli closed the Jazz Forum to guests, but was livestreaming performances of socially distanced musicians wearing masks in the club. After resuming in-person shows, the club continued to livestream shows of different acts, but shifted them from weekends to Thursday nights; the livestream shows ended after December 16, 2021. Morganelli reopened his Jazz Forum after fifteen months closed to in-person audiences. The first indoor show with an audience—requiring proof of vaccination, masks, and reduced capacity—was Friday, May 28, 2021, and featured Brazilian jazz with Hélio Alves's Quartet that included Duduka Da Fonseca, Steve Wilson, and Peter Washington. The group's first in-person shows were a month earlier, in Brooklyn under Da Fonseca's name and with Adnet on vocals, and at Small's jazz club in Manhattan under Alves's name. Not quite ninety days and fifty miles. Live performances happened all summer, following Covid protocols depending on location and venue; musicians were gradually posting to social media photos of rehearsals, concerts, and tours as they had done before the pandemic. In August 2021, Trio da Paz returned to Dizzy's Club with Adnet, Harry Allen, and Joe Locke. By December 2021, the Omicron variant of the virus increased Covid cases in the New York region to the point that Morganelli paused in-door shows for the weeks around New Year's Eve 2022. The club resumed shows in early 2022 with top acts, notably Eliane Elias. Recovery would be an up-and-down process, but clearly the venue owners and musicians, along with state and local authorities, were actively navigating the changing crisis aided by mass vaccination campaigns that differed by country and public acceptance.

Conclusion

Working, creating, cultivating, collaborating, networking, navigating, and circulating are among the activities that musicians and music industry professionals in this book do on a regular basis. They have applied their natural talents, personal determination, the support of family or others, and decades of hard work to pursue their aesthetic interests and career goals. A demographically diverse scene of musicians in New York City has been creating and performing Brazilian-jazz fusions, primarily within the structure of the jazz industry, performing locally and touring nationally and internationally. The book focused on bossa nova and samba jazz, while recognizing other approaches to Brazilian-jazz fusions. Societal inequities based on race, class, gender, and nationality have limited the collection of musicians who have been able to move to New York City and play Brazilian jazz professionally. Half the musicians are from Brazil, a quarter are US-born, and the rest immigrated from elsewhere. The white and male musicians have benefited from the support of social structures and economic forces, which have hindered others; however, a minority of female musicians and musicians of color have navigated those entrenched discriminatory barriers to become professional musicians in New York.

As discussed in this chapter, the business activities of musicians and industry personnel show how individuals exercise creative agency as they interact with powerful capitalist forces; in doing so, they can affect markets in subtle ways. With paradigm shifts in the music industry, changing business practices of music venues and record labels during the 2010s contrast with the situations in the preceding two decades: especially the major transitions from CDs to purchased downloads and then to streaming music services. During the height of the Covid-19 pandemic, beginning in 2020, the experiences of musicians and presenters exemplified contrasting ways they adopted new technologies and pivoted their business.

Similarly, the other chapters have explained individual innovations and shared practices in Brazilian-jazz fusions. In gradual steps and sometimes leaps, musicians are continually developing new approaches to music, within and between established genres, creating fusions with different, though sometimes related, musical ingredients. In turn, audiences have benefited from the chance to enjoy their musical creativity and potentially to learn from them. Because the musicians in this book have pursued deep relationships with Brazilian jazz, their prolonged activities, continual growth, and artistic creations are both polymusical and transnational. As musicians develop competencies in music and other cultural domains associated with multiple countries—what this book described as transnational polymusicalities—their experiences, knowledge, empathy, and growth nurture their musical creations and self-identities, and those of others.

Notes

1. Eduardo "Duduka" Da Fonseca, interview with author, July 22, 2016.
2. Nilson Matta, interview with author, March 3, 2020.
3. Daniella Thompson, "An American Malandro: Rick Warm's Record Label Is the Hardest-Working Malandro Around," *Brazzil* (webzine), April 2001, http://www.brazzillog.com/pages/musap r01.htm.
4. Jane Stein, interview with author, June 15, 2017.
5. Nicki Parrott, personal communication, Ramapo College, February 26, 2016.
6. Maurício Zottarelli, interview with author, December 11, 2019.
7. Romero Lubambo, interview with author, January 23, 2018.
8. Samba Meets Jazz Workshops, website, http://sambameetsjazz.com/, accessed March 21, 2022.

9. See McCann 2019.
10. Lubambo, interview.
11. Jassvan de Lima, interview with author, August 4, 2022.
12. Cyro Baptista, interview with author, June 7, 2016.
13. DeVeaux and Giddins 2019, 338.
14. Jackson 2012, 89–90; Greenland 2016, 92.
15. Jackson 2012, 72–73.
16. Taylor 2016, 2, 6, 11.
17. Burnett 1996, 30–32, 41–42; Negus 1999, 14–19; Taylor 2016; Ritchey 2019.
18. Adorno 1991.
19. Toynbee 2000, 3–6; Taylor 2016, 8; Ritchey 2019, 9.
20. Adorno 1991, 106.
21. Negus 1999, 14, 19.
22. Negus 1999, 5–6, 34; Toynbee 2000; Gosling 2004; Taylor 2016, Chapter 5; Whitmore 2020.
23. Hietanen and Rokka 2015.
24. Goldschmitt 2020, 15.
25. Taylor 2016, 14.
26. Burnett 1996, 6; Negus 1999, 7–8, 31; Toynbee 2000, 5, 8.
27. Toynbee 2000, xx–xxi.
28. Margolis 2013, 8, 16–22.
29. Goldschmitt 2020, 140, 172.
30. Greenland 2016, 88–89; Ritchey 2019.
31. Goldschmitt 2020, 140.
32. Annette A. Aguilar, interview with author, July 11, 2019.
33. Mark Morganelli, interview with author, January 7, 2018; Michael Solomon, personal communication.
34. Greenland 2016, 83.
35. Greenland 2016, 84, 93, 105.
36. Greenland 2016, 86.
37. Greenland 2016, 97.
38. Greenland 2016, 109.
39. Frith 1981, 92; Negus 1999, 18, 176–178; Shuker 2001, 34.
40. Heller 2017, 180–181.
41. Morganelli, interview.
42. Billy Newman, interview with author, January 26, 2018.
43. Giovanni Russonello, "Cornelia Street Café, a Pillar of Greenwich Village Experimentation, Closes Its Doors," *New York Times*, January 4, 2019, https://www.nytimes.com/2019/01/04/arts/music/cornelia-street-cafe-closes.html.
44. Newman, interview.
45. Greenland 2016, 89.
46. For a graphic summary, see Paul Resnikoff, "Music Industry, 1973-2013," Digital Music News, August, 26, 2014, https://www.digitalmusicnews.com/2014/08/26/music-industry-1973-2013/, accessed June 4, 2024.
47. Drott 2024, 1; International Federation of the Phonographic Industry, *Global Music Report: State of the Industry*, 2024, 11.
48. Millard 2005, 388–402; Morton 2006, 189–194; Kot 2010, Chapter 4.
49. Kot 2010, 49, 55.
50. Byrne 2012, 241.
51. Eumir Deodato, interview with author, August 11, 2011.
52. Taylor 2016, 127; Drott 2024, 2–3; International Federation of the Phonographic Industry, *IFPI Global Music Report*, 2020, 66.
53. Mulligan 2014; Seabrook 2015, 15–16.
54. International Federation of the Phonographic Industry, *IFPI Digital Music Report*, 2015, 38–39.
55. Byrne 2012, 239–244; Mulligan 2014; Taylor 2016, 127; Drott 2024, 4.
56. Goldschmitt 2020, 171, 184–187; also see the Digital Media Association, *Streaming Forward*, Annual Music Report, March 2018, 11, https://dima.org/wp-content/uploads/2018/04/DiMA-Streaming-Forward-Report.pdf, accessed June 4, 2024.
57. Anat Cohen, interview with author, June 14, 2017.

58. Deanna Witkowski, interview with author, March 19, 2019.
59. David Chesky, interview with author, January 12, 2018.
60. François Zalacain, interview with author, January 19, 2018.
61. Maúcha Adnet, interview with author, June 13, 2016.
62. Adnet, interview; Nanny Assis, interview with author, January 15, 2020.
63. Scott Feiner, interview with author, July 24, 2015.
64. In May 2021, the reported percentages of national populations that had been vaccinated were 39% in the US, 34% in Great Britain, 4.4% in Canada, and 8.9% in Brazil. Josh Horder, "Tracking Coronavirus Vaccinations Around the World," *New York Times*, last updated March 13, 2023, https://www.nytimes.com/interactive/2021/world/covid-vaccinations-tracker.html, accessed May 25, 2021 and June 10, 2024.
65. For example research about professional musicians and the live music industry during 2020 and 2021 of the pandemic, see Cohen and Ginsborg 2021; Flynn and Anderson 2021; Fram et al. 2021; Brooks and Patel 2022; Carr 2022; Dowd, Tai, and Zaras 2022; Haynes and Woodword 2022. For news articles from 2020 relevant to musicians and the jazz scene in New York City, see David Peisner, "Concerts Aren't Back. Livestreams Are Ubiquitous. Can They Do the Job?" *New York Times*, July 21, 2020, https://www.nytimes.com/2020/07/21/arts/music/concerts-livestreams.html; Ben Sisario and Giovanni Russonello, "Jazz Lives in Clubs. The Pandemic Is Threatening Its Future," *New York Times*, September 8, 2020, https://www.nytimes.com/2020/09/08/arts/music/jazz-clubs-coronavirus.html; Patricia Cohen, "A 'Great Cultural Depression' Looms for Legions of Unemployed Performers," *New York Times*, December 26, 2020, https://www.nytimes.com/2020/12/26/arts/unemployed-performer-theatre-arts.html; Matt Fripp, "Jazz Rebounds: Int'l players surveyed on Covid-19 impact," *Jazz Journalists Association News*, October 20, 2020, https://news.jazzjournalists.org/jazz-rebounds-intl-players-surveyed-on-covid-19-impact/. Articles accessed on November 23, 2021.
66. Thanks to Joshua Graff-Zivin for this point.
67. A mixed-method study of a hundred musicians in the United States and Canada found that after the initial month of isolation, musicians generally used technology to try resuming their prior collaborative practices (Fram et al. 2021). See also Manley-Muller 2021; and Flynn and Anderson 2021.
68. Haynes and Woodword 2022, 2.
69. In June 2020, I emailed thirty-five of my interviewees to see how they were during the pandemic; twenty-two responded with updates. In 2021, I interviewed sixteen professionals, diversifying participants based on their emailed experiences, types of work, age, gender, and location. These included musicians living in New York, New Jersey, Florida, Illinois, northern and southern California, and also those who left the United States for Brazil and the Caribbean; I also interviewed a presenter. I had also heard from New York musicians who relocated to Israel and Japan. To interview the musicians, I used a script of common questions, from open-ended to specific, which I first vetted with help from friends with expertise: violinist Jeremy Brown and health economist Joshua Graff-Zivin. Some musicians suggested additional questions during interviews. Most of my interviewees are white and from upper-middle-class families. Missing are musicians from working-class backgrounds, except for one Black Bahian from a poor family; musicians from more provincial parts of Brazil; and musicians with dependents to support.
70. A study of 385 British performing-arts professionals during the first months of the pandemic also found heightened levels of anxiety: "53% reported financial hardship, 85% reported increased anxiety, and 63% reported being lonelier than before the crisis. 61% sought support on finances while only 45% did so on health and wellbeing." (Spiro et al. 2020).
71. A literature review of research about performing artists during the pandemic who live mainly in Europe, the United States, and Canada, as well as Brazil, Israel, and China, concludes with a mixture of setbacks and benefits of remote work: "Whilst many negative psychological effects of lockdown were experienced, including anxiety and poor sleep, participants also reported positive effects, and described personal and professional opportunities the pandemic had brought, such as experiencing less pressure, enjoyment of having time to spend with family, and time to spend pursuing new avenues, developing new skills or improving existing skills" (Brooks and Patel 2022).
72. Perhaps because of the limited class demographics of my interviewees, these only included young and single adults, in their twenties and thirties, who were in early processes of establishing their permanent residency in the United States. Sociologist Rachel Skaggs found that the

pandemic affected early-stage artists working in the US more negatively than established artists (Skaggs 2024).

73. Felipe Viegas, interview with author, April 2, 2021.
74. Eduardo Belo, interview with author, February 3, 2021.
75. Clarice Assad, email correspondence, April 3, 2021.
76. Vitor Gonçalves, interview with author, February 24, 2021.
77. Flynn and Anderson also found a wide range of creative activity among professional musicians, including those stifled by depression and new responsibilities (2021, 9–10).
78. Richard E. Miller, interview with author, March 25, 2021.
79. Vanessa Falabella, interview with author, March 2, 2021.
80. Among my interviewees, Clarice Assad and Rafael Piccolotto de Lima made particularly creative music videos with socially-distanced musicians during the pandemic, available on YouTube or their websites. Omer Leshem researched the challenges of group interaction and improvisation for jazz musicians in New York City who made asynchronous recordings during the pandemic (2023).
81. Keith Spera, "Peek Inside: Sheraton New Orleans Downtown Opens a New Live Jazz Club," *NoLa.com*, May 6, 2021, https://www.nola.com/entertainment_life/keith_spera/article_21641 a38-acfc-11eb-ad61-6fef2c4b5a5e.html?fbclid=IwAR2jn8qi16OZ9ny7StaXTEclN7ZsB3fRVJn O5QbPtKXw3g-lObH5pFCUl5A. Email confirmation with Mark Morganelli, May 21, 2021.
82. Nanny Assis, telephone conversation, May 21, 2021.

List of Interviews

Adnet, Maúcha; voice; June 13, 2016
Aguilar, Annette A.; percussion, curator; July 11, 2019
Almeida, Lívio; woodwinds; January 13, 2016; February 19, 2021
Assad, Clarice; voice, piano, composer; August 6, 2015
Assis, Nanny; voice, guitar, percussion; January 15, 2020; March 5, 2021
Baptista, Cyro; percussion; June 7, 2016
Belo, Eduardo; bass; April 11, 2020; February 3, 2021
Boukas, Richard; voice, guitar, composer; July 21, 2015
Brandão, Itaiguara; bass; November 28, 2018
Bryant, Freddie; guitar; March 5, 2021
Cantuária, Vinícius; voice, guitar; August 14, 2015
Chesky, David; piano, composer, producer; January 12, 2018
Cohen, Anat; woodwinds; June 14, 2017
Continentino, Jorge; woodwinds; August 24, 2015
Costa, Amarildo; percussion; July 17, 2015
d'Affonseca, Junia Flavia; flute, promoter; June 8, 2016
Da Fonseca, Eduardo "Duduka"; drums, percussion; July 22, 2016
da Silva, Edson "Café" Aparecido; percussion, voice; January 24, 2020
Da Souza, Gene; presenter (in Florida); May 12, 2021
de la Corte, Rubens; guitar, composer; January 5, 2021
de Lima, Jassvan; radio host, producer; August 4, 2022
Deodato, Eumir; keyboards, composer, arranger, producer; August 11, 2011; August 26, 2013
Dreyer, Laura; woodwinds; January 13, 2020
Falabella, Vanessa; voice; March 19, 2019; March 2, 2021
Feiner, Scott; percussion; July 24, 2015
Fernandez, Ana; voice; May 28, 2021
Gonçalves, Vitor; piano, accordion, composer; July 24, 2015; February 24, 2021
Kettner, Scott; drums, percussion, producer; September 18, 2019
Krakowski, Sergio; pandeiro; April 20, 2020
Lubambo, Romero; guitar; January 23, 2018
Macedo, Jailton "Dendê"; percussion, singer, composer; October 10, 2013
Malmed Macedo, Leslie; manager, presenter; October 10, 2013
Matta, Nilson; bass; March 3, 2020
Miller, Richard E.; guitar; March 25, 2021
Morgan, Gary; composer, bass, woodwinds; August 8, 2015
Morganelli, Mark; trumpet, presenter; January 7, 2018
Nash, Ted; saxophone; May 5, 2021
Newman, Billy; guitar; January 26, 2018
Nobuzane, Miho; piano, voice, composer; August 11, 2015
Ogawa, Keita; percussion; January 13, 2016
Oliveira, José Luis "Zé Luis" Segneri; woodwinds, producer; August 20, 2015
Oliveira, Monika; voice, composer; September 30, 2016
Peixoto, Ricardo; guitarist (in California); March 26, 2021
Pereira, Susan; voice, piano, percussion, composer; August 8, 2015

Pereira, Vanderlei; drums, percussion, composer; August 8, 2015
Piccolotto de Lima, Rafael; composer, conductor; April 20, 2021
Porto, Telmo "Portinho"; drums, percussion; August 4, 2022
Ruzza, Amanda; bass; August 26, 2015; February 10, 2021
Saci, Fernando; drums, percussion; May 21, 2021
Salvador, Dom; piano, composer; January 4, 2018; April 1, 2020
Shimizu, Masa; guitar; February 5, 2016
Souza, Luciana; voice, composer; May 18, 2021
Stein, Jane; presenter; June 15, 2017
Teixeira, Cidinho; piano, composer; September 27, 2019
Viegas, Felipe; piano; April 2, 2021
Watanabe, Mamiko; piano, composer; August 10, 2015
Witkowski, Deanna; piano, voice; March 19, 2019
Zalacain, François; producer; Jan 19, 2018
Zottarelli, Maurício; drums, percussion; December 11, 2019

Selected Discography of Brazilian Jazz in New York, 2000–2020

Adnet, Maúcha, and Hélio Alves. 2013. *Milagre*. Zoho Music LLC. ZM 201302.

Aguilar, Annette A., and StringBeans. 2010. *The Day Waits for Nobody: Latin Jazz Brasilian*. Self-produced.

Almeida, Lívio. 2016. *Action & Reaction*. Self-produced.

Alves, Hélio. 2010. *Música*. Jazz Legacy. JLP 1001010.

Andrade, Leny, and Roni Ben-Hur. 2014. *Alegria De Viver*. Motéma Music. MTA-CD-165.

Assad, Clarice. 2016. *Live at the Deer Head Inn*. Deer Head Records. DH007.

Assis, Nanny. 2006. *Double Rainbows*. Blue Toucan Music. BT27109.

Baptista, Cyro. 2008. *Banquet of the Spirits*. Tzadik. TZ 7624.

Boukas, Richard, and Quarteto Moderno. 2016. *Live! Ao Vivo!* Self-produced.

Brandão, Itaiguara. 2015. *Awakening*. Audio & Video Labs, Inc. 5638482098.

Brazilian Trio: Hélio Alves, Duduka Da Fonseca, Nilson Matta. 2008. *Forests*. Zoho Music. ZM 200806.

Cantuária, Vinícius. 2012. *Indio de Apartamento*. Naïve Jazz. NJ 621811.

Cohen, Anat. 2015. *Luminosa*. Anzic Records. ANZ-CD-0050.

Continentino, Jorge. 2005. *Portrait*. Self-produced.

Da Fonseca, Duduka. 2012. *Samba Jazz—Jazz Samba*. Anzic Records. ANZ-CD-0041.

De La Corte, Rubens. 2015. *Nomad*. Self-produced.

Deodato, Eumir. 2010. *The Crossing*. Soul Trade.

Dreyer, Laura. 2000. *Mysterious Encounter*. Lavasphere.

Elias, Eliane. 2015. *Made in Brazil*. Concord Jazz. CJA-36693-02.

Feiner, Scott, and Pandeiro Jazz. 2013. *A View from Below*. Self-produced.

Fleurine. 2018. *Brazilian Dream*. Sunnyside. SSC 4031

Forro in the Dark. 2006. *Bonfires of São João*. Nublu Records. NUB00009.

Galvão, Sergio. 2013. *Phantom Fish*. Pimenta Music. Pimenta Music 102.

Gilberto, Bebel. 2007. *Momento*. Six Degrees Records. 657036 1133-2.

Gonçalves, Vitor. 2017. *Vitor Gonçalves Quartet*. Sunnyside. SSC1462.

Krakowski, Sergio. 2016. *Pássaros: The Foundation of the Island*. Ruweh Records. Ruweh 002.

Lubambo, Romero. 2014. *Só: Brazilian Essence*. Sunnyside. SSC1381.

Mariano, Cesar Camargo, and Romero Lubambo. 2003. *Duo*. Trama. T004/625-2.

Mateus, Abelita. 2017. *Vivenda*. Self-produced.

Matta, Nilson. 2013. *Nilson Matta's Black Orpheus*. Motéma. MTM-103.

Mueller, Klaus. 2016. *Village Samba*. Self-produced.

Meurkens, Hendrik. 2007. *New York Samba Jazz Quintet*. Zoho Music. ZM 200701

Morgan, Gary, and Panamericana! 2007. *Felicidade*. Consolidated Artists Productions. CAP 1014.

Morganelli, Mark, and the Jazz Forum All-Stars. 2019. *Brasil!* Self-produced.

Nation Beat (featuring Cha Wa). 2015. *Carnival Caravan*. Self-produced.

Nobuzane, Miho. 2014. *Simple Words (Jazz Loves Brazil)*. Self-produced.

Oliveira, Monika. 2017. *Zum Zum Zum*. Carioca NYC.

Oliveira, Zé Luis. 1999. *Guarani Banana*. Malandro Records. MAL 71010.

Ruzza, Amanda. 2012. *This Is What Happened*. Pimenta Music.

Panettieri, Greta. 2011. *Brazilian Nights: Live at Zinc Bar NYC*. Self-produced.

Passos, Rosa, and Ron Carter. 2003. *Entre Amigos*. Chesky Records.

Pereira, Susan, and Sabor Brasil. 2007. *Tudo Azul*. Riony Records. RIONY 8320.

Pereira, Vanderlei, and Blindfold Test. 2020. *Vision for Rhythm*. Jazzheads. JH1242.

Pizzarelli, John (featuring Daniel Jobim). 2017. *Sinatra & Jobim @ 50*. Concord Jazz. CJA00055.

Portinho Trio. 2008. *Vinho do Porto*. MCG Jazz. MCGJ1033.

Roditi, Claudio. 2011. *Bons Amigos*. Resonance Records. HCD 2010.

Salvador, Dom. 2010. *The Art of Samba Jazz*. Salmarsi Records. 884501439282.

Sanfonya Brasileira: Vitor Gonçalves, Eduardo Belo, Vanderlei Pereira (featuring Steve Wilson). 2018. *Sanfonya Brasileira*. Self-produced.

Santos, Adriano. 2010. *In Session*. Self-produced.

Sganga, Mark. 2010. *An Evening in Rio*. Self-produced.

Silberstein, Yotam. 2011. *Brasil*. Jazz Legacy Productions.

Sorce, Richard. 2017. *Samba para a Vida*. EverJazz Records.

Souza, Luciana. 2002. *Brazilian Duos*. Biscoito Fino. 532.

Teixeira, Cidinho, Leco Reis, and Edson Ferreira. 2016. *Brazzamerica*. Self-produced.

Trio da Paz. 2016. *30*. Zoho Music. ZM201602.

Watts, Débora. 2010. *Débora*. Self-produced.

Zottarelli, Maurício. 2009. *7 Lives*. Self-produced.

Bibliography

Adachi, Nobuko. 2004. "Japonês: A Marker of Social Class or a Key Term in the Discourse of Race?" *Latin American Perspectives* 31 (3): 48–76.

Adachi, Nobuko. 2014. "Japanese Brazilians: A Positive Ethnic Minority in a Racial Democracy." *Studies on Asia, Series IV* 4 (2): 31–74.

Adorno, Theodor W. 1991. "Culture Industry Reconsidered." In *The Culture Industry: Selected Essays on Mass Culture*, edited by Theodor W. Adorno and J. M. Bernstein, 98–106. London: Routledge.

Aebersold, Jamey. 2000. *Antonio Carlos Jobim.* Vol. 98, *Jamey Aebersold Play-a-Long.* New Albany, IN: Jamey Abersold Jazz.

Alexander, Jeffrey C. 2006. *The Civil Sphere.* New York: Oxford University Press.

Anderson, Benedict. 1991. *Imagined Communities: Reflections on the Origin and Spread of Nationalism.* Revised Edition. London: Verso.

Andrade, Mário de. 1999. *Dicionário musical brasileiro.* Edited by Oneyda Alvarenga and Flávia Camargo Toni. Belo Horizonte: Editora Itatiaia.

Andrews, George Reid. 2004. *Afro-Latin America, 1800–2000.* New York: Oxford University Press.

Appadurai, Arjun. 2013. *The Future as Cultural Fact: Essays on the Global Condition.* London: Verso.

Appert, Catherine M. 2016. "On Hybridity in African Popular Music: The Case of Senegalese Hip Hop." *Ethnomusicology* 60 (2): 279–299.

Appert, Catherine M., and Sidra Lawrence. 2020. "Ethnomusicology beyond #MeToo: Listening for the Violences of the Field." *Ethnomusicology* 64 (2): 225–253.

Atkins, E. Taylor. 2001. *Blue Nippon: Authenticating Jazz in Japan.* Durham, NC: Duke University Press.

Atkins, E. Taylor, ed. 2003. *Jazz Planet.* Jackson: University Press of Mississippi.

Avelar, Idelber, and Christopher Dunn. 2011. "Introduction. Music as Practice of Citizenship in Brazil." In *Brazilian Popular Music and Citizenship*, edited by Idelber Avelar and Christopher Dunn, 1–27. Durham, NC: Duke University Press.

Baily, John. 2001. "Learning to Perform as a Research Technique in Ethnomusicology." *British Journal of Ethnomusicology* 10 (2): 85–98.

Baily, John. 2008. "Ethnomusicology, Intermusability, and Performance Practice." In *The New (Ethno)musicologies*, edited by Henry Stobart, 117–134. Lanham, MD: Scarecrow Press.

Baily, John, and Michael Collyer. 2006. "Introduction: Music and Migration." *Journal of Ethnic and Migration Studies* 32 (2): 167–182.

Baran, Michael D. 2007. "'Girl, You Are Not Morena. We Are Negras!': Questioning the Concept of 'Race' in Southern Bahia, Brazil." *Ethos* 35 (3): 383–409.

Bares, William. 2009. "Eternal Triangle: American Jazz in European Postmodern." PhD diss., Music, Harvard University.

Barsalini, Leandro. 2009. "As Sínteses de Edison Machado: Um Estudo sobre o Desenvolvimento de Padrões de Samba na Bateria." MA thesis, Music, Universidade Estadual de Campinas.

Barzel, Tamar. 2015. *New York Noise: Radical Jewish Music and the Downtown Scene.* Bloomington: Indiana University Press.

Béhague, Gerard. 1973. "Bossa & Bossas: Recent Changes in Brazilian Urban Popular Music." *Ethnomusicology* 17 (2): 209–233.

Bennett, Andy, and Richard A. Peterson. 2004. "Introducing Music Scenes." In *Music Scenes: Local, Translocal and Virtual*, edited by Andy Bennett and Richard A. Peterson, 1–15. Nashville: Vanderbilt University Press.

Berendt, Joachim-Ernst, and Günther Huesmann. 2009. *The Jazz Book: From Ragtime to the 21st Century*. Chicago: Lawrence Hill Books.

Berliner, Paul. 1994. *Thinking in Jazz: The Infinite Art of Improvisation*. Chicago: University of Chicago Press.

Beserra, Bernadete. 2008. "In the Shadow of Carmen Miranda and the Carnival: Brazilian Immigrant Women in Los Angeles." In *Becoming Brazuca: Brazilian Immigration to the United States*, edited by Clémence Jouet-Pastré and Leticia J. Braga, 57–79. Cambridge, MA: Harvard University Press.

Bishop-Sanchez, Kathryn. 2016. *Creating Carmen Miranda: Race, Camp, and Transnational Stardom*. Nashville: Vanderbilt University Press.

Boeyink, Natalie. 2022. "Jazzwomen in Higher Education: Experiences, Attitudes, and Personality Traits." In *The Routledge Companion to Jazz and Gender*, edited by James Reddan, Monika Herzig, and Michael Kahr, 348–358. London: Routledge.

Bohlman, Philip Vilas. 2011. "When Migration Ends, When Music Ceases." *Music and Arts in Action* 3 (3): 148–165.

Bohlman, Philip Vilas. 2016. "Jazz at the Edge of Empire." In *Jazz Worlds/World Jazz*, edited by Philip Vilas Bohlman and Goffredo Plastino, 153–180. Chicago: University of Chicago Press.

Bohlman, Philip Vilas, and Goffredo Plastino, eds. 2016. *Jazz Worlds/World Jazz*. Chicago: University of Chicago Press.

Borge, Jason. 2018. *Tropical Riffs: Latin America and the Politics of Jazz*. Durham, NC: Duke University Press.

Born, Georgina, and David Hesmondhalgh. 2000. "Introduction: On Difference, Representation and Appropriation in Music." In *Western Music and Its Others: Difference, Representation, and Appropriation in Music*, edited by Georgina Born and David Hesmondhalgh, 1–58. Berkeley: University of California Press.

Botelho, Paula. 2008. "Brazilian Music in the *New York Times*: Sites for the Production of Representations of U.S. Dominance and the Consumption of Brazilian Popular Culture." PhD diss., Language Literacy and Culture, University of Maryland Baltimore County.

Brazilian Institute of Geography and Statistics. 1999. "What Color Are You?" In *The Brazil Reader: History, Culture, Politics*, edited by Robert M. Levine and John J. Crocitti, 386–390. Durham, NC: Duke University Press.

Brinner, Benjamin Elon. 1995. *Knowing Music, Making Music: Javanese Gamelan and the Theory of Musical Competence and Interaction*. Chicago: University of Chicago Press.

Brooks, Samantha K., and Sonny S. Patel. 2022. "Challenges and Opportunities Experienced by Performing Artists during COVID-19 Lockdown: Scoping Review." *Social Sciences & Humanities Open* 6 (1), article 100297, 1–13.

Brunet, Carla Sacon. 2012. "Carnaval, Samba Schools and the Negotiation of Gendered Identities in São Paulo, Brazil." PhD diss., Music, University of California at Berkeley.

Burnett, Robert. 1996. *The Global Jukebox: The International Music Industry*. London: Routledge.

Butterfield, Matthew. 2010. "Race and Rhythm: The Social Component of the Swing Groove." *Jazz Perspectives* 4 (3): 301–335.

Butterfield, Matthew. 2011. "Why Do Jazz Musicians Swing Their Eighth Notes?" *Music Theory Spectrum* 33 (1): 3–26.

Byrne, David. 2012. *How Music Works*. San Francisco: McSweeny's.

Campos, Daniel Ribeiro. 2014. "Os trios brasileiros da década de 1960: aspectos da condução do contrabaixo." MA thesis, Music, Institute of Arts, Universidade Estadual de Campinas.

Carlson, James C. 1968. "Implications of Programmed Instruction for a World Study of Music." International Society for Music Education, Dijon, France.

Carr, Paul. 2022. "Introduction: Covid Recovery and Early Covid Music Literature." *Journal of World Popular Music* 9 (1–2): 5–30.

Castaneda, Ramsey, and Amanda Quinlan. 2022. "Picturing Women in Jazz: An Analysis of Three Jazz History Textbooks." In *The Routledge Companion to Jazz and Gender*, edited by James Reddan, Monika Herzig, and Michael Kahr, 265–277. London: Routledge.

Castro, Ruy. 2000. *Bossa Nova: The Story of the Brazilian Music That Seduced the World.* Chicago: A Cappella.

Castro, Ruy. 2017. *A onda que se ergueu no mar: novíssimos mergulhos na bossa nova.* 2nd ed. São Paulo: Companhia das Letras.

Chen, Jacqueline M., Maria Clara P. de Paula Couto, Airi M. Sacco, and Yarrow Dunham. 2018. "To Be or Not to Be (Black or Multiracial or White): Cultural Variation in Racial Boundaries." *Social Psychological and Personality Science* 9 (7): 763–772.

Clark, Andrew, ed. 2001. *Riffs & Choruses: A New Jazz Anthology.* London: Continuum.

Cohen, Susanna, and Jane Ginsborg. 2021. "The Impact of COVID-19 on Mid-career Freelance Self-employed Orchestral Musicians in the UK." *Journal of Music, Health, and Wellbeing* (Autumn): 1–16.

Coimbra, Natalia de Sá. 2015. "Northeastern Brazilian Music in New York City: Representations between Brazil and the United States." In *Made in Brazil: Studies in Popular Music*, edited by Martha Tupinambá de Ulhôa, Cláudia Azevedo, and Felipe Trotta, 202–212. New York: Routledge.

Connell, Andrew Mark. 2002. "Jazz Brasileira? Música Instrumental Brasileira and the Representation of Identity in Rio de Janeiro." PhD diss., Ethnomusicology, UCLA.

Corona, Ignacio, and Alejandro L. Madrid. 2008. "Introduction: The Postnational Turn in Music Scholarship and Music Marketing." In *Postnational Musical Identities: Cultural Production, Distribution, and Consumption in a Globalized Scenario*, edited by Ignacio Corona and Alejandro L. Madrid, 3–22. Lanham, MD: Lexington Books.

Corossacz, Valeria Ribeiro. 2017. *White Middle-Class Men in Rio de Janeiro: The Making of a Dominant Subject.* Lanham, MD: Lexington Books.

Cottrell, Stephen. 2007. "Local Bimusicality among London's Freelance Musicians." *Ethnomusicology* 51 (1): 85–105.

Da Fonseca, Eduardo "Duduka," and Bob Weiner. 1991. *Brazilian Rhythms for Drumset.* Van Nuys, CA: Alfred Music.

Daniel, Yvonne. 2005. *Dancing Wisdom: Embodied Knowledge in Haitian Vodou, Cuban Yoruba, and Bahian Candomblé.* Urbana: University of Illinois Press.

Davis, Darién J. 1997. "The Brazilian-Americans: Demography and Identity of an Emerging Latino Minority." *Latino Review of Books*, Spring/Fall, 8–15.

Davis, Darién J. 2008. "Before We Called This Place Home: Precursors of the Brazilian Community in the United States." In *Becoming Brazuca: Brazilian Immigration to the United States*, edited by Clémence Jouet-Pastré and Leticia J. Braga, 25–55. Cambridge, MA: Harvard University Press.

Davis, Martha Ellen. 1994. "'Bi-Musicality' in the Cultural Configurations of the Caribbean." *Black Music Research Journal* 14 (2): 145–160.

DeCoste, Kyle. 2017. "Street Queens: New Orleans Brass Bands and the Problem of Intersectionality." *Ethnomusicology* 61 (2): 181–206.

Deschênes, Bruno. 2018. "Bi-musicality or Transmusicality: The Viewpoint of a Non-Japanese Shakuhachi Player." *International Review of the Aesthetics and Sociology of Music* 49 (2): 275–294.

DeVeaux, Scott. 1997. *The Birth of Bebop: A Social and Musical History.* Berkeley: University of California Press.

DeVeaux, Scott. 1998. "Constructing the Jazz Tradition." In *The Jazz Cadence of American Culture*, edited by Robert G. O'Meally, 483–512. New York: Columbia University Press.

DeVeaux, Scott, and Gary Giddins. 2019. *Jazz: Essential Listening.* 2nd ed. New York: W. W. Norton.

Diamond, Jody. 1998. "Review: Out of Indonesia: Global Gamelan." *Ethnomusicology* 42 (1): 174–183.

Díaz, Juan Diego. 2014. "Orkestra Rumpilezz: Musical Constructions of Afro-Bahian Identities." PhD thesis, Faculty of Graduate and Postdoctoral Studies (Ethnomusicology), University of British Columbia.

Díaz, Juan Diego. 2021. *Africanness in Action: Essentialism and Musical Imaginations of Africa in Brazil.* New York: Oxford University Press.

Dixon, Kwame, and Ollie A. Johnson III. 2018. "Introduction: Comparative Racial Politics in Latin America—Black Politics Matter." In *Comparative Racial Politics in Latin America*, edited by Kwame Dixon and Ollie A. Johnson III, 1–14. New York: Routledge.

Drott, Eric. 2024. *Streaming Music, Streaming Capital.* Durham: Duke University Press.

Doubleday, Veronica. 2008. "Sounds of Power: An Overview of Musical Instruments and Gender." *Ethnomusicology Forum* 17 (1): 3–39.

Dowd, Timothy J., Yun Tai, and Dimitrios Zaras. 2022. "The Sounds of Silence: Concerts, Musicians, and COVID-19." In *Remaking Culture and Music Spaces: Affects, Infrastructures, Futures*, edited by Ian Woodward, Jo Haynes, Pauwke Berkers, Aileen Dillane, and Karolina Golemo, 102–120. London: Routledge.

Dunn, Christopher. 2016. *Contracultura: Alternative Arts and Social Transformation in Authoritarian Brazil.* Chapel Hill: University of North Carolina Press.

Evans, Nicholas M. 2000. *Writing Jazz: Race, Nationalism, and Modern Culture in the 1920s.* New York: Garland.

Faria, Nelson. 2005. *The Brazilian Guitar Book: Samba, Bossa Nova and Other Brazilian Styles.* Petaluma, CA: Sher Music.

Faria, Nelson, and Cliff Korman. 2001. *Inside the Brazilian Rhythm Section.* Petaluma, CA: Sher Music.

Faudree, Paja. 2012. "Music, Language, and Texts: Sound and Semiotic Ethnography." *Annual Review of Anthropology* 41: 519–536.

Feld, Steven. 1996. "Pygmy POP: A Genealogy of Schizophonic Mimesis." *Yearbook for Traditional Music* 28: 1–35.

Feld, Steven. 2012. *Jazz Cosmopolitanism in Accra: Five Musical Years in Ghana.* Durham, NC: Duke University Press.

Fellezs, Kevin. 2011. *Birds of Fire: Jazz, Rock, Funk, and the Creation of Fusion.* Durham, NC: Duke University Press.

Fernández, Raúl A. 2003. "'Si no tiene swing no vaya' a la rumba': Cuban Musicans and Jazz." In *Jazz Planet*, edited by E. Taylor Atkins, 3–18. Jackson: University Press of Mississippi.

Figueiredo, Vera, and Daniel Oliveira. 2009. *Vera Cruz Island: Brazilian Rhythms for Drumset.* Lavallette, NJ: Hudson Music.

Flood, Liza Sapir. 2017. "Instrument in Tow: Bringing Musical Skills to the Field." *Ethnomusicology* 61 (3): 486–505.

Floyd, Samuel A., Jr. 1991. "Ring Shout! Literary Studies, Historical Studies, and Black Music Inquiry." *Black Music Research Journal* 11 (2): 265–287.

Flynn, Mathew, and Richard Anderson. 2021. "Playing In: Exploring the Effect of COVID-19 on Music Makers across the Liverpool City Region." *Journal of Music, Health, and Wellbeing* (Autumn): 1–18.

Fram, Noah R., Visda Goudarzi, Hiroko Terasawa, Jonathan Berger. 2021. "Collaborating in Isolation: Assessing the Effects of the Covid-19 Pandemic on Patterns of Collaborative Behavior Among Working Musicians." *Frontiers in Psychology* 12, article 674246, 1–16.

Freeman, Peter. 2019. *The Music of Antônio Carlos Jobim.* Bristol: Intellect.

Friberg, Anders, and Andreas Sundström. 2002. "Swing Ratios and Ensemble Timing in Jazz Performance: Evidence for a Common Rhythmic Pattern." *Music Perception: An Interdisciplinary Journal* 19 (3): 333–349.

Friedwald, Will. 1996. *Jazz Singing: America's Great Voices from Bessie Smith to Bebop and Beyond.* New York: Da Capo Press.

Frith, Simon. 1981. *Sound Effects: Youth, Leisure, and the Politics of Rock'n'Roll*. New York: Pantheon Books.

Fujita, Yuiko. 2009. *Cultural Migrants from Japan: Youth, Media, and Migration in New York and London*. Lanham, MD: Lexington Books.

Gates, Henry Louis, Jr. 2011. *Black in Latin America*. New York: New York University Press.

Gerard, Charley. 1998. *Jazz in Black and White: Race, Culture, and Identity in the Jazz Community*. Westport, CT: Praeger.

Gerischer, Christiane. 2006. "*O Suingue Baiano*: Rhythmic Feeling and Microrhythmic Phenomena in Brazilian Percussion." *Ethnomusicology* 50 (1): 99–119.

Gerstin, Julian. 2017. "Comparisons of African and Diasporic Rhythm: The Ewe, Cuba, and Martinique." *Analytical Approaches to World Music* 5 (2): 1–90.

Gevers, Jeroen. 2010. "Reinterpreting Bossa Nova: Instances of Translation of Bossa Nova in the United States, 1962–1974." MA thesis, Research Institute for History and Culture, Utrecht University.

Gidal, Marc. 2010. "Contemporary 'Latin American' Composers of Art Music in the United States: Cosmopolitans Navigating Multiculturalism and Universalism." *Latin American Music Review* 31 (1): 40–78.

Gidal, Marc. 2016a. "Catholic Music in Lusophone New Jersey: Circum-Atlantic Music, Intergroup Dynamics, and Immigrant Struggles in Transnational Communities." *American Music* 34 (2): 180–217.

Gidal, Marc. 2016b. *Spirit Song: Afro-Brazilian Religious Music and Boundaries*. New York: Oxford University Press.

Gidal, Marc. 2018. "Transnationalising Brazilian Ritual Music: Quimbanda in Argentina and Charismatic Catholicism in the USA." *Civilisations* 67: 111–128.

Giller, Marília. 2018. "Breve panorama histórico del jazz en Brasil." *Revista Musical Chilena* 72 (229): 33–56.

Gilroy, Paul. 1993. *The Black Atlantic: Modernity and Double Consciousness*. Cambridge, MA: Harvard University Press.

Gioia, Ted. 2015. *Love Songs: The Hidden History*. New York: Oxford University Press.

Glick Schiller, Nina, and Andrew Irving. 2015. *Whose Cosmopolitanism?: Critical Perspectives, Relationalities and Discontents*. New York: Berghahn Books.

Goldschmitt, K. E. 2020. *Bossa Mundo: Brazilian Music in Transnational Media Industries*. New York: Oxford University Press.

Gomes, Marcelo Silva. 2010. "Samba-jazz aquém e além da Bossa Nova: Três Arranjos para Céu e Mar de Johnny Alf." PhD thesis, Music, Universidade Estadual de Campinas.

Gomes, Rafael Tomazoni. 2012. "O Samba para piano solo de Cesar Camargo Mariano." MA thesis, Music, Universidade do Estado de Santa Catarina.

Gomes Maia Tomé Pimentel, Lucas. 2019. "Brazilian Rhythms on the Drum Set: Stylizations of Baião, Frevo and Maracatu by Drummers Airto Moreira, Nene and Marcio Bahia." MM thesis, School of Music, University of Louisville.

Gosling, Tim. 2004. "'Not for Sale': The Underground Network of Anarcho-Punk." In *Music Scenes: Local, Translocal and Virtual*, edited by Andy Bennett and Richard A. Peterson, 168–183. Nashville: Vanderbilt University Press.

Greenland, Thomas H. 2016. *Jazzing: New York City's Unseen Scene*. Urbana: University of Illinois Press.

Gridley, Mark C. 1988. *Jazz Styles: History and Analysis*. 3rd ed. Englewood Cliffs, NJ: Prentice Hall.

Hagedorn, Katherine J. 2001. *Divine Utterances: The Performance of Afro-Cuban Santería*. Washington, DC: Smithsonian Institution Press.

Hargreaves, Wendy Louise. 2014. "Jazz Improvisation: Differentiating Vocalists." PhD thesis, Queensland Conservatorium, Griffith University.

Harris, Jerome. 2000. "Jazz on the Global Stage." In *The African Diaspora: A Musical Perspective*, edited by Ingrid T. Monson, 103–134. New York: Garland.

Hayes, Essie. 2006. "A Brazilian Master Speaks: Dom Salvador's Lyrical Life." *Allegro*, February.

Haynes, Jo, and Ian Woodword. 2022. "Introduction: Making Sense of Culture and Music Space During and Beyond the Pandemic." In *Remaking Culture and Music Spaces: Affects, Infrastructures, Futures*, edited by Ian Woodward, Jo Haynes, Pauwke Berkers, Aileen Dillane, and Karolina Golemo, 1–18. London: Routledge.

Heller, Michael C. 2017. *Loft Jazz: Improvising New York in the 1970s*. Oakland: University of California Press.

Henry, Clarence Bernard. 2008. *Let's Make Some Noise: Axé and the African Roots of Brazilian Popular Music*. Jackson: University Press of Mississippi.

Hersch, Charles. 2017. *Jews and Jazz: Improvising Ethnicity*. New York: Routledge.

Hertzman, Marc A. 2013. *Making Samba: A New History of Race and Music in Brazil*. Durham, NC: Duke University Press.

Herzig, Monika. 2022. "Sheroes: The Role of All-Women Groups." In *The Routledge Companion to Jazz and Gender*, edited by James Reddan, Monika Herzig, and Michael Kahr, 468–477. London: Routledge.

Hietanen, Joel, and Joonas Rokka. 2015. "Market Practices in Countercultural Market Emergence." *European Journal of Marketing* 49 (9/10): 1563–1588.

Higgins, Niko. 2016. "In Search of Compatible Virtuosities: *Floating Point* and Fusion in India." In *Jazz Worlds/World Jazz*, edited by Philip Vilas Bohlman and Goffredo Plastino, 338–363. Chicago: University of Chicago Press.

Holt, Fabian. 2007. *Genre in Popular Music*. Chicago: University of Chicago Press.

Holt, Fabian. 2016. "Jazz and the Politics of Home in Scandinavia." In *Jazz Worlds/World Jazz*, edited by Philip Vilas Bohlman and Goffredo Plastino, 51–78. Chicago: University of Chicago Press.

Hood, Mantle. 1960. "The Challenge of 'Bi-Musicality'." *Ethnomusicology* 4 (2): 55–59.

Jackson, Travis A. 2002. "Jazz as Musical Practice." In *The Cambridge Companion to Jazz*, edited by Mervyn Cooke and David Horn, 83–95. Cambridge: Cambridge University Press.

Jackson, Travis A. 2012. *Blowin' the Blues Away: Performance and Meaning on the New York Jazz Scene*. Berkeley and Chicago: University of California Press; Center for Black Music Research, Columbia College.

Jacobson, Matthew Frye. 1999. *Whiteness of a Different Color: European Immigrants and the Alchemy of Race*. Cambridge, MA: Harvard University Press.

Jeffri, Joan. 2003. *Changing the Beat: A Study of the Worklife of Jazz Musicians*. Washington, DC: National Endowment for the Arts, Research Center for Arts & Culture.

Johnson, Aaron J. 2022. "Trumpet Men: Performances of Masculinity in Jazz." In *The Routledge Companion to Jazz and Gender*, edited by James Reddan, Monika Herzig, and Michael Kahr, 69–80. London: Routledge.

Johnson, Bruce. 2002. "The Jazz Diaspora." In *The Cambridge Companion to Jazz*, edited by Mervyn Cooke and David Horn, 33–54. Cambridge: Cambridge University Press.

Johnson, Bruce. 2022. " 'The Frivolous, Scantily Clad "Jazzing Flapper," Irresponsible and Undisciplined': Jazz as a Feminine Domain." In *The Routledge Companion to Jazz and Gender*, edited by James Reddan, Monika Herzig, and Michael Kahr, 3–14. London: Routledge.

Jones, LeRoi. 1963. *Blues People: Negro Music in White America*. New York: W. Morrow.

Joseph, Tiffany D. 2015. *Race on the Move: Brazilian Migrants and the Global Reconstruction of Race*. Stanford, CA: Stanford University Press.

Jouët-Pastré, Clémence, and Leticia J. Braga, eds. 2008. *Becoming Brazuca: Brazilian Immigration to the United States*. Cambridge, MA: Harvard University Press.

Karns, Keith. 2022. "Hard Bop Cool Pose: Bebop, the Blues, and Masculinity in the Music of Lee Morgan." In *The Routledge Companion to Jazz and Gender*, edited by James Reddan, Monika Herzig, and Michael Kahr, 81–91. London: Routledge.

Kassell, Matthew. 2018. "A Legend's Long Trail." *New York Times*, November 1.

Kendi, Ibram X. 2021. "Progress." In *The 1619 Project: A New Origin Story*, edited by Nikole Hanna-Jones and The New York Times Magazine, 421–440. New York: One World.

Kettner, Scott. 2022. *The Essential Pandeiro Method*, edited by Barri Anne Brown. Self-published.

Kettner, Scott, Aaron Shafer-Haiss, and Michele Nascimento. 2013. *Maracatu for Drumset and Percussion: A Guide to the Traditional Brazilian Rhythms of Maracatu de Baque Virado*. Milwaukee: Hal Leonard.

Kingsbury, Henry. 1988. *Music, Talent, and Performance: A Conservatory Cultural System*. Philadelphia: Temple University Press.

Kisliuk, Michelle. 1997. "(Un)doing Fieldwork: Sharing Songs, Sharing Lives." In *Shadows in the Field: New Perspectives for Fieldwork in Ethnomusicology*, edited by Gregory F. Barz and Timothy J. Cooley, 23–44. New York: Oxford University Press.

Klotz, Kelsey. 2023. *Dave Brubeck and the Performance of Whiteness*. New York: Oxford University Press.

Kot, Greg. 2010. *Ripped: How the Wired Generation Revolutionized Music*. New York: Scribner.

Kraidy, Marwan M. 2002. "Hybridity in Cultural Globalization." *Communication Theory* 12: 316–339.

Krüger, Simone, and Ruxandra Trandafoiu. 2014. "Introduction: Touristic and Migrating Musics in Transit." In *Globalization of Musics in Transit*, edited by Simone Krüger and Ruxandra Trandafoiu, 1–31. New York: Routledge.

Kubik, Gerhard. 1999. *Africa and the Blues*. Jackson: University Press of Mississippi.

Kubik, Gerhard. 2010. *Theory of African Music*. Vol. 2. Chicago: University of Chicago Press.

Kubik, Gerhard. 2017a. *Jazz Transatlantic*. Vol. 1, *The African Undercurrent in Twentieth-century Jazz Culture*. Jackson: University Press of Mississippi.

Kubik, Gerhard. 2017b. *Jazz Transatlantic*. Vol. 2, *Jazz Derivatives and Developments in Twentieth-century Africa*. Jackson: University Press of Mississippi.

Kuper, Adam. 1999. *Culture: The Anthropologists' Account*. Cambridge, MA: Harvard University Press.

LaFevers, Cory James. 2018. "Embodying Brazilianness: Performing Race and Place in Austin, Texas." PhD diss., Music, University of Texas at Austin.

Lapidus, Benjamin L. 2021. *New York and the International Sound of Latin Music, 1940–1990*. Jackson: Unversity Press of Mississippi.

Legg, Benjamin. 2015. "The Bicultural Sex Symbol: Sônia Braga in Brazilian and North American Popular Culture." In *Performing Brazil: Essays on Culture, Identity, and the Performing Arts*, edited by Severino João Medeiros Albuquerque and Kathryn Bishop-Sanchez, 202–223. Madison: University of Wisconsin Press.

Leshem, Omer. 2023. "Musical Collaborations During Covid-19–How the Remote Music-Making Process Affected Jazz Musicians' Communication, Social Dynamics, and Musical Decisions." PhD diss., New School for Social Research.

Lena, Jennifer C. 2012. *Banding Together: How Communities Create Genres in Popular Music*. Princeton, NJ: Princeton University Press.

Lesser, Jeff. 2013. *Immigration, Ethnicity, and National Identity in Brazil, 1808 to the Present*. New York: Cambridge University Press.

Levine, Lawrence. 1998. "Jazz and American Culture." In *The Jazz Cadence of American Culture*, edited by Robert G. O'Meally, 431–447. New York: Columbia University Press.

Levinson, Jerrold. 2013. "Jazz Vocal Interpretation: A Philosophical Analysis." *Journal of Aesthetics and Art Criticism* 71 (1): 35–43.

Lewis, George E. 2004a. "Improvised Music after 1950: Afrological and Eurological Perspectives." In *The Other Side of Nowhere: Jazz, Improvisation, and Communities in Dialogue*, edited by Daniel Fischlin and Ajay Heble, 131–162. Middletown, CT: Wesleyan University Press.

Lewis, George E. 2004b. "Afterword to 'Improvised Music after 1950': The Changing Same." In *The Other Side of Nowhere: Jazz, Improvisation, and Communities in Dialogue*, edited by Daniel Fischlin and Ajay Heble, 163–172. Middletown, CT: Wesleyan University Press.

Lidskog, Rolf. 2016. "The Role of Music in Ethnic Identity Formation in Diaspora: A Research Review." *International Social Science Journal* 66: 23–38.

Lindsay, K., and P. Nordquist. 2007. "Pulse and Swing: Quantitative Analysis of Hierarchical Structure in Swing Rhythm." *Journal of the Acoustical Society of America* 122: 2945–2946.

Lis, Eduardo. 1996. "Creating a New Tradition: The Brazilian Jazz Experience in North America." MA thesis, Music, York University.

Livingston-Isenhour, Tamara Elena, and Thomas George Caracas Garcia. 2005. *Choro: A Social History of a Brazilian Popular Music.* Bloomington: Indiana University Press.

Lobo, Arun Peter, and Joseph J. Salvo. 2013. "A Portrait of New York's Immigrant Mélange." In *One out of Three: Immigrant New York in the Twenty-First Century*, edited by Nancy Foner, 35–63. New York: Columbia University Press.

Lopes, Denilson. 2008. "Transnational Soundscapes: Ambient Music and Bossatrônica." In *Postnational Musical Identities: Cultural Production, Distribution, and Consumption in a Globalized Scenario*, edited by Ignacio Corona and Alejandro L. Madrid, 209–218. Lanham, MD: Lexington Books.

Lopes, Thely Carvalho. 2009. "Shifting Identities in the Brazilian Restaurants of New York City." PhD diss., Latin American, Caribbean, and U.S. Latino Studies, SUNY, Albany.

Lund, Martin. 2022. *Whiteness.* Cambridge, MA: MIT Press.

Madrid, Alejandro L. 2011. "Transnational Musical Encounters at the U.S.-Mexico Border: An Introduction." In *Transnational Encounters: Music and Performance at the U.S.-Mexico Border*, edited by Alejandro L. Madrid, 1–16. New York: Oxford University Press.

Madrid, Alejandro L., and Robin D. Moore. 2013. *Danzón: Circum-Caribbean Dialogues in Music and Dance.* New York: Oxford University Press.

Magaldi, Cristina. 2008. "Before and after Samba: Modernity, Cosmopolitanism, and Popular Music in Rio de Janeiro at the Beginning and End of the Twentieth Century." In *Postnational Musical Identities: Cultural Production, Distribution, and Consumption in a Globalized Scenario*, edited by Ignacio Corona and Alejandro L. Madrid, 173–184. Lanham, MD: Lexington Books.

Magaldi, Cristina. 2009. "Cosmopolitanism and World Music in Rio de Janeiro at the Turn of the Twentieth Century." *Musical Quarterly* 92: 329–364.

Maia, Suzana. 2012. *Transnational Desires: Brazilian Erotic Dancers in New York.* Nashville: Vanderbilt University Press.

Manley-Muller, Gwen. 2021. "Remote Musical Collaboration During the COVID-19 Pandemic." *Journal of Music, Health, and Wellbeing* (Autumn):1–12.

Margolis, Maxine L. 2008. "Brazilian Immigration to the United States: Research and Issues for the New Millennium." In *Becoming Brazuca: Brazilian Immigration to the United States*, edited by Clémence Jouet-Pastré and Leticia J. Braga, 339–363. Cambridge, MA: Harvard University Press.

Margolis, Maxine L. 2009. *An Invisible Minority: Brazilians in New York City.* Rev. ed. Gainesville: University Press of Florida.

Margolis, Maxine L. 2013. *Goodbye, Brazil: Émigrés from the Land of Soccer and Samba.* Madison: University of Wisconsin Press.

Mateus, Abelita Brandão. 2014. "The Influences Contributing to the 'Samba Jazz Feel' of Cesar Camargo Mariano's Piano Trio Style." MM thesis, Music, William Paterson University of New Jersey.

Maultsby, Portia K. 2017. "The Politics of Race Erasure in Defining Black Popular Music Origins." In *Issues in African American Music: Power, Gender, Race, Representation*, edited by Portia K. Maultsby and Mellonee V. Burnim, 47–65. New York: Routledge.

McCann, Bryan. 2004. *Hello, Hello, Brazil: Popular Music in the Making of Modern Brazil.* Durham, NC: Duke University Press.

McCann, Bryan. 2007. "Blues and Samba: Another Side of Bossa Nova History." *Luso-Brazilian Review* 44 (2): 21–49.

McCann, Bryan. 2015. "Maurício Einhorn: Musical Crossings." In *Performing Brazil: Essays on Culture, Identity, and the Performing Arts*, edited by Severino João Medeiros Albuquerque and Kathryn Bishop-Sanchez, 170–182. Madison: University of Wisconsin Press.

McCann, Bryan. 2019. *João Gilberto and Stan Getz's Getz/Gilberto. 33 1/3 Brazil.* New York: Bloomsbury Academic.

McCann, Bryan. forthcoming. "David and Steve Sacks: Navigating Brazilian Jazz and Bossa Nova in New York in the 1970s–80s." In *Brazil's Northern Wave: Bossa Nova Fifty Years after Carnegie Hall*, edited by Jason Stanyek and Frederick Moehn. New York: Oxford University Press.

McDonnell, Judith, and Cileine de Lourenço. 2008. "Brazilian Immigrant Women: Race, Ethnicity, Gender, and Transnationalism." In *Becoming Brazuca: Brazilian Immigration to the United States*, edited by Clémence Jouet-Pastré and Leticia J. Braga, 151–174. Cambridge, MA: Harvard University Press.

McGee, Kristin. 2022. "Gendered Interventions in European Jazz Festival Programming: Keychanges, Stars, and Alternative Networks." In *The Routledge Companion to Jazz and Gender*, edited by James Reddan, Monika Herzig, and Michael Kahr, 190–204. London: Routledge.

McGowan, Chris. 2012. *The Brazilian Music Book: Brazil's Singers, Songwriters and Musicians Tell the Story of Bossa Nova, MPB, and Brazilian Jazz and Pop*. Santa Monica, CA: Culture Planet.

McGowan, Chris, and Ricardo Pessanha. 2009. *The Brazilian Sound: Samba, Bossa Nova, and the Popular Music of Brazil*. Rev. ed. Philadelphia: Temple University Press.

Meadows, Eddie S. 2003. *Bebop to Cool: Context, Ideology, and Musical Identity*. Westport, CT: Praeger.

Mercier, Catherine G. 2013. "Interpreting Brazilianness: Reception and Representation in the Brazilian Music Scenes of Toronto and Montreal." PhD diss., Ethnomusicology, University of Toronto.

Middleton, Richard. 2012. "Introduction: Music Studies and the Idea of Culture." In *The Cultural Study of Music: A Critical Introduction*, edited by Martin Clayton, Trevor Herbert, and Richard Middleton, 1–14. New York: Routledge.

Millard, Andre. 2005. *America on Record: A History of Recorded Sound*. 2nd ed. Cambridge: Cambridge University Press.

Moehn, Frederick. 2012. *Contemporary Carioca: Technologies of Mixing in a Brazilian Music Scene*. Durham, NC: Duke University Press.

Monk, Ellis, Jr. 2013. "Color, Bodily Capital, and Ethnoracial Division in the U.S. and Brazil." PhD diss., Sociology, University of California at Berkeley.

Monk, Ellis, Jr. 2021. "The Unceasing Significance of Colorism: Skin Tone Stratification in the United States." *Daedalus* 150 (2): 76–90.

Monson, Ingrid T. 1995. "The Problem with White Hipness: Race, Gender, and Cultural Conceptions in Jazz Historical Discourse." *Journal of the American Musicological Society* 48 (3): 396–422.

Monson, Ingrid T. 1996. *Saying Something: Jazz Improvisation and Interaction*. Chicago: University of Chicago Press.

Monson, Ingrid T. 1999. "Riffs, Repetition, and Theories of Globalization." *Ethnomusicology* 43 (1): 31–65.

Monson, Ingrid T., ed. 2000. *The African Diaspora: A Musical Perspective*. New York: Garland.

Monson, Ingrid T. 2002. "Jazz Improvisation." In *The Cambridge Companion to Jazz*, edited by Mervyn Cooke and David Horn, 114–132. Cambridge: Cambridge University Press.

Monson, Ingrid T. 2004. "Preface." In *The Other Side of Nowhere: Jazz, Improvisation, and Communities in Dialogue*, edited by Daniel Fischlin and Ajay Heble, xi–xiv. Middletown, CT: Wesleyan University Press.

Monson, Ingrid T. 2007. *Freedom Sounds: Civil Rights Call Out to Jazz and Africa*. Oxford: Oxford University Press.

Morton, David. 2006. *Sound Recording: The Life Story of a Technology*. Baltimore: Johns Hopkins University Press.

Mulligan, Mark. 2014. "The Death of the Long Tail: The Superstar Music Economy." MIDiA Consulting [Media Insights & Decisions in Action]. www.midiaconsulting.com.

Murphy, John P. 2006. *Music in Brazil: Experiencing Music, Expressing Culture*. Global Music Series. New York: Oxford University Press.

Naveda, Luiz, Fabien Gouyon, Carlos Guedes, and Marc Leman. 2011. "Microtiming Patterns and Interactions with Musical Properties in Samba Music." *Journal of New Music Research* 40 (3): 225–238.

Negus, Keith. 1999. *Music Genres and Corporate Cultures*. London: Routledge.

Nestrovski, Livia Scarinci. 2013. "Sambop: o scat singing brasileiro a partir da obra de Leny Andrade (1958–1965)." MA diss., Music, Universidade Federal do Estado do Rio de Janeiro.

Nettl, Bruno. 2005. *The Study of Ethnomusicology: Thirty-One Issues and Concepts*. New ed. Urbana: University of Illinois Press.

Newman, Billy. 2002. *Brazil: Your Passport to a New World of Music*. Van Nuys, CA: Alfred Music.

Nicholson, Stuart. 2002. "Fusions and Crossovers." In *The Cambridge Companion to Jazz*, edited by Mervyn Cooke and David Horn, 217–252. Cambridge: Cambridge University Press.

Omi, Michael, and Howard Winant. 2015. *Racial Formation in the United States*. 3rd ed. New York: Routledge.

Ong, Aihwa. 1999. *Flexible Citizenship: The Cultural Logics of Transnationality*. Durham, NC: Duke University Press.

Owensby, Brian P. 1999. *Intimate Ironies: Modernity and the Making of Middle-Class Lives in Brazil*. Stanford, CA: Stanford University Press.

Ozkirimli, Umut. 2000. *Theories of Nationalism: A Critical Introduction*. New York: St. Martin's Press.

Pacini Hernandez, Deborah. 2010. *Oye Como Va!: Hybridity and Identity in Latino Popular Music*. Philadelphia: Temple University Press.

Packman, Jeff. 2021. *Living from Music in Salvador: Professional Musicians and the Capital of Afro-Brazil*. Middletown, CT: Wesleyan University Press.

Patel, Aniruddh D. 2008. *Music, Language, and the Brain*. New York: Oxford University Press.

Pellegrinelli, Lara. 2005. "The Song Is Who?: Locating Singers on the Jazz Scene." PhD diss., Music, Harvard University.

Pellegrinelli, Lara. 2008. "Separated at 'Birth': Singing and the History of Jazz." In *Big Ears: Listening for Gender in Jazz Studies*, edited by Nichole T. Rustin and Sherrie Tucker, 31–47. Durham, NC: Duke University Press.

Pellegrinelli, Lara, Shannon J. Effinger, Jordannah Elizabeth, Kira Grunenberg, Rachel Horn, Georgia Sebesky, and Natalie Weiner. 2021. "Equal at Last? Women in Jazz, by the Numbers." *NPR Music*, January 12.

Perlman, Marc. 1994. "American Gamelan in the Garden of Eden: Intonation in a Cross-Cultural Encounter." *Musical Quarterly* 78 (3): 510–555.

Perrone, Charles A. 1989. *Masters of Contemporary Brazilian Song: MPB, 1965–1985*. Austin: University of Texas Press.

Picaud, Myrtille. 2016. "'We Try to Have the Best': How Nationality, Race and Gender Structure Artists' Circulations in the Paris Jazz Scene." *Jazz Research Journal* 10 (1–2): 126–152.

Piedade, Acácio Tadeu de Camargo. 2003. "Brazilian Jazz and Friction of Musicalities." In *Jazz Planet*, edited by E. Taylor Atkins, 41–58. Jackson: University Press of Mississippi.

Piedade, Acácio Tadeu de Camargo. 2005. "Jazz, música brasileira e fricção de musicalidades." Anais do XV Congresso da Associação Nacional de Pesquisa e Pós-Graduação em Música (ANPPOM), UFRJ, Rio de Janeiro.

Piedade, Acácio Tadeu de Camargo, and Marina Bastos. 2007. "Análise de improvisações na música instrumental: em busca da retórica do jazz brasileiro." *Revista Eletrônica de Musicologia* 11. http://www.rem.ufpr.br/_REM/REMv11/04/04-bastos-jazz.html.

Pinckney, Warren R., Jr. 2003. "Jazz in India: Perspectives on Historical Development and Musical Acculturation." In *Jazz Planet*, edited by E. Taylor Atkins, 59–80. Jackson: University Press of Mississippi.

Plastino, Goffredo. 2016. "Jazz Napoletano: A Passion for Improvisation." In *Jazz Worlds/World Jazz*, edited by Philip Vilas Bohlman and Goffredo Plastino, 309–337. Chicago: University of Chicago Press.

Plastino, Goffredo, and Philip Bohlman. 2016. "Introduction." In *Jazz Worlds/World Jazz*, edited by Philip Vilas Bohlman and Goffredo Plastino, 1–48. Chicago: University of Chicago Press.

Polak, Rainer, and Justin London. 2014. "Timing and Meter in Mande Drumming from Mali." *Music Theory Online* 20 (1). https://mtosmt.org/issues/mto.14.20.1/mto.14.20.1.polak-london.html.

Pond, Steven F. 2005. *Head Hunters: The Making of Jazz's First Platinum Album*. Ann Arbor: University of Michigan Press.

Pravaz, Natasha. 2012. "Performing *Mulata*-ness: The Politics of Cultural Authenticity and Sexuality among Carioca Samba Dancers." *Latin American Perspectives* 39 (2): 113–133.

Pravaz, Natasha. 2013. "Transnational Samba and the Construction of Diasporic Musicscapes." In *The Globalization of Musics in Transit: Music Migration and Tourism*, edited by Simone Krüger and Ruxandra Trandafoiu, 272–297. New York: Routledge.

Pressing, Jeff. 2002. "Black Atlantic Rhythm: Its Computational and Transcultural Foundations." *Music Perception: An Interdisciplinary Journal* 19 (3): 285–310.

Provost, Sarah Caissie. 2022. "Accessing Jazz's Gendered Places and Spaces." In *The Routledge Companion to Jazz and Gender*, edited by James Reddan, Monika Herzig, and Michael Kahr, 423–434. London: Routledge.

Putnam, Erin. 2012. "World Music and the Individual: The Negotiation of Cultural Capital and Identity through Bossa Nova in the United States." MA thesis, Music, UCSB.

Quintero, Michael Birenbaum, Jason Stanyek, Melissa Gonzalez, Jorge Arévalo Mateus, Mario Rey, Sydney Hutchinson, Lois Wilcken, Roberto Avant-Mier, John Koegel, and Edgardo Díaz Díaz. 2014. "Latino Music." In *Grove Music Online*, Oxford University Press.

Ramnarine, Tina K. 2007. "Musical Performance in the Diaspora: Introduction." *Ethnomusicology Forum* 16 (1): 1–17.

Ramos-Zayas, Ana Y. 2012. *Street Therapists: Race, Affect, and Neoliberal Personhood in Latino Newark*. Chicago: University of Chicago Press.

Ratliff, Ben. 2015. "Resurrecting the Barreling Sound of a Samba-Jazz Band from the '60s." *New York Times*, November 30, 2015.

Ray, William. 2001. *The Logic of Culture: Authority and Identity in the Modern Era*. Oxford: Blackwell.

Reddan, James, Monika Herzig, and Michael Kahr, eds. 2022. *The Routledge Companion to Jazz and Gender*. London: Routledge.

Reily, Suzel Ana. 1996. "Tom Jobim and the Bossa Nova Era." *Popular Music* 15 (1): 1–16.

Reily, Suzel Ana, and Katherine Brucher, eds. 2018. *The Routledge Companion to the Study of Local Musicking*. New York: Routledge.

Resler, Chloe. 2022. "The Rise of Queermisia in Jazz: Medicalization, Legislation, and Its Effects." In *The Routledge Companion to Jazz and Gender*, edited by James Reddan, Monika Herzig, and Michael Kahr, 119–130. London: Routledge.

Reynolds, Dean S. 2017. "Jazz and Recording in the Digital Age: Technology, New Media, and Performance in New York and Online." PhD diss., Music, City University of New York.

Rice, Timothy. 2003. "The Ethnomusicology of Music Learning and Teaching." *College Music Symposium* 43: 65–85.

Ritchey, Marianna. 2019. *Composing Capital: Classical Music in the Neoliberal Era*. Chicago: University of Chicago Press.

Robbins, Bruce, and Paulo Lemos Horta, eds. 2017. *Cosmopolitanisms*. New York: New York University Press.

Roberts, Dorothy. 2021. "Race." In *The 1619 Project: A New Origin Story*, edited by Nikole Hanna-Jones and The New York Times Magazine, 45–61. New York: One World.

Roberts, John Storm. 1999. *Latin Jazz: The First of the Fusions, 1880s to Today*. New York: Schirmer Books.

Roberts, Tamara. 2016. *Resounding Afro Asia: Interracial Music and the Politics of Collaboration*. New York: Oxford University Press.

Roediger, David R. 2005. *Working toward Whiteness: How America's Immigrants Became White: The Strange Journey from Ellis Island to the Suburbs*. New York: Basic Books.

Rogers, Richard A. 2006. "From Cultural Exchange to Transculturation: A Review and Reconceptualization of Cultural Appropriation." *Communication Theory* 16: 474–503.

Roth-Gordon, Jennifer. 2016. *Race and the Brazilian Body: Blackness, Whiteness, and Everyday Language in Rio de Janeiro*. Oakland: University of California Press.

Rustin, Nichole T., and Sherrie Tucker, eds. 2008a. *Big Ears: Listening for Gender in Jazz Studies*. Durham, NC: Duke University Press.

Rustin, Nichole T., and Sherrie Tucker. 2008b. "Introduction." In *Big Ears: Listening for Gender in Jazz Studies*, edited by Nichole T. Rustin and Sherrie Tucker, 1–28. Durham, NC: Duke University Press.

Sandroni, Carlos. 2000. "Le tresillo: Rythme et 'Métissage' dans la musique populaire latino-américaine imprimée au XIXe siècle." *Cahiers de musiques traditionnelles* 13: 55–64.

Sandroni, Carlos. 2021. *A Respectable Spell: Transformations of Samba in Rio de Janeiro*. Translated by Michael Iyanaga. 2nd ed. Urbana: University of Illinois Press.

Saraiva, Joana Martins. 2007. "A invenção do sambajazz: discursos sobre a cena musical de Copacabana no final dos anos 1950 e início dos anos 1960." MA thesis, Pontifícia Universidade Católica do Rio de Janeiro.

Schuller, Gunther. 1989. *The Swing Era: The Development of Jazz, 1930–1945*, Vol. 2: *The History of Jazz*. New York: Oxford University Press.

Seabrook, John. 2015. *The Song Machine: Inside the Hit Factory*. New York: W. W. Norton.

Seigel, Micol. 2009. *Uneven Encounters: Making Race and Nation in Brazil and the United States*. Durham, NC: Duke University Press.

Shelemay, Kay Kaufman. 2006. "Ethiopian Musical Invention in Diaspora: A Tale of Three Musicians." *Diaspora* 15 (2/3): 303–320.

Shipton, Alyn. 2001. *A New History of Jazz*. London: Continuum.

Shuker, Roy. 2001. *Understanding Popular Music Culture*. 2nd ed. London: Routledge.

Siegel, Joel E. 2000. "Jazz Singing: Between Blues and Bebeop." In *The Oxford Companion to Jazz*, edited by Bill Kirchner, 220–234. New York: Oxford University Press.

Silva, Graziella Moraes, and Marcelo Paixão. 2014. "Mixed and Unequal: New Perspectives on Brazilian Ethnoracial Relations." In *Pigmentocracies: Ethnicity, Race, and Color in Latin America*, edited by Edward Eric Telles and Project on Ethnicity and Race in Latin America, 172–217. Chapel Hill: University of North Carolina Press.

Silverman, Carol. 1995. "Learning to Perform, Performing to Learn." *Journal of American Folklore* 108 (3): 307–316.

Silverman, Carol. 2012. *Romani Routes: Cultural Politics and Balkan Music in Diaspora*. New York: Oxford University Press.

Skaggs, Rachel. 2024. "Socially Distanced Artistic Careers: Professional Social Interactions in Early, Established, and Late Career Stages during COVID-19." *Poetics* 103: 1–13.

Skidmore, Thomas E. 1993. "Bi-Racial U.S.A. vs. Multi-Racial Brazil: Is the Contrast Still Valid?" *Journal of Latin American Studies* 25 (2): 373–386.

Slobin, Mark. 2012. "The Destiny of 'Diaspora' in Ethnomusicology." In *The Cultural Study of Music: A Critical Introduction*, edited by Martin Clayton, Trevor Herbert, and Richard Middleton, 118–128. New York: Routledge.

Smith, Anthony D. 2010. *Nationalism: Theory, Ideology, History*. 2nd ed. Cambridge, UK: Polity Press.

Smith, Cristen A. 2016. *Afro-Paradise: Blackness, Violence, and Performance in Brazil*. Urbana: University of Illinois Press.

Snyder, Andrew. 2022. *Critical Brass: Street Carnival and Musical Activism in Olympic Rio de Janeiro*. Middletown, CT: Wesleyan University Press.

Solomon, Thomas. 2015. "Theorizing Diaspora and Music." *Urban People/Lidé Města* 17 (2): 201–219.

Spiro, Michael. 2006. *The Conga Drummer's Guidebook*. Petaluma, CA: Sher Music.

Spiro, Neta, Rosie Perkins, Sasha Kaye, Urszula Tymoszuk, Adele Mason-Bertrand, Isabelle Cossette, Solange Glasser, and Aaron Williamon. 2020. "The Effects of COVID-19 Lockdown 1.0 on Working Patterns, Income, and Wellbeing Among Performing Arts Professionals in the United Kingdom (April–June 2020)." *Frontiers in Psychology* 11, article 594086, 1–17.

Spitzberg, Brian H., and Gabrielle Changnan. 2009. "Conceptualizing Intercultural Competence." In *Sage Handbook of Intercultural Competence*, edited by Darla K. Deardorff, 2–52. Thousand Oaks, CA: Sage.

Stanyek, Jason. 2004. "Transmissions of an Interculture: Pan-African Jazz and Intercultural Improvisation." In *The Other Side of Nowhere: Jazz, Improvisation, and Communities in Dialogue*, edited by Daniel Fischlin and Ajay Heble, 87–130. Middletown, CT: Wesleyan University Press.

Stanyek, Jason. 2011. "Choro do Norte: Improvising the Transregional Roda in the United States." *Luso-Brazilian Review* 48 (1): 100–129.

Stanyek, Jason, and Frederick Moehn, eds. forthcoming. *Brazil's Northern Wave: Bossa Nova Fifty Years after Carnegie Hall*. New York: Oxford University Press.

Starr, Larry, and Christopher Alan Waterman. 2010. *American Popular Music from Minstrelsy to MP3*. 3rd ed. New York: Oxford University Press.

Stewart, Alex. 2007. *Making the Scene: Contemporary New York City Big Band Jazz*. Berkeley: University of California Press.

Stokes, Martin. 2004. "Music and the Global Order." *Annual Review of Anthropology* 33: 47–72.

Stowe, David W. 1994. *Swing Changes: Big-band Jazz in New Deal America*. Cambridge, MA: Harvard University Press.

Suzuki, Yoko. 2011. "'You Sound Like an Old Black Man': Performativity of Gender and Race Among Female Jazz Saxophonists." PhD diss., Music, University of Pittsburgh.

Taylor, Timothy Dean. 2016. *Music and Capitalism: A History of the Present*. Chicago: University of Chicago Press.

Teixeira, Cidinho. 2011. *Brazilian Rhythms on the Keyboard*. Edited by Janet Lemansky and Pedro Bermudez. Rottenburg: Advance Music.

Telles, Edward Eric. 2014. "The Project on Ethnicity and Race in Latin America (PERLA): Hard Data and What Is at Stake." In *Pigmentocracies: Ethnicity, Race, and Color in Latin America*, edited by Edward Eric Telles and Project on Ethnicity and Race in Latin America, 2–35. Chapel Hill: University of North Carolina Press.

Tenzer, Michael. 2011. "Integrating Music: Personal and Global Transformations." In *Analytical and Cross-Cultural Studies in World Music*, edited by Michael Tenzer and John Barlow Roeder, 357–387. New York: Oxford University Press.

Thayler, Allen. 2011. "Right at Home." *Wax Poetics* (48), 44–52, https://magazine.waxpoetics.com/article/dom-salvador-right-at-home/.

Titon, Jeff Todd. 1995. "Bi-musicality as a Metaphor." *Journal of American Folklore* 108 (429): 287–297.

Tokita, Alison. 2014. "Bi-musicality in Modern Japanese Culture." *International Journal of Bilingualism* 18 (2): 159–174.

Town, Sarah. 2019. "'Timbeando en Nueva York': Cuban *Timba* Takes Root Abroad." *Ethnomusicology* 63 (1): 105–136.

Toynbee, Jason. 2000. *Making Popular Music: Musicians, Creativity and Institutions*. New York: Oxford University Press.

Treece, David. 2013. *Brazilian Jive: From Samba to Bossa and Rap*. London: Reaktion Books.

Trimillos, Ricardo D. 2004. "Subject, Object, and the Ethnomuisicology Ensemble: The Ethnomusicological 'We' and 'Them.'" In *Performing Ethnomusicology: Teaching and*

Representation in World Music Ensembles, edited by Ted Solís, 23–52. Berkeley: University of California Press.

Tsing, Anna Lowenhaupt. 2005. *Friction: An Ethnography of Global Connection*. Princeton, NJ: Princeton University Press.

Tucker, Sherrie. 2000. *Swing Shift: "All-Girl" Bands of the 1940s*. Durham, NC: Duke University Press.

Tucker, Sherrie. 2004. "Bordering on Community: Improvising Women-in-Jazz." In *The Other Side of Nowhere: Jazz, Improvisation, and Communities in Dialogue*, edited by Daniel Fischlin and Ajay Heble, 244–267. Middletown, CT: Wesleyan University Press.

Tucker, Sherrie. 2008. "When Did Jazz Go Straight? A Queer Question for Jazz Studies." *Critical Studies in Improvisation / Études critiques en improvisation* 4 (2): 1–16.

Turino, Thomas. 2000. *Nationalists, Cosmopolitans, and Popular Music in Zimbabwe*. Chicago: University of Chicago Press.

Turino, Thomas. 2008. *Music as Social Life: The Politics of Participation*. Chicago: University of Chicago Press.

Vertovec, Steven. 2009. *Transnationalism*. London: Routledge.

Vianna, Hermano. 1999. *The Mystery of Samba: Popular Music and National Identity in Brazil*, edited and translated by John Charles Chasteen. Chapel Hill: University of North Carolina Press.

Wade, Bonnie C. 2013. *Thinking Musically: Experincing Music, Expressing Culture*. 3rd ed. New York: Oxford University Press.

Wade, Peter. 2009. *Race and Sex in Latin America*. London: Pluto Press.

Wade, Peter. 2017. "Racism and Race Mixture in Latin America." *Latin American Research Review* 52 (3): 477–485.

Walser, Robert, ed. 1999. *Keeping Time: Readings in Jazz History*. New York: Oxford University Press.

Washburne, Christopher. 1998. "'Play It *Con Filin*?' The Swing and Expression of Salsa." *Latin American Music Review* 19 (2): 160–185.

Washburne, Christopher. 2020. *Latin Jazz: The Other Jazz*. New York: Oxford University Press.

Weidman, Amanda. 2014. "Anthropology and Voice." *Annual Review of Anthropology* 43: 37–51.

Weinstein, Barbara. 2011. "Postcolonial Brazil." In *The Oxford Handbook of Latin American History*, edited by Jose C. Moya, 212–256. New York: Oxford University Press.

Weiss, Sarah. 2014. "Listening to the World but Hearing Ourselves: Hybridity and Perceptions of Authenticity in World Music." *Ethnomusicology* 58 (3): 506–525.

Werbner, Pnina, ed. 2008. *Anthropology and the New Cosmopolitanism: Rooted, Feminist and Vernacular Perspectives*. New York: Berg.

Whitmore, Aleysia K. 2020. *World Music & The Black Atlantic: Producing & Consuming African-Cuban Musics on World Music Stages*. New York: Oxford University Press.

Willard, Patricia. 2000. "Ella Fitzgerald, Sarah Vaughan, and Billie Holiday." In *The Oxford Companion to Jazz*, edited by Bill Kirchner, 235–249. New York: Oxford University Press.

Williams, Linda F. 2003. "Interpreting the Creative Process of Jazz in Zimbabwe." In *Jazz Planet*, edited by E. Taylor Atkins, 81–99. Jackson: University Press of Mississippi.

Wilson, Olly. 1974. "The Significance of the Relationship between Afro-American Music and West African Music." *Black Perspective in Music* 2 (1): 3–22.

Wilson, Olly. 1998. "Black Music as an Art Form." In *The Jazz Cadence of American Culture*, edited by Robert G. O'Meally, 82–101. New York: Columbia University Press.

Winant, Howard. 1999. "Racial Democracy and Racial Identity: Comparing the United States and Brazil." In *Racial Politics in Contemporary Brazil*, edited by Michael George Hanchard, 98–115. Durham, NC: Duke University Press.

Witzleben, J. Lawrence. 2010. "Performing in the Shadows: Learning and Making Music as Ethnomusicological Practice and Theory." *Yearbook for Traditional Music* 42: 135–166.

Wong, Patrick C. M., Anil K. Roy, and Elizabeth Hellmuth Margulis. 2009. "Bimusicalism: The Implicit Dual Enculturation of Cognitive and Affective Systems." *Music Perception: An Interdisciplinary Journal* 27 (2): 81–88.

Woolner, Christina J. 2021. "'Out of Time' and 'Out of Tune': Reflections of an Oud Apprentice in Somaliland." *Ethnomusicology* 65 (2): 259–285.

Young, James O. 2011. "Appropriation and Hybridity." In *The Routledge Companion to Philosophy and Music*, edited by Theodore Gracyk and Andrew Kania, 176–186. Abingdon: Routledge.

Zheng, Su. 2010. *Claiming Diaspora: Music, Transnationalism, and Cultural Politics in Asian/Chinese America*. New York: Oxford University Press.

Zola, Rebecca. 2022. "Women in Jazz: A Failed Brand." In *The Routledge Companion to Jazz and Gender*, edited by James Reddan, Monika Herzig, and Michael Kahr, 412–422. London: Routledge.

Index